DAVID HARE

Plays One

Slag

Teeth 'n' Smiles

Knuckle

Licking Hitler

Plenty

Introduced by
the Author

faber and faber

LONDON · BOSTON

This collection first published in 1996 by
Faber and Faber Limited
3 Queen Square London WC1N 3AU

Photoset by Parker Typesetting Service, Leicester
Printed in England by Clays Ltd, St Ives plc

In *Teeth 'n' Smiles* the chorus from the song 'How Do You Do It?' by Mitch
Murray is reprinted by kind permission of Dick James Music Ltd. © 1962;
the lines from Cole Porter's 'You're the Top' from the musical production of
Anything Goes are used by permission of Harms Inc. Chappell & Co.
© 1934; details of the bombing of the Café de Paris can be found in
The Blitz by Constantine Fitzgibbon.

All rights whatsoever in these plays are strictly reserved and applications for
permission to perform them must be made in advance, before rehearsals
begin, to Casarotto Ramsay Ltd, National House, 60–66 Wardour Street,
London W1Z 3HP

A CIP record for this book is available from the British Library

ISBN 0-571-17741-7

2 4 6 8 10 9 7 5 3 1

Contents

Introduction

*The editors at Faber and Faber talk to the author
about the plays in this collection.*

Q: *Was* Slag *the first full-length play you wrote?*
Yes. I wrote it in 1969, with the typewriter on my knees,
while travelling in a van with an itinerant theatre group
Tony Bicât and I had founded called Portable Theatre. I'd
started the company one year earlier, as a director in fact.
A playwright let us down and we were left with a gap in
our programme, so I was forced to write a one-act play at
short notice. The piece was as silly as you'd expect of
something concocted in four days by someone who'd
never really thought about writing a play before. It was a
primitive satire on the unlikelihood of revolution in Britain
– this was the late sixties, remember – but it did attract
Michael Codron's attention. He immediately asked me to
write a full-length play. *Slag* was produced originally at
Hampstead in 1970. It was then revived a year later by the
Royal Court who had a gap in their programme. They
therefore picked it up and put in a starrier, though equally
excellent, cast. Michael went on to be involved with my
first four plays.

Q: *You could also call* Slag *a satire.*
Oh certainly. By one of those coincidences of timing that
have been a feature of my life as a writer, I had started
reading some of the wilder feminist writings of the period,
and in between the time when I began writing the play and
its subsequent production the whole subject of women's
liberation had become hotly topical. Germaine Greer had
been clever enough to corral some of the ideas that were in
the air and impose her extraordinary intellectual discipline
on them to write *The Female Eunuch*. It was both a

wonderful and a popular book. This meant by the time the audience reached the theatre, they were, if you like, ready for the fun.

Q: *You have said* Slag *is about your own schooldays.*
The most useless advice any writer can be given is: write about what you know. How can a writer do otherwise? Perhaps a better injunction might be: write about what you know, but make sure you transform it. Fiction is only interesting if it involves a true act of imagination. Noël Coward made me laugh when he described *Slag* as five very good scenes and one bad one. I'm afraid he was being generous. But what dreamlike vitality the play does have is entirely from my imagining something about which, by definition, I can know nothing: what it's like to be in an all-female community.

Q: *Did you imagine at that time you were going, primarily, to be a comic writer?*
I honestly didn't think about it. In all the plays I wrote in the seventies there is a powerful element of scorn. Scorn, I'd say, rather than anger, because I was impatient with an old England which had transparently collapsed, and yet the illusion of which still gripped our thinking and feeling. And, of course, scorn is best expressed comically. I love satire because I think it's so good for you. Derisive public laughter is powerfully democratic. I was delighted with a recent humourless academic publication, claiming to be about my plays. It reviles them on the wonderful grounds that they're full of jokes. I loved that. Nothing threatens the ivory tower more than a good laugh. But it was a confusion about whether I was indeed a satirist or something else which led to my meeting Peggy Ramsay, who became my agent, and, I would say, the formative influence on my playwriting life.

Recently, I've read Harold Bloom's book, *The Western Canon*, which asserts that any serious writer belongs consciously to a tradition and feels him or herself to be in some sort of direct dialogue with the great Western writers. I must admit I have no sense of this. When I am asked to name playwrights who have been an influence on me, I am stumped to name any. If that seems immodest, then I can only say, on the contrary, I admire plenty of playwrights – and a good many among my contemporaries – yet it seems to me the more you admire a writer, the less you want to imitate them. The least attractive part of Shaw or Joyce or Tolstoy is the part that feels itself in competition with Shakespeare. And indeed those playwrights in my lifetime who have sought, say, a deliberately Shakespearian dimension to their work seem to me to have gone alarmingly astray. What influences me in my writing is not literature but life. And nobody has ever given me more courage to write than Peggy.

Q: *What do you mean by that?*
Well, I wrote three plays – all satires – before I wrote *Knuckle*. Admittedly it's still pastiche. It's based on the idea of re-setting an American thriller in the deepest Home Counties of England. Nevertheless, it does have, distinctively, the first stirrings of a slightly different voice, a voice which is in earnest. The play has a morality. The hero doesn't get the girl precisely because he behaves badly. My first agent, who had taken me on in the hope that I would rip merry hell out of contemporary society, was horrified by the play. He told me that I should stick to writing jokes. It was his reaction that impelled me to give the play to Peggy Ramsay. Peggy was an ex-opera singer – very brilliant, very forthright. In the fifties she had started a literary agency which was run with a carefree kind of vigour and enthusiasm which was unique in theatrical London. When she read *Knuckle* she was so excited she broke her lifetime rule. She put her own money into a client's production. It was a play she was determined to fight for.

I have to make clear I think Peggy the most impassioned and literate fighter of the post-war British theatre. Alongside Joan Littlewood, John Osborne and George Devine, she is one of its unequivocal heroes, though perhaps the least known. There are at least a dozen writers, the most famous of them Joe Orton, who owe a good part of their prosperity to her championship. She was never better, or livelier, than when defending an author who was ahead of public taste. So when *Knuckle* finally opened, disastrously, in the week after Edward Heath's election called to decide 'Who Runs Britain', it was Peggy who steadied my nerve and kept me writing through the distinctly choppy months that followed.

Q: *The critics hated it?*
Not entirely. It had one or two powerful advocates, including the late Harold Hobson in the *Sunday Times*. One or two critics, like Irving Wardle, who then wrote for *The Times*, were kind enough later publicly to admit that they'd misjudged the play on first viewing. But there's no doubt that the whole venture of producing a play which attacked the capitalist system in a West End theatre had a symbolic significance which somewhat obscured the text. It evoked responses which were, shall we say, not entirely literary. Through all the resulting disappointment, it was Peggy who constantly reassured me that it's not finally very important how any individual play in a writer's life is received. The long run is what matters. She always told me she believed I would still be writing in twenty years' time. If I am, it is, in part, thanks to her. She had a perspective and a *sang froid* which I entirely lacked.

Reading it now, of course, the play does seem modestly prophetic. It is organized round the two types of British capitalism which ten years later were to clash so violently: the paternalistic kind with its old social networks and its spurious moralizing, and the new aggressive, shameless variety which would gain such ascendancy in the 80s.

Knuckle is a director's piece and is still revived all over the world by directors who imagine they can solve its stylistic demands. They're usually wrong. The stagecraft is immature. There are too many scenes and too many of them are set in the same places. The only excuse I have for its clumsiness is that I was writing with such political urgency I neglected the craft. Or maybe I just didn't possess it in the first place. Anyway, the cliché that is always advanced about my work is that I try to use the language of the cinema in the theatre. It's not true. Any such aim would be doomed. More properly, when writing epic plays, you should try to develop a theatrical language which parallels the cinema's freedom, but which necessarily uses different techniques. You have to find equivalents. Too much of Knuckle is in mid-shot.

Q: Teeth 'n' Smiles *was a much less contentious play.*
Indeed. I've been involved in a couple of these ephemera – plays which seem to have their success because they are mysteriously in touch with the mood of a particular time. They then just disappear into the theatre annuals. Certainly I haven't heard of anyone doing Teeth 'n' Smiles in the last ten years. I directed this one – as I now did all my plays for the next ten years – and I remember it as one of the really blessed times I've had in the theatre. 1975 was a very hot summer. This wonderful rock music was pounding out of the Royal Court Theatre into Sloane Square. Malcolm McClaren had just opened the boutique Sex some way down the Kings Road. And, somehow, everything was set fair for a sloppy, dirty, funny play about hippies behaving badly through a long night in Cambridge. I think Peter Brook says somewhere that theatre is partly fashion and anyone who doesn't accept that is going to get their heart broken. But, on the other hand, anyone who, having accepted it, doesn't then

instantly forget it, is going to be a bad playwright. He's right.

Q: *It has a very original use of music.*
I had hated the way the theatre tried to emulate pop music in the sixties. Theatre people envied its popularity, so they tried to hitch a ride on pop music's vitality. 'Oh if only the theatre could be like rock music', they'd say. Whereas I liked both. But I liked them because they were different. I've never been a great fan of the musical theatre. Only the very greatest musicals avoid generality. Most of them just jump straight in to trying to yank at your emotional levers without doing the work of involving you in the first place. Opera, on stage at least, leaves me cold. Dramatically, it's so slow. But in *Teeth 'n' Smiles* we had the idea that the music would actually be part of the drama, that it would develop character, that it would tell a story. In other words, it would be justified naturalistically. And I think the idea works.

Q: Knuckle *had introduced Kate Nelligan to the West End stage and she went on to appear in several other of your plays* – Licking Hitler, Plenty *and* Dreams of Leaving. There's an interesting remark by Evelyn Waugh where he says that at the age of forty every British writer either becomes a prophet or finds a style. For me, it was when I was approaching thirty that I began to realize that the rhythm in which you write is as important as the apparent meaning – that the rhythm indeed is part of the meaning. By rhythm, I don't just mean rhythm of dialogue, but the sense of the beat both in the language itself and in its interplay with the action. It was at the time that I was beginning to tighten and refine the tension of my dialogue – I wanted it as distinctively strung and taut as I could make it – and at the same time it happened that I had the great good fortune to meet Kate.

  I've worked with some actors, good actors – in other

peoples' work I've seen them to be excellent – and yet
somehow they instinctively don't hear my lines. Sadly,
these actors might as well go home on the first day.
They're in for weeks of torture. Because, frankly, you
either hear the music or you don't. Kate had not just a
faultless ear for my lines, but a very extraordinary tension
in her physicality as well. This made her the near-perfect
player of my work. She was always compelling. The fact
she was Canadian also gave her an edge in playing these
very English plays. People used to think I wrote parts for
her, which I never did. But undoubtedly her fearlessness
and her ambition helped me to develop my ambition as
well. I like to think we grew together.

Q: *The TV film,* Licking Hitler, *is based on a real
operation?*
I discovered by chance about the Black Propaganda Units
which had done their best to disorient the German war
effort with highly personalized disinformation. I wouldn't
say they had remained a secret after the war. After all,
there was a book by the man who had run them, Sefton
Delmer, called *Black Boomerang*, which is some sort of
record of his peculiar work. But nobody before had quite
seized on the significance of what these units were up to. I
was inspired in this idea of re-thinking some parts of the
war effort by Angus Calder's great book, *The People's
War*. This pointed out that it was the Second World War
itself which educated the people towards the great Labour
victory of 1945. The rejection of Churchill was not the
anomaly or betrayal of popular, patriotic history. Far from
it. It was the logical result of an army coming home and
expressing their feelings about their own experiences by
demanding change.

A lot of people were kind enough to write to me, asking
how I had so accurately imagined events which had
happened before I was born. They thought it was eerie.

DAVID HARE

But I've often said guesswork is the writer's basic skill. If you can't guess, don't write. Immediately after *Licking Hitler*, there was a flood of films and plays, as if a lot of other writers suddenly realized what fun this business of re-interpreting the war was going to be. Yet when I watch *Licking Hitler* today, there is, both in the script and the playing, a mixture of hurt and bewilderment and downright innocence which I don't think any of its imitators either caught or understood.

Q: *And* Plenty, *presumably, was written at the same time?*
That's right. They're twin works. I just remember writing in my diary the words 'A woman over Europe', and then having the visual image of a woman sitting in an overcoat on a packing case, rolling herself a cigarette, with her husband lying naked at her feet. It all grew from there.

Q: *It took some time for* Plenty *to catch on?*
Although I had worked at the National Theatre since 1971 in one capacity or another, *Plenty* was my first play to be done there. This was 1978. The board asked Peter Hall to take it off after several weeks on the grounds that it was not playing to full houses. Peter said if they could not play work they believed in, then there was no real point in having a National Theatre. Thanks to his loyalty, the play stayed on. The audiences grew, and as the run went on, the play began to sell out and to acquire the reputation which moved it to Broadway, and which led eventually to the movie being made. In America, it's still the play by which I'm best known. As the National Theatre has gone on to produce ten of my plays, I always think of Peter's faith in the play in its early days as something which turned out to be crucial in my life.

Q: *Did you feel it was the play towards which you'd been working since you became a playwright?*

Most certainly. It has the balance I want. It shows a woman, Susan Traherne, choosing to live her life in dissent. And it allows that dissent full range. It revels in her power. But it also shows the price she pays. What's more, it shows the effect of her anger on another person's life. In this way, two choices are contrasted. Susan chooses dissent, but Brock chooses assimilation. The audience is left to consider the advantages and drawbacks of both. It sets me off on what I suppose became the intention of a great deal of my later work: to show the way moral decisions in real life involve far more complex motivations and effects than are usually allowed in fiction. I ceased trying to bully the audience's reactions to what I portrayed, to demand a particular response from them, and instead let them decide for themselves what their feelings about the characters and their choices were.

Q: *Is that your ideal?*
My ideal is to create a tension. Theatre is a moral form. In telling a story it is almost impossible to stop the audience drawing moral implications. You can fight it as hard as you like. Some of our most distinguished playwrights – like Wilde, like Beckett – are seen to try and avoid that moment at which the audience inevitably asks, 'So what's he trying to say here?' I fully understand their irritation with that question, because I too hate plays where the author offers too easy a diagram. I hate to see the real difficulties of life programmatically reduced – as they are, say, in melodrama. Yet on the other hand, audiences do draw moral conclusions from plays. They just do. And anyone who frustrates the audience's needs by lack of clarity equally quickly comes to grief.

Q: *But* Plenty, *for instance, provoked a whole variety of reactions. It can't be reduced to one meaning.*
Not at all. Nor would I wish it to be. The whole point of writing plays is to express things which cannot be reduced.

In America *Plenty* was widely seen as a play about the Vietnam war. In Japan it was seen as a play about the superiority of women to men. In England it was seen as post-war history by some and as a play about a debilitating neurosis by others. In Israel, I am told the movie was watched every week on a kibbutz, whether from choice or necessity I don't know.

Q: *It was the end of nearly ten years' work?*
You could say. The day after it opened in London, I went to live abroad. I couldn't go fast enough. And it was over four years before I wrote another stage play.

David Hare
London
September 1995

SLAG

For Margaret

Characters

Joanne, twenty-three
Elise, twenty-six
Ann, thirty-two

The play is written deliberately with as few stage and acting instructions as possible. Blackouts should be instant, gaps between scenes brief, and scenery minimal.

Slag was first performed at the Hampstead Theatre Club, London, on 6 April 1970 with the following cast:

Joanne Rosemary McHale
Elise Marty Cruickshank
Ann Diane Fletcher

Designed by John Halle
Directed by Roger Hendricks-Simon

Revived at the Royal Court Theatre, London, on 24 May 1971 with the following cast:

Joanne Lynn Redgrave
Elise Barbara Ferris
Ann Anna Massey

Designed by John Gunter
Directed by Max Stafford-Clark

SCENE ONE

Common Room. They are standing formally with hands raised.

Joanne I, Joanne.

Elise I, Elise.

Ann I, Ann.

Joanne Do solemnly promise.

Elise and Ann Do solemnly promise.

Joanne For as long as I know Elise and Ann.

Elise For as long as I know Joanne and Ann.

Ann For as long as I know Joanne and Elise.

Joanne To abstain from all forms and varieties of sexual intercourse.

Elise and Ann All forms and varieties of sexual intercourse.

Joanne To keep my body intact in order to register my protest against the way our society is run by men for men whose aim is the subjugation of the female and the enslavement of the working woman.

Elise and Ann The working woman.

Joanne All forms of sex I therefore deny myself in order to work towards the establishment of a truly socialist society.

Ann breaks away.

Ann Oh, come on.

Joanne What?

Ann I've come along with you so far, but . . . socialist society!

Joanne All right, you may dissent at this point but the essential commitment is made. All sex I deny.

Ann Can we not drop the subject now once and for all?

Elise No one's going to test our determination anyway.

Joanne Is there any coffee?

Ann No. No one's going to be much deprived.

Elise It's not as if we ever saw men except parents, and it's very unlikely we'll ever see any more of those.

Ann It wasn't really that bad.

Joanne It was a disaster.

Exit Elise.

Ann They were a little conscious of the lack of numbers. Who wouldn't be? A chill in the air of Great Hall.

Joanne The singing of the Internationale should have warmed them up.

Ann That was a singularly silly gesture on your part. Nobody knew the tune anyway. But your stupidity at least managed to unite them. We've been through the very worst that we can know, and now it'll be time to rebuild.

Joanne When Robinson Crusoe landed on a desert island, his first instinct was to create a perfect embryo of the society he had escaped from.

Ann Thank you, Joanne, but can we leave politics out of this? We will build a new sort of school where what people feel for people will be the basis of their relationships. No politics.

Joanne In Buñuel's version – 1952, I think, anyway his Mexican period, the part of Robinson Crusoe was played by . . .

Re-enter Elise.

Elise Coast's clear. They've gone.

Joanne The part of Crusoe was played by . . .

Elise For Christ's sake shut up.

Ann Let's not talk like that.

Joanne You started it.

Ann What's the point?

Joanne She was getting at me.

Ann Divided we fall.

Ann resumes chalking in the coloured parts of the blackboard. Elise starts knitting.

Elise I've nearly finished another bootee. Its little feet are going to look so sweet.

Ann Lovely.

Joanne All you need now is a fuck.

Joanne picks up Sight and Sound.

Elise I'm sitting here and often I stop and think perhaps I've seen my very last man.

Ann Tradesmen.

Elise I mean real men. I can't quite grasp what that means. Ann, Joanne, imagine it.

Joanne Tremendous.

Elise No more men.

Joanne The ideal.

Ann We're perfectly well used to it. I've been two years without now and I tell you I feel better.

Elise You don't look any better.

Ann I eat better.

Elise Repulsive.

Joanne goes to the window where something has caught her attention. She screams out.

Ann I've taken off weight and I don't have my skin trouble any longer.

Joanne Stop buggering about, you vile little child.

Ann I don't doubt, Elise, that men will some time reappear in your life.

Joanne That's better.

Ann And you will be happy. But until then we must spend the time creatively.

Elise Hurrah.

Ann We will build a new Brackenhurst.

Joanne When Robinson Crusoe landed on a desert island his first instinct . . .

Ann Well what would you do?

Joanne Do as you like. You're in charge.

Ann You find it so easy to criticize. What would you do?

Joanne I don't know.

Ann Really? Elise?

Elise What?

Ann Do I have to do all the thinking?

Elise Mm.

Joanne (*back at window*) Take that thing out of your mouth.

A bell rings incredibly loud.

Ann There's no time to be lost.

Joanne Incidentally, I'm fed up with my room.

Ann Your room will be seen to.

Joanne When I was a projectionist . . .

Elise We don't want to know.

Joanne Do you know the last film I saw?

Elise *Touch of Evil*, Orson Welles, 1957.

Joanne Stupid to claim it's a great film, but it does contain the most wonderful camera-work.

Elise The last film I saw was *Look at Life*.

Ann I haven't been for years.

Elise Called *Loads on Roads*.

Joanne That's late '68 *Look at Life*. Not a very great period at all. Very facile camera-work.

Elise I enjoyed it.

Joanne Crap.

Elise I thought it assured.

Joanne I thought it crap.

Elise I had a really good time.

Joanne What are you trying to get at?

Ann And I never saw it.

Elise You'd have liked it, Ann.

Joanne What are you trying to prove?

Ann Girls, my girls.

Joanne (*faintly*) Oh yes.

> *Ann gets up, throws the chalk into the air. The bell rings again. Yells across the room out of the window*

Ann Get into class.

Joanne Who's teaching?

Elise I am.

Ann Why aren't you in there?

Elise I've given them reading. I put that bossy one in charge.

Ann Is that a sign of a good schoolteacher?

Elise We're appalling schoolteachers.

Ann Come, come.

Joanne Are you going to teach?

Elise No.

Joanne I think I will, then.

> *Exit Joanne.*

Ann I won't have that said.

Elise Why have we only got eight pupils then?

Ann Eleven paid.

Elise Eight stayed.

Ann The eight are very happy.

Elise Freaks.

Ann You're as responsible as anyone.

Elise Agreed.

Ann Though not as responsible as her.

Elise She's not harming anyone.

Ann She's harming my girls. My beautiful girls. I'm sentimental perhaps but I do think girls should be spared her sort of nonsense.

Elise It does them good.

Ann Stop expressing your opinions. They don't help.

Elise Leave off.

Ann You're such a hopeless person. As a person. Don't you wish anything for yourself?

Elise In the words of Isadora Duncan, I would like to be remembered as a great dancer but I fear I will only be remembered as a good bang.

Bell rings yet more insistently.

That's all. The whole thing can probably be blamed on some childhood vitamin deficiency. Or a great rush of air to my legs that sucks men to me. I'm chilly.

Ann It is chilly.

Elise Stop staring at me.

Ann Window.

Elise shuts the window.

Do you think things are very far gone?

Elise Of course.

Ann The parents were not impressed. What do you think of Joanne's plans?

Elise Ridiculous.

Ann She's renamed her study the Women's Liberation Workshop. She says she's teaching dialectics this week instead of gym.

Elise You'll have to fight back.

Ann What do you think of my plans?

Elise Hopelessly naïve.

Ann I like the idea of a new cricket pavilion.

Elise Hopeless optimism.

Ann I'd like a new row of baths.

Elise Hopeless incompetence.

Ann They're currently filthy.

Elise The girls tell me they find it exciting to smoke cigarettes in their baths, the height of decadence.

Ann I'd prefer you didn't talk about the girls smoking in front of me.

Elise You know they smoke.

Ann I do not know they smoke. I don't know that at all. And if they do, Elise, I want it reported to me properly, not slipped into our conversation by subterfuge. I'm only trying my best. (*no response*) There are sixteen too many milk bottles coming every day. This has been going on for nine days. There are 144 spare bottles of milk in various shades of cheese.

Elise Joanne is domestic science.

Ann Joanne is.

Elise She's a constant reproach.

Ann I've told her.

Elise I told her to love life. If you come to Brackenhurst unused, you are sure to be unused for life.

Ann It's not that bad. Fancy a game?

Elise Thank you, no.

Ann Just because you always lose.

Ann is bouncing a ping-pong ball on her bat.

Elise I lose at all the games I play from ping-pong upwards and at Brackenhurst as there's nothing else to do it makes for a very fine time.

Ann starts thwacking the ball hard against the back wall and leaping and grunting to return it.

Ann And that. And that. And that.

Elise If the governors see fit to close the school, we'll all be out of a job.

Ann And that.

Elise Are they all relations of yours?

Ann Mostly.

Elise Look at this dress. Do you think it suits me?

Ann stops ping-ponging. Elise walks manneredly round the room, head high, legs in a straight line.

Ann I've seen it so often I can't tell.

Elise I should have been a model. I would have shown clothes to advantage. I would have loved it. I should have been an actress.
'Thou know'st the mask of night is on my face

Else would a maiden blush bepaint my cheek
For that which thou has't heard me speak tonight.'
Acting. That was Acting.

Ann has returned to her blackboard.

(*loud and black*) O Desdemona!

Ann Look, I think it's all in, come and see.

Elise Where? It looks very nice.

Ann It's taken me four hours that. The children need colour to help them learn.

Elise Why don't you get rid of Joanne?

Ann I am responsible as much to my staff as to the children in my care. I have to think on everyone's behalf.

Enter Joanne.

You're meant to be teaching. Why have you left?

Joanne I got bored. Your children are so stupid. I was reading Schopenhauer at 10 but this lot can't manage an alphabet.

Ann Who's looking after them?

Joanne I left that bossy one in charge – Lucrecia Bourgeois as I call her. She's loving it.

Ann You're the worst of the lot.

Joanne There's a dog, incidentally, crapping on your tennis courts.

Exit Ann fast to tennis courts.

You were talking about me.

Elise Rubbish.

Joanne You changed the subject.

Elise I bet there's nothing on the courts.

Joanne Flabby cow. The jerk. Go and look.

Elise Doesn't bother me.

Joanne Flabby cow.

Elise Child.

Joanne Tit. Withered tit.

Enter Ann.

Elise Well?

Ann There's nothing there.

Joanne You've hardly looked.

Ann I've looked enough.

Joanne The dog's probably gone by now but I doubt if the crap will have fled.

Ann I've looked once.

Joanne Take a proper look.

Ann No.

Joanne Do you want to warp my development or something?

Ann OK.

Exit Ann.

Elise What's out there?

Joanne If she can't see it, that's her problem.

Elise Invention.

Joanne In a situation like this, anything is possible. The ascendant triumph of the mind. The battle pitched in heaven and in hell.

Elise You mean there's nothing out there?

Joanne You must allow for things beyond your understanding.

Elise You mean there's nothing out there.

Joanne The inner eye.

Elise You don't impress me with these antics and you only lose the sympathy of Ann.

Joanne The revolutionary consciousness – my own – admits of no limitation to possible fields of vision. The world is infinite. As soon as anything may be said to have revolutionary essence, it may be said to exist.

Elise Do dogs' stools have revolutionary essence?

Joanne The case of the dogshit is marginal and particular.

Ann is back.

Ann What is the point of all this? You send me hunting . . . I really don't understand you.

Joanne There are things about you I dislike.

Ann Let's simply talk about it.

Joanne It's there if you look for it.

Ann I don't know.

Joanne This is a woman's world.

Ann and Elise reel.

Elise Again!

Ann Nothing to do with it.

Joanne I'm sick of you stamping about like a man gone wrong.

Elise So what?

Joanne If men reappear, if we ever see men again at Brackenhurst, they will have to be fey imitations of women to make any impact at all. Let me tell you this –

Elise Again.

Joanne No, really, listen. Brackenhurst inches the world forward. Brackenhurst is sexual purity. Brackenhurst is the community of women. Nothing is pointed, nothing perverts.

Elise She's off her tiny tits.

Ann Politics again. I've told you about politics.

Joanne I'm talking about women being women.

Elise There are some things a woman doesn't talk about.

Joanne Yes?

Elise And her rights are one.

Ann Her rights is one.

Joanne I'm talking about women being really women, being different from men.

Ann When I edited my school magazine, we made the rule you could write about anything you wanted except sex, religion and politics. I've tried to stick to that rule in life.

Joanne And the dog's crap?

Ann The original point.

Joanne Yes.

Ann Wasn't there. You don't have any respect at all.

Joanne It was there.

Ann There are old-fashioned values and discipline is one.

Joanne Please look again.

Ann If you people wash away the old-fashioned values, what happens to the old-fashioned people who happen to believe in them?

Elise You're not old-fashioned.

Ann There are people riding on the back of those values. You can't shoot the horse away from under them.

Elise It doesn't make sense.

Joanne I've long since lost track.

Ann If I can't discipline my staff into abandoning superficial left-wing feminist nonsense –

Joanne The point of the conversation . . .

Elise (*to Ann*) You don't *have* any values.

Joanne I'm trying to get through to you.

Ann You're just using me.

Joanne Forget it.

> *Pause.*

Ann It's not there. I've combed the ground.

Joanne Thank you.

Elise How did we get into this conversation?

Joanne Forget it.

> *Joanne goes to pour out a Scotch. Pause.*

Ann Feminist nonsense.

Joanne You've never listened, how do you know?

> *Pause.*

Ann In three weeks the chairman of the Governors comes to inspect and we're far from ready.

Elise We ought to have something special to show her.

Ann Let's paint the hall.

Joanne Are you determined to ignore me?

Ann Oh, shut up.

Joanne I won't be ignored.

Elise Does she know there are only eight pupils?

Ann Everyone knows.

Elise Could we keep it from her? Does she know we've lost the Royal child?

Ann Everyone knows.

Joanne It left a damn sight better off.

Ann It hardly profited from the particular trick you taught it.

Joanne Everyone should know.

Ann What you taught that child was not on the syllabus. It was not royal either.

Joanne Royal children are just the same as any others. They should know how to masturbate. It's instinctive.

Ann If it's instinctive, you didn't need to induce it.

Joanne I did not demonstrate, nor did I make any physical gesture of demonstration. I lent it some elementary literature.

Ann Put about by your bloody feminists.

Joanne Masturbation is the only form of sexual expression left to the authentic woman.

Ann I don't see the value of the act.

Joanne There are three of us here. For five hundred, five thousand, five million years, the inferior sex, the sex used, used for their sex: the fingers of the nation sidling for the clit, fingers of power and of government. At Brackenhurst there are only women. Brackenhurst is a new way of life.

Elise Brackenhurst has everything but men.

Joanne Exactly. Brackenhurst inches the world forward. Here at least is a pure ideal. No men.

Ann There are no men here because they might savage the children. It's nothing to do with sexual abstinence.

Elise I'm a normal sort of woman.

Ann I want this to be a tight-knit community.

Elise I am normal.

Joanne This is the battle-ground of the future. From the start there were those who said marry, infiltrate, get in there, and a different crowd who argued – separate, the divorce is total. It's between intercourse or isolation. I favour isolation. After black power, woman power.

Sound of children off has grown audible. Rowdy cheers as if they could hear what Joanne was saying and approved.

Ann Disorder!

Ann stomps to the common-room door, yells out.

If I catch anyone talking, I'll have them on oats and water for a week.

Silence. Ann closes the door very slowly.

Elise That bossy one can't keep order.

Ann All I care about is that you lost us our best pupil.

Joanne The child had asked to be taken away long before it wanked itself off.

Ann Don't be so vulgar.

Joanne I read the letter it wrote a week before it left. It said mummy the dormitory walls are wet and I want out of this hole.

Ann Cruel. Really.

Joanne pours out another Scotch.

Elise She was peculiarly our own.

Joanne She paid the fees.

Ann Her mother paid.

Joanne Her mother was a fool.

Ann Her mother was a queen.

Elise Her father was a bit odd.

Joanne Her father was the queen. He's the only one I admire in this whole rotten business.

Elise It was your fault.

Joanne I hate children anyway.

Elise They sense that.

Joanne They hate me.

Ann They think you're working class.

Joanne I am working class.

Elise Cheltenham's only member of the working class.

Joanne It doesn't mean I'm not.

Ann No more politics. I've had enough.

Elise If you're working class, I'm Brigitte Bardot.

Joanne We're all in the same frig.

Elise And other platitudes.

Joanne Will you stop getting at me?

Elise I won't let you rest until . . .

Joanne Ann, will you tell your assistant to shut up, I'm taking to drink.

Another Scotch

Ann Elise, shut up –

Elise Don't do what she says.

Joanne Have you checked recently for the revolutionary turd?

Ann Of course I have.

Another Scotch

Joanne Then now I'd like you to look for that leak on the roof.

Elise You don't know there's anything there.

Joanne If my bedroom walls are wet, it's a good bet to hunt on the roof for the reason.

Ann You should refer it to the Building Maintenance Committee.

Joanne We are the committee.

Elise We're not in session.

Joanne I'm for your going up.

Elise I'm against it.

Ann I'm chairman.

Joanne Which means you have to vote for. Chairman always does.

Ann Very well, I see I shall have to go, but if this is another of your damnfool tricks . . .

Elise She's having you on.

Joanne I would never . . .

Ann Getting me up on the roof.

Joanne Up, up and to the roo-oof.

Elise It's undemocratic.

Ann I'll do it to keep the peace. I'll do anything to make you happy.

Exit Ann to roof.

Elise You've no right to upset her.

Joanne Let her face facts.

Elise Women's Liberation Workshop!

Joanne She's spent her whole life pretending she's a man. Deserves what's coming to her.

Elise She's just a dear, sweet middle-class girl. Like us all.

Joanne No such thing as middle class. In a capitalist economy, there are only two functions – labour and the organization of labour. People often refer to something called a middle class which suffers mythically from a middle-class morality but there's no such thing. There's the controllers and the controlled.

Elise You don't believe that.

Joanne I do.

Elise And which category do Cheltenham girls fit into?

Joanne That's nothing to do with it. All women are controlled. It's no longer a matter of birth. There's a new system of privilege based on intelligence – or rather a certain sort of acquisitive masculine intelligence that would bend in any direction to smother alternatives. In this society where an active, probing, hopeful intelligence is the sign of being a good bloke, women are valued for one thing – their reproductive facility. They bang like shithouse doors. The alternative society that we create may be black or it may be crippled or it may, let's hope, be female – but it is an alternative. There'll be no moral judgements, or processes of consultation, or export drives, or balance of payments. There is independence of mind and body. The alternative cannot be defined.

Elise Why not?

Joanne By escaping definition it escapes parody and defeat. Brackenhurst is the first real experiment in all-female living.

Elise And this is it? This is it?

Joanne Yes.

Elise This is all-female living? This is the revolution?

Joanne Yes.

Elise What we've got now?

Joanne Yes.

Elise I'd rather not.

Joanne It's only in embryo. We've scarcely begun. I anticipate communal female living on a massive scale – independence of thought among teachers and pupils. I've already begun. I've told the children that you and Ann haven't yet grasped the concept. I teach them to despise Ann because she wants to make Brackenhurst like other societies.

Elise What about me?

Joanne I tell them you're immature because you still want to give your cunt to capitalism.

Elise I've never thought of it that way.

Joanne Do.

Elise I never could. Men are just men to men and there it is.

Ann goes flying down outside the window and lands unseen with a thump.

My God!

Elise makes to dash across the room to the window. Joanne grabs at her and stops her getting there.

She's hurt herself.

Joanne Leave her.

Elise She's fallen off the roof.

Joanne Don't help her, for God's sake, we want a crisis.

Elise Let go of me.

Joanne forces Elise on to the ground and sits on top of her.

Joanne Any intermediate action that serves to reinforce the status quo rather than to restructure the whole system must by very definition be wrong.

Elise Get fucking off me.

Joanne The present situation must be allowed to develop

to a crisis point in order to emphasize to all the needs for the complete overall destruction of the present scheme of things. Let her lie there a bit.

Elise forces Joanne off her and rushes up.

Elise Fucking maniac.

Joanne Liberty! Equality! Sisterhood!

Elise rushes to the window, opens it.

Elise Are you all right?

Ann Slight fall. Nothing at all.

Ann is seen to get up, completely unscathed. Climbs in the window.

Foot must have slipped.

Elise Let me get you a drink.

Ann Please don't bother.

Ann rubs her ankle, but seems unbruised.

I was stretching for the drainpipe when my foot slipped.

Elise You could have been hurt.

Ann I'm pretty tough. I'll go back up.

Ann gets up to go out.

Elise You can't go up now.

Ann Why not?

Elise You've just had a fall.

Joanne Finish the job.

Ann I'll find out what's up there.

Joanne Did you find anything?

Elise You can't go up again right after falling down. It's very dangerous.

Ann Nonsense.

Elise You can't possibly go back.

Ann I promise you it's OK.

Elise (*vehement*) I forbid you.

Ann Elise.

Elise (*still vehement*) There's nothing wrong with the pipe. Stay where you are.

Ann Really, I can't deal with both your tempers.

Elise What are you going up for? Her?

Ann I said I'd have a look.

Elise Her bedroom walls are perfectly dry. I've felt them. Do you know what she's just told me? Do you know what she tells the children?

Joanne goes and pours another drink.

Ann I can imagine.

Elise I wouldn't repeat the things she says about us.

Ann She's free to say what she likes. She's a member of my staff.

Joanne Are you going up on the roof or not?

Ann Of course.

Joanne You'd better go up before it's dark.

Elise Don't you dare.

Ann What?

Elise I suppose you believe this stuff about how she's

miserable at night.

Ann I'd do the same for you.

Elise Kiss my foot.

Ann Huh.

Joanne Let's get on. It must be lovely on the roof.

Ann I'm bound to protect her.

Elise I accept that, Ann, and will you lick my big toe?

Ann Don't be so silly. Ha ha.

Elise Cut my toenails with your teeth.

Ann Don't be so silly.

Elise Cut my toes.

Ann Please let's be friends.

Elise Toes.

Joanne Isn't that sunset beautiful?

Elise Put my toes in your mouth.

Ann Out of sheer embarrassment.

Elise Go on.

Ann You don't . . .

Elise Go on.

Joanne Isn't that the most beautiful sunset?

Ann Come.

Elise Ann.

Ann Elise.

Elise Do what you say.

Ann kneels down and bites the nail off Elise's toe.

Fantastic.

Ann bounds back and away, smiling.

Joanne A girl could almost be happy.

Elise Now lick.

Ann Come.

Elise Lick my toes.

Ann licks Elise's toes.

Joanne Absurd. Ludicrous. Are we meant to take that seriously?

Ann That was nothing.

Ann gets up.

Joanne Why can't people think of anything else when they think of women?

Ann That proved nothing.

Joanne They think of sex.

Ann It doesn't mean anything, Elise. It's quite without significance.

Elise Now do it again but with more tact.

Joanne Lick a toe with tact.

Elise Again.

Joanne How can you lick a toe with tact?

Elise Don't be difficult.

Ann Tact isn't in it.

Elise Don't be difficult.

Ann licks again.

Exactly.

Ann Absolutely.

Joanne Fucking ridiculous.

Ann It just felt good.

Joanne is pouring out another drink.

I'll have a drink, Joanne.

Joanne Get it yourself.

Ann I take it from you now, Joanne, but I'm hard put to take it when the girls are around.

Joanne Some kind of imaginative gleam in me upsets you.

Exit Elise quietly at this line.

Ann I have some status here.

Joanne You know I'm an artist.

Ann I know.

Ann goes to get a drink.

Joanne Not the kind of artist that actually has anything to do with art. I wouldn't touch it eeurch. Culture eeurch. But an artist in the way I am. I want gold cherubs blowing trumpets over my bed and an ivory bathtub to wash in.

Ann Anything.

Joanne Not dripping polystyrene.

Ann It's tiled over to keep it warm.

Joanne It gives me hay fever. I trip daily over those stringy raffia mats on the slippery path to the bathroom, where the basin is slimy with a coat of old toothpaste, other people's spittings of toothpaste and saliva. In this state I fall downstairs to teach eight benighted little sods what – you change the time-table so often I'm doing woodwork when I should be teaching chemistry. I want out of it, my love.

Ann There's nothing I can do.

Joanne I'm determined to leave.

Ann Of course.

Joanne gets two drinks, one for Ann.

Joanne Here at Brackenhurst, a distinctive sound. The heavy breathing that means nothing is happening. At Brackenhurst nothing ever happens. The tedium is quite a challenge, quite an experience. The distinctive English sight of nothing happening and nothing going to happen.

Ann Nothing ever happens at Brackenhurst.

Joanne What was the point of that game with the toes?

Ann That was Elise's idea.

Joanne Ah.

From the nearby classroom, sound of children singing 'The Lord is my Shepherd' in agonized treble.

Ann Elise is teaching again. She has the knack of making them happy. She's a superior teacher. When the Governors come, I'll expect you to behave. I'll expect you to be a positive person.

Joanne You're poisoning me.

Ann I'm quite without malice.

Joanne I've had stomach cramps all week. There's poison in my food.

Ann You must complain to the kitchens.

Joanne You are the kitchens.

Music stops.

Ann You're a child and you're lucky to be here, and it's only because Elise and I love you and look after you that you are able to face life at all, and it's only because we want you to be happy that we protect you. You're a parasite and depend on us, and every night I pray for you, and I'd maybe like you to be somewhat grateful.

Joanne My arse.

Ann You're a schizophrenic, Joanne.

Joanne Cow, flabby cow.

Ann The doctor said you ought to be told.

Joanne Sodden flabby cow.

Ann I'm tired of having to love you.

Joanne I'm sick of your motherly concern.

Ann Schizophrenic garbage.

Joanne Cow.

Blackout on the last word.

During the scene change: 'The Lord Is My Shepherd'

SCENE TWO

Brackenhurst playing-fields. Bright day. Glare. Ann and Elise are lounging in deckchairs, with a high wire fence behind them. They watch the game intensely. Immediately the lights come up they clap.

Ann Very good.

Elise Good.

Ann Very good.

Elise Shot.

Ann She's got a lovely cover drive.

Elise Shot.

Ann Don't let her catch you. Run, for God's sake, run.

Sounds of the game very low.

Elise She's all right.

Ann She will not play off her back foot. She will not move on to it.

Elise I've told her often enough.

Ann I've told her again and again.

Elise The visitors are good. They're undeniably good.

Ann Doesn't it make you glad to be alive? What is it Wordsworth says?

Elise Dunno.

Ann Ah.

Enter Joanne dressed in white.

Joanne God, it's hot.

Ann It's hot or it's cold, you always complain.

Joanne It's a man's game anyway, it's quite wrong for women to play it at all.

Ann They're not a match for our first eleven.

Joanne What eleven? There *are* only eight.

Ann Seven. Another dropped out this morning. The chauffeur came to remove her.

Elise (*gets up*) I can't see why we're so bad at this business.

Ann We're not bad.

Joanne takes Elise's seat.

Elise I know I'm not very clever and, Joanne, you're controversial, Ann, you're a little scaring to the young, but we're no worse than most.

Ann D'you think Benenden has this trouble?

Elise They seem to hold on to their pupils.

Ann You think we're doing something wrong?

Elise There seems to be something missing. The schizophrenic's got my chair.

Joanne It's mine.

Elise We're rather short on facilities.

Ann Oh well done. What a good shot. That was good. I still say a pavilion. That's where we fall down. Everyone should get a prize on Sports Day – things like that. Class tells.

Elise Men in the dormitories.

Ann Elise.

Elise I am pornography.

Ann I am cricket.

They laugh.

Joanne I want to go and see a film. Take your filthy seat.

Elise takes Joanne's seat.

Ann The bus went hours ago and there's not one back today.

Joanne I'll go tomorrow.

Ann No bus tomorrow because it's Thursday.

Joanne I'm walking tomorrow.

Ann It's eighteen miles.

Joanne I'll cycle.

Ann The tyres are flat.

Joanne I want to see a fucking film.

Ann Don't swear.

Elise Shot.

Joanne I'm sick of looking at things live. I want to see them second hand.

Ann When D. H. Lawrence went to the cinema for the first time he found it so – vulgar – he vomited.

Joanne You mean old snipcock.

Elise Joanne.

Ann Lawrence was the most wonderful man of our age.

Joanne Lawrence never got over his amazement that the bits slotted together.

Ann Lawrence loved truth and beauty. Stop this filthy talk. (*Pause.*) Stupid girl has run herself out.

   They clap.

Elise Well played.

Ann Good innings.

Elise Well done.

Ann Very good.

Elise How ugly she is.

Joanne She can't help that.

Elise Never said she could.

Joanne Why pick on me all the time?

Joanne gets up and walks off towards the returning batswoman offstage.

I say, Sarah.

Exit Joanne.

Ann Now.

Elise replaces her own chair with an old deckchair she gets from the fence and sits down in another spot with her original chair.

Elise There.

Ann That one?

Elise It'll do what's required. I prepared it.

Ann It's hardly fair to her.

Elise Don't weaken now.

Ann Excellent. I have very high hopes of this joke.

Elise This is awfully good fun.

Ann Who is in now?

Elise points.

Oh, it's her. She won't score anything.

Elise I hate her.

Ann She's not much.

Joanne enters.

Joanne I said well done to that girl and she said that was no compliment coming from me as I hate cricket.

Elise True.

Joanne I get easily upset. (*Joanne sits in the chair. It collapses.*)

Elise Hurrah, hurrah.

Ann She fell right into it.

Joanne What imagination.

Elise Don't be sarky. You fell right into it.

Joanne Imaginative.

Elise Don't try and get out of it. You fell for it.

Joanne I'm suffering, damn you.

Ann Don't take it so seriously.

Elise Have a little fun.

Joanne Doesn't anyone realize how much I suffer?

Ann We can see.

Elise So can the whole school. All seven.

Joanne You will not take me seriously.

Elise No.

Joanne Isn't there a time to stop joking and –

Elise No.

Joanne You shun me, the girls shun me.

Ann You're making a ridiculous exhibition of yourself. Shut up and sit down.

Joanne What have you got against me?

Elise Relax.

Ann You think we persecute you.

Joanne You poison my food.

Ann You think everyone hates you.

Joanne It's a pathetically ineffective way of poisoning anyone to put arsenic in their food, because it starts coming out in their hair. Look.

Joanne gets up, shakes her head down and runs her fingers through her hair.

Elise Dandruff.

Joanne Arsenic.

Ann We love you.

Joanne You collapse my deckchair.

Elise Joke.

Joanne It's not just you, it's the girls.

Ann You think everyone is against you.

Joanne Let me make myself clear. I didn't come here to be liked. I came for different reasons and it wasn't to entertain you or fartarse on your behalf. I was wrong to be sidetracked. I'm tough as leather as the children say – they hate me. OK. What I set out to do was educate this mob to be themselves. I'm here to teach isolation so I resent the fact I have to mix with you at all. I want every child to know that it's a girl and different for being a girl and better for being a girl. I want a separate culture. I want a different way of life. We're too far gone to want anything but everything – all the way out. I want a self-sufficient child. I want an alternative to everything men are. I left everything I loved, I haven't been to the cinema for I don't know how long, to come to Brackenhurst, to work in a community that was feminine by necessity and make it feminine by choice. You should want to be women. And I found – what did I find – Elise whose idea of the sexual revolution is to open her legs and say AAAAAH and Ann – what can I say? And a combined ability that keeps a tenuous grasp on just seven children. I'll teach them all they need and I don't care if you hate me for it.

Elise It's gone right past square leg.

Ann Oh well hit.

Elise And you teach them – sleight of hand.

Ann Not that incident again.

Elise You teach them dexterity with the Mum rollette.

Joanne What a squalid mind you have.

Ann Let me tell you something, Joanne, that I ought to have told you a long time ago.

Joanne What's that?

Ann No, I can't be bothered.

Joanne You have nothing to tell me.

Ann I'm putting you in charge of the School Corps.

Joanne Over my dead body.

Ann If necessary. I'm appointing you Sergeant Major. It's a position of some responsibility. At Brackenhurst we control the minds of the young. We have the influence to shape their lives. I have listened to you for some time now, Joanne. I've heard your views on power, responsibility, education, the British Press, constitutional monarchy, the race to the moon, the emancipation of women, Lord

Thomson, the Archbishop of Canterbury, cricket, dancing, smoking and masturbation and I'm glad having listened to judge your opinions pure balls and your mind irretrievably shallow.

Elise That's strongly put.

Ann I'm so tired of the political mind.

Joanne breaks away fast to the back.

Joanne Where's the gap in this bloody thing?

Joanne darts back and forth, gives up trying to find a gap, throws herself up on to the wire instead. Ann gets up.

Ann Come back here.

Joanne I'm getting out.

Joanne clambers up towards the top. Ann pursues, catches her leg, pulls at it, brings her to the ground. Joanne up on her feet launches at Ann. Ann throws her over her shoulder to the ground. Helps her up, leads her forward.

Ann Karate specialist, you see. Simple skill worth knowing.

Joanne is sat down gently.

Joanne You hurt me.

Ann Everyone tries a breakout at one time or another.

Elise The third mistress always tries.

Joanne You've let them go before.

Ann The mistresses, not the girls.

Elise The girls are easier to catch.

Ann One girl reached the village but the uniform gave her away.

Elise I thought this was meant to be the ideal community.

Joanne If we are to be grouped together for some social purpose . . .

Elise Social theory.

Joanne But this is a repressive . . .

Ann You are hardly likely to get any farther than anyone before you.

Joanne Masculine . . .

Elise Not on those legs!

Joanne Does no one listen to anything I say?

Elise No.

Joanne I feel victimized.

Ann This school . . .

Joanne Don't bother to go on.

Ann This school . . .

Joanne Don't bother to go on.

Ann This school . . .

Joanne I don't want to hear. We don't want to hear.

Ann This school . . .

Joanne Don't finish that sentence.

Ann This school . . .

Joanne I won't let you.

Ann This school . . .

Joanne You're not to.

Ann This school . . .

Pause. Surprise.

This school has some standards to keep up. And I will murder to maintain them.

Pause.

Joanne I think that sums up things pretty well. From now on war.

Joanne tries minimally to break again, but Ann is on her feet almost before she moves.

Vicious.

Joanne edges back towards Ann's old chair, which she moves away from the other two. Ann is left without one.

Ann Education should be lethal. I think of teaching as a knife.

Joanne Vicious.

Ann We must be very careful what they hear and see. The sight of you, Joanne, is therapeutic. They thank God they're not like you.

Elise It's true.

Ann I use you in my social adaptability classes. Some of the girls have very advanced theories about you.

Joanne Such as.

Ann I use you as an example of the modern woman.

Joanne What about her?

Elise Me?

Joanne Permissiveness.

Elise I wish it was.

Joanne Debauchery, love of body. Isn't she in your classes?

Ann Elise is the Assistant Headmistress.

Joanne That's not what it says on the lavatory wall.

Ann It is really of no consequence. You and I know that, Joanne. We are above such things. I look at Elise.

Elise Don't bother with me.

Ann And pity that pathetic dependence on the body.

Joanne Pathetic.

Elise I'm just backward.

Ann You shudder she's so retarded.

Elise I'm just backward, I like cricket and sex.

Ann Cricket, my God.

Ann runs out to the front of the stage, peers out. Sigh of relief. Claps.

I completely forgot.

Elise Shot.

Ann Very good.

Joanne Nothing has changed.

Elise Excellent.

Ann Excellent. Doesn't it make you glad to be alive? After all your bickering and complaint? It's criminal not to enjoy yourself. I'm so sorry for you, my love.

Joanne Forget it.

Ann But I must ask you to do your duty now. That dreadful woman is signalling which means you must go out and umpire.

Joanne I hate it.

Ann It's your turn.

Joanne I make all the wrong decisions. Everyone gets so angry with me.

Ann Quite right. It makes for a game of chance. Better by far for the character.

Elise I'm always fair.

Ann I always try to throw in some errors of judgement to spite all those frightful girls who are all skill and no charm.

Elise They think it's favouritism.

Ann I'll do your umpiring for you, Joanne, if you'll do my shower duty in return.

Joanne Thank you.

Exit Ann.

Joanne All right, tell me now.

Elise Do you really want to know?

Joanne She trusts you, doesn't she?

Elise She believes I love Brackenhurst.

Joanne It's all a bit improbable.

Elise I don't know the details but I can tell you this much. There are no men at Brackenhurst.

Joanne Tradesmen.

Elise Let's not get political. Tradesmen aren't real men.

Who comes here? A few corn and meat merchants, hardly virile, hardly material for Ann. But . . . she is definitely having an affair with the butcher.

Joanne The butcher!

Elise She says he has capable hands. I'd call them murderous. Real butcher's hands with black hairs on the finger joints – they attract her.

Joanne How disgusting it all is.

Elise She thinks of him a lot. He's called Haskins.

Joanne There's an alliance, a union?

Elise Of course.

Joanne Intercourse on some, on several occasions?

Elise Of course.

Joanne The pig.

Elise Ann told me he was an *energetic* man.

Joanne Things are definitely happening.

Elise Oh yes.

   Pause.

Joanne I knew that it would all come out.

Elise She's a woman of character.

Joanne I can see her across the field. Look, look. Everything other people would have wanted her to be. I daren't be too rude for fear you won't like me.

Elise It's all too far gone for that.

Joanne I feel silly.

Elise It's never stopped you before.

47

Joanne You don't like me anyway.

Elise I do.

Joanne She's capable, lovable, would even be a good mother to a child. She's a fool because she wants to be, like so many old people.

Elise She's 32.

Joanne She's old. Why do they all choose to be like that? The trouble with Ann –

Elise Tell me the trouble with Ann.

Joanne The trouble with Ann –

Elise The trouble with Ann is the trouble with most people. Her life stopped at the age of 18.

Minor uproar on the field.

What's happening?

Joanne Hard to say. I think Ann called a no-ball some time after one of our lot was caught.

Elise Typical decision.

Joanne We must never accept things, never give in.

Elise What use is Ann to you?

Joanne No use. What's the time?

Elise Tea time.

Joanne I haven't worked everything out yet. You must remember I have survived an English education. To have any plan of action at the end of an English education is a triumph.

Elise But you don't have a plan for Ann?

Joanne Brackenhurst is a pure ideal, pure idealism. I had a dream last night. It concerned you. Would you like to hear it?

Elise No.

Joanne I'll tell you.

Elise I should think it was a ballet dancer in flames or a snake in a custard pie.

Joanne Not quite. This was the dream. You were about to have a child, and the rest of us – there were a lot of us – gathered round a table and waited for you to give birth. You were not much inflated, simply we knew you were pregnant. You didn't look it. We knew it in the way you can be sure in dreams. You suddenly asked to be excused, to slip out for a few moments, but I protested. I took an active part because I felt involved which is unusual. I felt so strongly, not towards you, but about you. I wanted to *see* you have the child. You lay down on the table and the first animal came out. There was some discussion among us as to who should have the first bite, but a man interrupted and ate your first child which was a chicken. The second was a fish and I had some. You lay on the table and the wet animals came regularly from you. And we all ate.

Elise You really are a fraud.

Joanne It's true.

Elise You muck around stamping about in our lives.

Joanne I'm just trying to help.

Elise Listen, help yourself.

Joanne How?

Elise Ann's changed. She's gone weak in the heart from knowing Haskins . . . He's your man.

Joanne I want to get at her somehow.

Elise Use the butcher.

Joanne Yes.

Elise The butcher's knife. Look, they're coming in.

Applause.

Joanne It looks like *Accident*. Joseph Losey, 1967. The great Dirk Bogarde.

Elise In for tea.

Joanne They look so fucking happy.

Elise Rah! Rah!

Enter Ann in a white coat.

Ann Smashing game.

Blackout, end of scene.

During the scene change Helen Shapiro sings 'Walking Back To Happiness'.

SCENE THREE

A row of baths in a white-tiled room. Elise alone. She dances a few steps of her 'Walking Back to Brackenhurst' routine in complete silence but with facial expression. Runs suddenly to behind a tiled shower wall. Enter Joanne. A bucket falls on her head. Pain. She jumps up and down once or twice holding her head, hopping ludicrously. Turns. Sees Elise.

Joanne A bucket just fell on my head.

Elise No sense of humour.

Joanne Tit.

Elise I didn't do it.

Joanne Bloody Ann did it. They're out to get me. Last night the chandelier that's over my bed crashed down as I was getting in. It's getting so I daren't move.

Elise It's all in your imagination.

Joanne It was a vow we all took, remember? And it was inherent in the vow that we'd all love each other a little more.

Elise It wasn't specified.

Joanne And we will stick to that?

Elise Yes.

Joanne And there will be a little more – love.

Elise Give me a hand.

Joanne I've a yoyo here I want to mend.

Elise Eh, lass.

Joanne It's not running properly.

Elise Thou wer't born idle and thou shal't cum to nowt.

Joanne That's very good.

Elise It should be. I was born there.

Joanne You come from the North?

Elise Of course.

Joanne I never knew. Was your father a miner?

Elise No.

Joanne Not the other side, not a millowner?

Elise Of course not.

Joanne And you were poor?

Elise Very.

Joanne And did you eat chip butties and go to chapel?

Elise Incessantly.

Joanne Oh, Elise I never guessed you were working class. Why's your name Elise?

Elise They mis-spelt Elsie on the birth certificate.

Joanne And when you were young was it all day trips to Bingley and Huddersfield and Salford and Leeds? Is that how it really was? I see it so clearly. Did your parents fuck loudly in upstairs rooms?

Elise The only person who fucked was my sister. She married early and they came to live with us in the room next door to me. And at nights before I really knew what was happening, she used to cry out suddenly when she reached her orgasm – 'Eh, by gum.'

Joanne How splendid!

Elise It was wonderful. I used to lie there and imagine what it would be like to have a real vaginal orgasm.

Joanne No such thing.

Elise There is.

Joanne Isn't.

Elise Is.

Joanne All orgasms are the same in the female. The idea that there are two kinds has been put about by oppressive males determined to deny women their rightful clitoral pleasures.

Elise Nonsense.

Joanne It's true. Men have consistently attempted to downgrade the clitoris. They claim it is just a withered penis. What arrogance! A withered penis! The clitoris has been scientifically established as having the greatest concentration of sensory nerve endings of any part of a human body, male or female. More than this.

Elise There's more?

Joanne It has also, inch for inch, measure for measure, a far greater erectile capacity than the comparatively dull, insensitive, numb male organ.

Elise Is that really true?

Joanne The satisfaction of the female is correspondingly greater than that of the male. The penis is a poor blunt instrument beside the sensitivity of the delicate amazing clitoris.

Elise Are you a virgin?

Joanne Of course.

Elise Then you don't know what you're talking about.

Joanne You don't have to have felt a penis to know these things. You can make your mind up perfectly adequately from descriptions and drawings.

Elise Help me clean the baths.

Joanne No.

Elise There's an inspection in half an hour. As soon as the Greek dancing's over. And I've got my song to rehearse.

Joanne (*sitting*) Now give us a song!

Elise Do you want to see?

Joanne Please.

Elise For the Governors of Brackenhurst a song, in the modern idiom.

Joanne Come on.

Elise Give us a chance.
Walking back to Brackenhurst
Ump a o ye ye
Had enough of loneliness
Ump a o ye ye
Brackenhurst's the place for me
It's the only place to be.

> *Elise re-practises getting the dance right that goes with it.*

How was it?

Joanne Dreadful.

Elise Why?

Joanne What does it mean? It doesn't mean anything.

Elise I've always wanted to entertain. I'm going to try showbiz when I get out.

Joanne (*up*) Is it easy to do that walk?

Elise Nothing simpler.

Joanne and Elise (*together*)
Walking back to Brackenhurst
Ump a o ye ye
Had enough of loneliness
Ump a o ye ye
Brackenhurst's the place for me
It's the only place to be.

Joanne I'm coming along.

Elise Very good.

Joanne (*singing*) 'I'm Singing In The Rain'. Gene Kelly.
1951. I never thought to have any talent. Look, I'll show
you how to do the Gene Kelly.

She dances, rather slowly, but with some beauty.

Elise I've got work to do.

Joanne (*snatching the brush*) Let someone else do the
work.

Elise Give me that. I've got to do it.

Joanne Why?

Elise Ann told me to.

Joanne So?

Elise I'll report you.

Joanne What do you think you're doing, Elise, obeying
her?

They process round with Elise trying to get the brush.

Are you really going to spend your entire life imagining
penises of amazing thrust and magnitude – phantom
penises – alternately fucking and obeying, laying down
under men whatever they say? Lying down under Ann?

Elise Give me the brush.

Joanne Use your claws. And counting your shares? You
see, I've found out about the shares in Shell Oil and ICI
and Marks and Spencer and –

Elise Good shares!

Joanne Class traitor – a working-class girl with shares in
Dow Chemicals. A very good share the napalm share as
long as the war holds. Supply and demand – very much a

seller's market nowadays in napalm.

Elise I'm putting it aside for my old age.

Joanne tosses her the brush.

Joanne Quite so.

Elise sets to work cleaning one bath while filling another with water.

Elise You've been hunting through my papers.

Joanne I'm fascinated by your private life. I find it studded with young bucks.

Elise You have read everything in my room.

Joanne Everything. If we're to live together, make this community work, then we must know everything about each other, so we're strong in each other.

Elise Not much strength in my things.

Joanne I don't know.

Elise Quite the opposite. I don't like you hunting about, trying to make me political.

Joanne Make you? We're all political. We're in politics up to our eyeballs, in the shit, God help us.

Joanne throws Ajax over the floor as she speaks.

Elise What's that for? Help me scrub.

Joanne No.

Elise Ann'll see to you. Wait till I tell her. What is that for?

Joanne It's for Ann to clean. Principles of guerrilla warfare. I am fighting back where least expected.

Ann enters in Greek costume.

Ann Did you grease the bottoms of the Greek dancers' shoes?

Elise Did she do that?

Joanne Not saying.

Ann They're falling about like skittles in there. I'm going to have a word or two to say. Free form and bodily expression it's meant to be, and you've got them tumbling about showing their knickers in front of the Governors. Clean up that mess on the floor, Joanne. If you won't help, then you'll have to go.

Joanne Suits me.

Ann Are these chairs not done, Elise, mercy, and the Governors not five minutes away?

Joanne From where I'm standing I can see the butcher calling at the door. He's knocked twice and looks like giving up.

Ann I'll go down and speak to him.

Joanne I think it's a delivery, I'll see to it.

Ann Please, I can manage.

Joanne I am Domestic Science, I can go.

Ann I am Kitchens, I will.

Joanne The Governors are waiting for you in the Hall.

Ann Out of my way.

Joanne Let me.

Ann Quick or he'll go.

Joanne Exactly. Back to the Greek dancing.

Ann I want to see the butcher.

She gets by.

Joanne There's nothing between his legs you couldn't find elsewhere.

Ann Vulgar. Heartless child.

Joanne So?

Ann You're fired.

Ann rushes out. Joanne yells after her.

Joanne If a lascivious and debauched headmistress can't even . . .

Elise drudges on. Joanne turns back.

I'm out of it. She's just let me go. And there's a Warner Brothers Retrospective at the National Film Theatre and I just couldn't be happier.

Elise What about our community?

Joanne The mistake of any doctrinal group is to render itself monolithic. In other words, intercourse or isolation? I'm leaving. I must take my practical experience of a feminist community – Brackenhurst – to my sisters in the outside world. Who can benefit from what I learnt here.

Elise She won't let you go.

Joanne To show women everywhere they don't have to lie down for anyone.

Elise You haven't done anything here. You haven't gone one inch towards helping any woman here.

Joanne I've got that woman on the run. This place'll never give off that dreadful masculine chill again. Look, she's chasing the butcher down the drive.

Elise You've closed the whole place down.

Joanne Well, that's good, isn't it? Are you going to run that bath all day? Dawn. An empty street. A delicatessen. Goldstein's delicatessen. A scrap of paper blowing down the cardboard street. A streetlight still lit. Two boys dressed in something like tweed and urchin caps, sly as hell with shining faces. A brick, a window, they throw it through, hands into the cooked meat counter but the alarm's gone and we're on our way into another Warner Brothers Retrospective season.

Elise has turned the bath off. Ann has entered. Joanne continues to fanfare the Retrospective.

Ann You know I don't mind about all the troubles, Joanne, that have set you aside from the rest of us, your being an artist and therefore different. But the point must be made. You live in a world of your own, and you must control your fantasies.

Ann throws her a leg of lamb. Joanne catches it.

You are Domestic Science.

Joanne You sacked me.

Ann That remains to be seen.

Joanne I'm dismissed. (*threatening with the joint*) I promise you.

Ann We need you far too much.

Elise Far too much.

Ann There's no need for that now, Elise. The Governors have gone.

Elise What about my song?

Ann Keep it for another time.

Elise My song.

Ann There are very few Governors left. A few more Governors than pupils in fact, but not very many all the same.

Ann has been standing at the back. She drops to her knees.

God, why I allow it I will never know.

Joanne (*gently*) Let me go. There are only five pupils. You don't need three teachers.

Ann Where would you go?

Joanne I'd work in the cinema again.

Ann You couldn't cope, it's become terribly hard work. They have seventy-millimetre equipment. That's man's work.

Joanne There's no ready reason . . .

Ann (*no longer resigned but really angry*) You're as much sold on this place as the rest of us. (*recovering*) Isn't she, Elise?

Elise Yes.

Joanne Why do you want me to stay?

Ann Because we love you.

Joanne Why do you love me?

Ann Because you're you. You're my testament to Brackenhurst, I remember the Princess said to me –

Joanne Snob.

Ann The Princess said – 'Why employ somebody with such a feeble grasp of reality?' She meant you. 'Your Highness,' I replied, 'here we care.' And her Highness answered and I was very moved by this, 'Perhaps in the

kingdom of the mind the sane are mad and the mad sane.'
Such a way she said it. And they say royalty aren't
intellectuals. They aren't in the way you are, Joanne:
neurotic and miserable, trying to make us all sad.

Joanne She still took her kid away.

Ann You drive everyone away. The Governors fled so fast
you might have thought the house was on fire. Your feminist
appeals strike no chord in women and simply repel men.

Joanne Good. It was a real disappointment to me when
you gave in. Chastity was something of a passion of mine.
To have held off for so long, Ann, and then to give in to
the butcher – a fine man, a working man, an artisan,
certainly. But not the man you deserve, through no fault of
his own a victim, poor sod, one of the sodding people.

Ann I'm a cumbersome performer. I don't count myself
very much. I haven't laid bare great golden fields of
happiness I'd care to tell you about. I don't have simple
sexual needs. No one who teaches at Brackenhurst does.
We're all in the Freud and underpant class. The men I've
known leave soon afterwards. But my experience of men is
what makes me a woman.

Joanne How grotesque.

Ann Grotesque it may be to you whose experience of sex
is the Brackenhurst changing-rooms in among the
brassières, but to those of us –

Elise Do keep it down –

Ann You're on my side.

*Joanne leaps on to the end of the bath facing the
audience.*

Joanne All my suffering! I shall crop my hair like Joan of
Arc. Dreyer 1926.

She falls face downwards into the water, comes up.

Extravagant gesture.

But Ann is over at the side of the tub and speaks at once.

Ann While you're there, Joanne, listen.

Elise takes Joanne's other arm and they support her head over the edge of the end of the bath.

The world is not divided into two. The bad and the good and the women and the men. Do you understand that? Do you understand?

Joanne I don't believe it.

Ann and Elise duck her head and hold it under the water.

Ann Can you hear me?

Ann and Elise lift her head out.

All right, do you feel better? You've caused a lot of trouble with your views. Let's get this straight. I am a woman and I'm inferior to men. The woman's place is below, beneath and under men.

Joanne It's not.

Ann and Elise duck her head and hold it under the water.

Ann I will fight to the death for my right to be inferior. Inferiority is a privilege I wish to preserve. I don't want to be equal. And I don't want my girls equal. And I don't want a socialist community.

Ann and Elise lift her head out.

Joanne Now it comes out.

Ann pushes her down repeatedly and hard into the water.

Ann See what I want? See what I want?

Elise Leave her alone.

Ann I'm losing my pupils, my Governors, my school, my self-respect.

Elise Leave her alone. Let's go for a drink.

Ann lets go of Joanne. Ann and Elise leave.

Ann (*as they go*) Yesterday she handed all the girls a jar of Vaseline.

Exeunt.
Joanne gets dripping out of the bath.

Joanne Very good, excellent.

Blackout, end of scene.

During the scene change: Henry Mancini.

SCENE FOUR

Common Room. Ann and Elise are at opposite ends of the room, well dressed. They're pissed, but elevated not slurring.

Ann Drink?

Elise You can take me out tonight.

Ann goes to get a drink.

With the present shortage of men you may take me out.

Ann Thank you.

Elise Don't be shy.

Ann What would you like?

Elise Scotch.

Ann Go mad and have a Campari.

Elise I'll have a Scotch.

Ann My first . . .

Elise What? Go on, say.

Ann (*mumbling*) Lovely dress.

Elise Thank you.

Ann Lovely.

Elise Huh huh.

Ann You've got the figure for it, too. So slim.

Elise Flat-chested. I've always had small breasts.

Ann I didn't imagine they'd shrunk.

Remark is unreasonably funny. They laugh.

Oh very good. So far very good.

Elise It doesn't convince me for a moment. I feel exceedingly foolish. I'd never laugh at a joke like that.

Ann I was perfectly well in there.

Elise It's not a bit realistic.

Ann I wish I had your breasts.

Elise You're welcome to them.

Ann I don't know what it is people like about big breasts.

Elise Don't be absurd. Absurd. If you ever talked like – a man would fly if you said that.

Ann Who's the man?

Elise You are.

Ann So?

Elise So . . .

Ann I make the rules.

Elise You can't have it both ways. Are you a man?

Ann I'm the bloody man.

Elise Then no breasts. Breasts are out. You may comment on mine but you may not refer to your own.

Ann I knew when I first met you that here was someone very warm, very responsive, who would understand the troubles – in my life immediately.

Elise A great improvement. Certainly . . .

Ann A lot of people want the physical thing.

Elise That's my experience.

Ann But when somebody special –

Elise Absolutely the same thing with me.

Ann Then there is an immediate – I want a word.

Elise Rapport –

Ann Rapport –

Elise Yes?

Ann It's going to be more than physical. Though of course it may be physical as well.

Elise As well. Of course.

Ann It will in fact be better for the physical thing will be based on something real.

Elise That's tremendously exciting.

Ann It will be based on our respect for each other's minds.

Elise Rather than our bodies.

Ann You know.

Elise I know.

Ann Don't you think we have something?

Elise Ann, I've no sooner sat down than –

Ann I don't mean to rush you.

Joanne enters unseen at the back of the stage, but they realize.

Elise And in front of Joanne.

Ann and Elise burst out laughing.

There've been others, Ann.

Ann I know.

Elise Oh I don't mean others physically, though there have been others – physically. I mean I'm not young enough to imagine . . . Let's say I've woken up more times than I've been to bed. I'm not young enough to think things will ever be different.

Ann I don't want to crowd you out.

Elise No.

Ann I mean it.

Elise Yes.

Ann No I mean –

Elise Listen.

Ann Yes.

Elise We'll have a go.

Joanne Is this a private game or can anyone join in?

Elise It is for two players.

Ann Elise and I.

Elise Love is not a game. The love of a man –

Ann Here played by me –

Elise For a woman –

Ann Elise –

Elise Is the yolk of the cosmic egg. The good bit.

Joanne I see you're going to be foolish all night.

Elise I've come from the graveyard where my father is buried into the light of a room where a man sits and waits not attending the service, not invited. His room has white walls and enough books to go round and – oh – he has, I cannot describe, it he has wise eyes and is peaceful and well liked and contented in the evening, and can forget, is able to forget.

Ann I'm walking with a dog across a hillside and can see the farm where he is mending a barn door at which he is hopeless, as he is at most practical things, but I keep it in me that I don't think he's very good at things, as he is nice and as he is a bit soulful.

Joanne I'm lying with my legs open being licked off by a dog. He is brave and nice and has wise eyes.

Ann Your hair's all wet.

Joanne I fell in the bath.

Ann I hope it taught you a lesson.

Elise Describe his prick.

Ann Uncircumcized.

Joanne You've got slovenly minds and worse bodies and why I should expend this energy on you I don't know. What's wrong is not the system but that you poor cheap victims of the thing should absurdly see yourself as winners.

Elise There's something in what she says.

Ann I admire her for saying it.

Elise She's certainly got guts.

Ann And a hell of a way with words.

Elise You've got to admire her.

Ann Now shut up.

Elise How long's his prick?

Ann Never measured it. Too satisfied to care.

Joanne If the length of a man's penis were the measure of his worth then life would fall very easily into place.

Elise At my husband's school –

Joanne Your what? Your husband?

Elise I am married, you know.

Joanne I never knew that.

Ann Roger.

Joanne You're married? And you persist in this fantasy that marriage is good and men were made for women?

Elise Like falling off a horse. You get back on again.

Joanne My God!

Elise You carry on. I've still got his shares. If the facts of all this depress you, let's stop now rather than carry on. Roger meant lots to me, more than you could guess from the transcript of the divorce proceedings which is in itself an unsung opera.

Ann If the memory of him obtrudes into our lovemaking.

Elise We must go on.

Ann Is Joanne in the way?

Elise Leave her.

Joanne Babylonian whore.

Ann If when I feel you you can feel no pain.

Elise Relax.

Ann Can we make it? Over the years and past the debris into the rosetrees and the valley.

Elise Over the hollyhocks and the chrysanthemums into the waterfall and the clearing past the breakfasts and the crying and the –

Ann Rosetrees.

Elise Past the rosetrees into a clearing. Help me into the clearing.

Ann Can we make it?

Elise (*loud and black*) O Desdemona! (*loud but not black*) Heaven forfend that I, to whom thou hast entrusted love, here, here on this teeming soil, that hast our meeting here entrusted to the earth, should, with mine own hand, pluck my dagger from my side, and with deliberate stealth make to plunder that which I have made my own.

Ann Hush sweet Ophelia, let not the ardour of thy love thy temper overthrow.

Elise If we settled in advance for less than what we wanted, admitted from the start it was impossible to do the thing properly, would that be more satisfactory?

Ann No.

Elise Is there a way, could there be a way of starting a relationship that wasn't going to end in confusion and turning away at parties to avoid the eye of the person who knew you?

Ann Maybe someone whose balls you've played with while they were asleep.

Elise Is there a way of coming to them and looking them in the eye and being honest and free?

Ann If I took you, if I took you inside me –

Elise Other way round.

Ann Sorry, if you took me inside you, would you wonder if I cried suddenly at night or fled to London or forgot a meeting.

Elise How can I tell you what an affair with a woman like me would be like? I'm flirtatious, horribly romantic and unreliable.

Ann And as a man, I'm prone to sudden anger, like a lion in the way I am.

Elise I'm like a cheetah.

Ann I'm like a lion.

Elise I'm like a gnu.

Ann I'm like a hippopotamus.

Elise If there were some way of expressing to you directly the likelihood, the probability of disaster, then you might back away and say you didn't want to get hurt.

Ann If you could see as I do the hope of the world lying in women being different from men, I've always put them on a pedestal – they're kinder and better able to cope.

Elise In this whirligig.

Ann In this vortex.

Elise In this whirligig there are no masters. There is man. There is woman.

Ann There is desert.

Elise Desert?

Ann Against the elements, man, woman.

Elise There is desert. I wish it were possible. What do you think?

Joanne I think you're nuts and we've been through this before.

Elise But this time a real relationship –

Joanne The number of times I've heard you say you were a gnu and Ann respond with the unlikely information that she's a hippopotamus are really beyond counting. If it ever came to anything, I wouldn't mind, but the evening drags on until the gnu turns to the hippopotamus and says shall we watch *News at Ten*?

Elise There ought to be a way of starting a relationship as you mean to go on. What happens now?

Ann I don't know. You've done more of this than I have.

Elise That's not a very nice thing to say.

Ann I'm sorry. I didn't mean it.

Elise Forget it.

Ann Elise, let it be now.

Elise Are you ready?

Ann I can't wait.

Elise I'm so scared at this stage.

Ann This is an inevitable stage. Think of it as expression.

Ann and Elise confront.

Elise.

Ann puts her hand on Elise's breast.

Joanne Stop.

The interjection is routine. Ann and Elise ignore it.

Stop.

Ann Why?

Joanne In front of me.

Ann Undress.

Ann steps back. Elise turns away from Joanne towards Ann and takes off the top of her dress. Her breasts are bare.

Incredible.

Elise turns round to Joanne, turning her back on the audience, lets the top drop to the floor. Pause. Joanne faints.

Blackout as she goes down. End of scene.

SCENE FIVE

Two beds, side by side, but not touching. Joanne is sitting up in one reading Sight and Sound. *Elise is buried invisibly deep in the other.*

Joanne 'The lyric fluency of Ozu is the nearest the Japanese cinema gets to Chekhov.' Discuss.

Elise grumbles in her sleep.

'Lee Marvin represents not just capitalist man in a state of repressed aggression, but the entire *Weltanschauung* of contemporary American life.' Oh yes.

Elise turns again.

Elise What time is it?

Joanne Five.

Elise Morning?

Joanne Afternoon.

Elise What's happening?

Joanne Ann is teaching chemistry. I am reading drivel. Are you feeling any better?

Elise No.

Elise comes up from under the covers, goes over to the mirror.

Joanne 'Donald Duck's dribblings of premature ejaculation symbolize the failure of Western man . . .'

Elise is looking at herself hard in the mirror and interrupts.

Elise Can you see anything?

Joanne No.

Elise It's coming all right. I have a sudden passion for pineapple. I'd really love a slice of pineapple.

Joanne Yesterday it's prunes, today it's pineapple. You don't fool anybody.

73

Elise Won't anyone believe me?

Elise exercises. Left hand to right foot, right hand to left foot

Joanne You'll damage the little bastard.

Elise Give it a lively ride.

Elise starts running on the spot.
singing as she runs:
We are from Roedean
Good girls are we
We take care of our virginity
And again and again
And again and again
Right Up Roedean School
Up School Up School

As Elise sings, Joanne draws the curtains and winter afternoon light pours into the dark room.

I'll make the little bastard glad he was born.

Joanne You're so sure it's a boy.

Elise I want a boy. You believe me then.

Joanne I think it shows great imagination.

Elise You believe it exists.

Joanne I think it's the most wonderful thing.

Elise goes back to bed.

Elise I don't want to do myself damage.

Joanne Of course not. (*Joanne tucks her in.*) I still say you've been screwed.

Elise And I say I haven't.

Joanne It doesn't happen like that.

Elise It happened this time.

Joanne You can't be pregnant if you haven't been laid. It's never happened before.

Elise Once.

Joanne That doesn't count.

Elise I may have a Messiah.

Joanne You'll never convince me. It was a vow, a vow mutually agreed. No men. Pure feminism, pure love. Brackenhurst inches the world forward. You agreed.

Elise I never agreed.

Joanne (*throwing away* Sight and Sound) I won't read this rubbish. It was agreed between us that it was possible to create a society of women. That was fine. As long as no one betrayed the ideal, I tolerated dissent. But then Brackenhurst fell apart. Brackenhurst is pure feminism. Brackenhurst inches the world forward. The falling apart was in this manner: Ann laid, Haskins responsible, retribution strangely transferred to you.

Elise She got the fun, I got the baby. She and I were very close.

Joanne Exactly.

Elise You don't resent us loving each other?

Joanne You're not in love. It is a conspiracy.

Elise There was very little else around.

Joanne I am very little else, I suppose.

Elise You're not really mature. And you seem to provide yourself with all the loving you need.

Joanne Brackenhurst inches the world forward. I've taken to smoking.

Joanne lights a cigarette.

Elise Not the only sign of decay.

Joanne My hair's falling out with arsenic poisoning and my nails have gone soft.

Elise It's all fantasy.

Joanne You thinking yourself pregnant and me thinking myself dead.

Elise Murdered.

Joanne Yes.

Elise Why should she want to kill you?

Joanne Why does she keep me here?

Elise You're her pupil, really. You're the only one now, apart from that one downstairs.

Joanne I always knew Bossy Lucrecia would outlive the rest.

Ann Ann has made her Head Girl.

Joanne As she's the only one, it's not much of an honour.

Elise Symbolic.

Elise takes out her knitting from under the covers.

Joanne Ugh, motherhood suits you. How can you?

Elise What?

Joanne Knit. Aren't you ashamed? Doesn't it mean anything to be cast in a forever and always role of the most blatant submission?

Elise I like it.

Joanne Have you never wanted to change?

Elise Women have babies.

Joanne So?

Elise It's biological. They dive for the breast.

Joanne But the care of babies? Is that all you look forward to?

Elise I spent the first half of my life on my back. I want something to show for it.

Joanne But the two should be connected. Years of indulgence – nothing. Then you stop and suddenly you're pregnant. Now you'll spend the rest of your life tending a kid while life happens around you.

Elise Nothing ever happens at Brackenhurst.

Joanne I don't mean Brackenhurst, I mean the world.

Elise Brackenhurst inches the world forward, Brackenhurst . . .

Joanne All right. That can't be all you want.

Elise My mother was a Communist. She had three houses, a large private income, a couple of scarcely literate novelist lovers and a small pink card that said she was a member of the Communist Party. My father had very little to do with her apart from their initial union, a policy he was wise to maintain for all his thirty-seven years. Spent mostly as a schoolteacher before his early death when a gold crucifix suspended from the ceiling of Chartres Cathedral fell on his head. Hence my hatred of religion. And of teaching. So I wasn't very political from the start. My mother's money was in patent medicine. My father's heart was in culture. Which is probably why I'm sick of watching you two fight it out. I've never seen the need to get that worked up.

Joanne I thought you were working class.

Elise I never said so. I shall devote my life to rearing children.

Joanne It soon won't be necessary. This might interest you.

Joanne has picked up a book from the side of her bed.

There are 46 chromosomes in each human cell. Did you know that? In each cell. Of these 46, two are the sex chromosomes, determining sex. Now both sexes have in common one X chromosome, and in the woman the other sex chromosome is an X as well. Whereas in the man it's a Y. The woman is XX, the man XY. That Y is an impurity, a biological accident that is being slowly eradicated by natural development, which is working towards the purest form. Pure XX – female as we call it today.

Elise Babies?

Joanne Some other method.

Elise A better method?

Joanne (*mocking*) Who knows?

Elise And will there still be love?

Joanne If you want it.

Elise Pleasures of the body?

Joanne Pleasures of the mind.

Elise I don't want your evolution.

Joanne No choice.

Elise And will we ever be happy?

Joanne Don't be trivial.

Elise I don't call it – ow, it kicked.

Elise shoots up to the top of the bed.

Joanne Impossible.

Elise I felt it.

Joanne I believe you felt it, but I don't believe it kicked. Taste this.

Elise What is it?

Joanne holds up a transparent bag of white stuff.

Joanne This is my mashed potato. We had it for lunch, I'd like you to try some. It's poisoned.

Elise Eugh, it's vile.

Joanne Taste some, titface.

Elise puts a finger in, scoops, and gingerly tastes.

Elise Mashed potato.

Joanne I said.

Elise I think it's very good.

Joanne Are you getting that bitter taste – acid tinge?

Elise No. How did you get it?

Joanne I scooped it off the plate when Ann wasn't looking. It's blatantly poisoned. I have to get rid of it.

Joanne throws it expertly out the window.

There's quite a pile out there, but no one ever notices. I wouldn't tell anyone but you.

Elise There's no one else to tell.

Joanne True.

Elise We ought to see more people.

Joanne I've suddenly seen what's dogged me all along. Ann is the father of your child.

Elise Hardly.

Joanne The X chromosome ascends.

Elise Ha ha.

Joanne I've been thinking all day about your story and there's one thing missing. Where's the man?

Elise Do you think I like being abnormal?

Joanne It's biologically possible. Ann is the father.

Elise When it first happened I was hell's ashamed. Who wants a baby and not know how?

Joanne It's obviously Ann's.

Elise You agree it exists.

Joanne I've changed my theory to fit the facts.

Elise How could Ann have done it?

Joanne You remember that night?

Elise I'm not asking when, I'm asking how.

Joanne What was that business about, the night I fainted? The night you did your act in front of me?

Elise Oh. Joke.

   Pause.

Joanne This child's not going to do what you want. It won't get you out of here. It is incestuous offspring of this place.

Elise It is the hope I have of happiness.

Joanne I'm sorry for you then. I'm changing for supper.

Joanne goes behind the screen.

Elise There's no need to dress behind there.

Joanne Doesn't matter.

Elise I wouldn't be embarrassed to see your body.

Joanne Please.

Elise I'd quite like it.

Joanne I don't want to be watched all the time.

Elise There's no need to be so prudish.

Joanne I am not a prude. I just –

Elise What?

Joanne For Christ's sake leave me alone.

Elise Body body body body body.

Joanne AAAAH!

Silence. Joanne still behind the screen

Elise Joanne. Joanne, are you all right? Are you OK in there?

Elise gets out of bed, goes towards the screen, passing the mirror, so she stops a second, stands sideways, looks to see if she's any fatter, pats her stomach, goes on, stops.

Joanne.

Elise goes behind the screen, as Joanne comes round the front unseen, creeping round to the very front, sits down on the floor.

Joanne.

Joanne And your child will very probably be stillborn.

Elise comes out from behind the screen.

Elise You worried me.

Joanne Not really.

Elise If I have a boy I'll call it Joseph, but if it's a girl Joanne.

Joanne Ha ha.

Elise I mean it. You don't know how much I love you.

Joanne Elise, will you please be quiet?

Elise You don't know how easy you are to upset. You're a joy.

Enter Ann.

Ann (*coming fast through*) Lucrecia's chemistry is definitely improving.

Ann goes immediately behind the screen.

Joanne Daddy!

Ann (*from behind the screen*) Are you any better, Elise?

Elise I'm sure I'm pregnant.

Ann comes out with a hypodermic needle with a little bottle of liquid on the end.

Ann I'm giving everyone flu injections this year to prevent the school grinding to a halt.

Ann holds the needle up to the light and pulls back the plunger.

Joanne Don't bring that thing near me.

Elise Nor me. In my condition it'll upset nature's balance.

Ann (*pointing to a pile of sheets in the corner of the room*) Joanne, I told you.

Joanne Very well.

Ann (*smiling*) Lucrecia –

> *Exit Ann.*
> *Joanne moves round to Elise's bed.*

Joanne Out of bed, earth mother, I've got to change your sheets.

Elise Do you think she's murdering our last pupil?

Joanne Pump her full of vitamins to keep her breathing, more like.

> *Joanne is changing the sheets on Elise's bed. Elise has gone to lie on the third [vacant] bed.*

Get off that bed, heffalump.

Elise Why?

Joanne (*moving to stand at the top of it*) It's mine.

Elise Pardon. (*Moves to centre bed.*)

> *Joanne goes back to changing the sheets on Elise's bed.*

I wonder if things will be better next term.

Joanne They'll never get better. There'll be no change. We could be shitting gold bricks here and no one would come to sweep up the dung after us. People don't like Brackenhurst. It's like all the other useless institutions – schools, ministries, theatres, museums, post offices – people will go a long way to avoid them. Look at those lawns and flowerbeds and fountains. Nobody wants to go where people gather. Who wants it?

Elise There's mud on my slippers, Joanne. On my slippers, mud.

Enter Ann, with a spent hypodermic. Heads behind screen to replace it.

Ann, there's mud on my slippers.

Ann Well, Sherlock, tell me what you think.

Elise I haven't been out of the house in them. (*picking some off*) Look.

Joanne is by now at work on the centre bed.

Joanne, did you borrow my slippers for your agricultural class?

Joanne Of course not. I mean, yes.

Ann No, you mean yes?

Joanne I admit it, yes.

Elise You planted vegetables in my slippers.

Joanne Not in them. Wearing them. That's how the mud got on them, sorry.

Elise The pom-poms will wilt if you get them wet.

Joanne It's all in the past.

Ann has joined Joanne working on centre bed. Pause.

Ann You're cheerful, Joanne.

Joanne I'm sorry, does that spoil the atmosphere?

Ann Not at all.

Pause.

Elise There's a trail of mud in fact right across the room.

Joanne It leads from the vegetable patch to your bed.

Elise Not that way it doesn't.

Joanne I'll do this bed, while you finish that.

Joanne is over at the third bed, taking with her all the dirty sheets which she puts down by the side of the bed.

Ann I'll help.

Joanne It's OK.

Ann Don't put those dirty sheets on the floor.

Joanne They're dirty.

Ann No need to make them dirtier.

To avoid Ann picking them up, Joanne chucks them over to Elise, who is back on her own bed.

Joanne You look after them.

Elise (*opening them out*) They're incredibly dirty.

Joanne (*moving to the far side*) I'll do this side.

Elise Joanne, have you been growing vegetables in your bed?

Joanne No.

Ann No you mean yes?

Joanne No I mean no.

Elise Well the world must be fighting its way through the floor.

Ann is by now at the bottom of the bed. She lifts up the bed, there's a muddy blanket underneath which she casts aside, then lifts up the floor. Reveals hole, shovel, etc.

Ann You're tunnelling your way out.

Joanne *The Great Escape*, John Sturges, 1963.

Ann You've ruined my parquet floor in your malicious attempt to escape.

Joanne I thought I'd get away with it.

Ann You thought I wouldn't notice great piles of earth you've been throwing out the window.

Joanne I've been trying to mix it with the soil.

Ann What about the great white patches of cold mashed potato, then?

Joanne That's poisonous potato. You can see the plants have died out there.

Ann The plants have suffocated under the weight of garbage you pour on to them.

Joanne It was the only place to put it.

Ann What were you doing in the first place?

Joanne I wanted out.

Ann You could have come and spoken to me. I would have listened.

Joanne I know.

Ann Quiet, wait till you're spoken to. *Expectavi orationem mihi vero querelam adduxisti.*

Ann moves to the downstage table and sits down. Joanne shrugs at the Latin.

Joanne Look how far I got, look how near I was to getting out.

Ann (*taking up her writing-pad*) I knew all the time.

Joanne Like that dog. You know about that.

Ann It's your fault walking in the grounds at night.

Joanne You didn't tell me you starved the thing. I was the first meat it had seen in weeks.

Ann Alsatians can go for long periods without food.

Joanne Just see how near I was.

Elise is knitting again.

Elise Second bootee finito. Leggings now.

Ann (*holding up the letter she's written*) 'Dear Mum, How are you? It's been a long time since I've written but we've been terribly busy this term – always like this in the Christmas term. I've hardly had time to sit down. What can I tell you about Brackenhurst?' (*Starts writing.*)

Joanne I thought the hols were very quiet. Through the summer months I dug so gently into the earth, towards great peacefulness, great rest.

Ann 'These are not days, mother, in which private education is much valued. I sometimes feel we are out of step with this generation. It is a constant struggle to keep in tune with new ideas. However, a new cricket pavilion will go some way . . .' (*She returns to writing.*)

Joanne I'm giving myself a time limit. If I'm not out of here by the time that child is born, I'll kill myself.

Elise Agreed.

Ann 'How is father? How is his face? Joanne and Elise send you their love. They are a constant source of help to me.'

Joanne I'm going to be sick. (*She rushes out.*)

Ann 'We have Mrs Reginald Maudling coming for speech day next year. Rather a catch. Love, Ann.' Elise, you remember mother?

Re-enter Joanne.

Joanne Poisoner.

Ann What?

Joanne You're poisoning me.

Ann How do you know?

Joanne Oesophagal pain, vomiting, bloody diarrhoea with traces of mucus, weakness, jaundice, restlessness, headache, dizziness, chills, cramps, irritability, paralysis, polyneuritis, anaesthesias, paresthesias, hyperceratosis of the palm and soles of the feet, cirrhosis of the liver, nausea, abdominal cramps, salivation, chronic nephritis in the cardiovascular system, dependent oedema, cardiac-failure.

Ann Remedy?

Joanne holds up a small bottle in her hand.

Joanne Dimercaprol. Complete recovery six months.

Blackout. End of Scene Five.

SCENE SIX

The Common Room, devastated in the cause of slipper hockey. A large table with a blackboard at the back covered in scores. Elise is umpiring at the back. All three are wearing tennis skirts.

Ann The hockey championships of Brackenhurst.

Joanne This is serious.

Ann The serious championship.

Joanne We need a fourth.

Elise I'm no good anyway, I'd as soon give up.

Joanne Certainly not. This is to the death.

Elise I can scarcely get across the pitch. I'm so far gone.

Joanne And here at Brackenhurst the tension is well nigh unbearable, with three prima donnas of the hockey circuit ranged in claw to claw fighting. Ann:

Ann Precision great maturity skill wonderful effortlessness.

Joanne Joanne:

Ann Brute power brilliant aim marvellous speed.

Joanne Elise:

Ann The odd fluke shot relieving general hopelessness.

Elise Thank you.

Joanne It would be much better if we had a fourth.

Elise Man.

A brief violent rally between Ann and Joanne.

Ann (*crying out*) Vigour and dash.

Joanne (*slamming*) *Con brio.*

Ann My goal.

Joanne That was practice. We hadn't started properly.

Ann That was not warming up. That was game. Elise?

Elise Wasn't watching.

Joanne That's right. Opt out.

Joanne whips off her cardigan very fast and we see her arms for the first time which are covered in scars and tattoos.

Ann What?

Elise Tattoos!

Joanne The criminal sisterhood: tattoos.

Ann And scars.

Joanne I cut my wrists.

Joanne hits viciously, Ann rushes for it but misses. Leaves it.

Ann When?

Joanne Some months ago.

Ann What happened?

Joanne Nothing. You've heard of haemophiliacs, well I'm a haemophobiac, couldn't keep the wretched stuff flowing. Come on, serve.

Ann The tattoos.

Joanne Everyone has them.

Ann Who?

Joanne In Holloway.

Ann In Holloway!

Joanne The prisoners tattoo their girlfriends' names on their arms; but when they get out their pimps are angry because they say it drives off custom.

Ann Let me see. (*Reads Joanne's arm.*) Ann. Elise.

Joanne Leave me alone. (*She breaks away.*)

Ann You've tattooed our names on your arm.

Joanne I'm taking a penalty. My pimp'll be angry when I get out.

Elise Five minutes' time.

Ann Plenty can still happen.

Elise We'll know in five minutes.

Joanne We've sat through this vast vacation waiting for damned anybody to enrol, face it, nobody's coming.

Ann Give it time. We are teachers first and foremost, you and I, plain strength it would be wrong to misapply.

Elise Five minutes and the term starts.

Joanne hits the slipper but Ann catches it with her hand.

Ann Unlock the doors.

Joanne Hardly any point. We know already.

Ann That's not true.

Joanne I think we'll be able to control the flow.

Ann You're really back on form.

Elise She got her confidence back.

Joanne I do feel secure.

Elise Do I chalk up that last goal or not?

Ann Let her have it.

Joanne (*bowing*) Madame.

Ann Bully.

Joanne I don't want to keep you from your duties, my dear.

Ann puts down her stick.

Ann I call it poor sportsmanship when you needle insidiously and scratch at subjects that are nothing to do with the game in hand.

Joanne We're only playing to pass the time, thanks to

your scholastic success. We should be out on cocoa duty in the normal way of things, or lugging trunks up abandoned staircases to the dorm, instead of staging the international championship of all time.

Ann We know why Brackenhurst has hit a poor patch. One person teaching knife throwing, Jew baiting, guerrilla antics and sexual self-help has sharply influenced enrolment figures.

Joanne Fire me.

Ann Quite. Service.

Ann serves and the ball is way out of line.

Joanne Your own goal.

Ann lays down her bat and stalks out.

Mark up that point, Elise.

Elise To you?

Joanne To me. She's mad. Give me the slipper.

Elise lumberingly serves. Joanne scores effortlessly. Elise trundles to get it, almost falls.

You look really ugly today. Ugly in some special way falling over yourself for that little thing.

The bell rings incredibly loud.

She's gone completely off her head.

Ann's voice comes over the loudspeakers.

Ann (*off*) Testing, testing 1-2-3-4-5 –

Elise It works.

Joanne Four weeks' work and it had better.

Ann (*off*) Testing. Report immediately to your

headmistress. Do not collect two hundred pounds, do not pass go.

Joanne makes huge gestures of insanity and gabbles.

(*sings – off*) What the world needs now is love, sweet love.

Joanne Give me another.

Joanne wins casually.

No fun with you. Look at your horrible body.

Elise My stomach is in a way very beautiful.

Joanne It would need a woman to fancy you. You really look revolting.

Elise Doesn't matter, you used to say, what women look like. Physical appearance was a snare, something men had invented to grade off women.

Joanne One day – all women – are going to be equal.

Elise It's not so much that women aren't equal. It's more that they're ugly.

Ann (*sings – off*) What the world needs now is love, sweet love.

Joanne Give over.

Elise When I first learnt I was pregnant and I didn't go to a doctor by the way, just stopped getting the curse and watched myself inflate, then I felt the joy of a way to leave Brackenhurst. Now I've had the bugger in my womb so long I feel I've lugged it from here to Singapore.

Joanne There are times when I feel I've suffered so much that the world has just got to move over and yield.

An enormous hymn comes flooding over the speakers, with the voices of 400 schoolgirls raised in song.

(*shouting through the din*) Where's it coming from?

Elise It's her.

Enter Ann, her hands raised as if at the head of a religious procession. Joanne dashes out, Ann bows slightly, smiling at Elise. The music ends very suddenly, the plug ripped out and Joanne's voice comes over the speakers.

Joanne (*off*) The revolutionary party has seized control of the radio station and therefore declares the revolution complete. End of revolution.

The speakers go dead.

Ann There's no one. Not even Lucrecia. There are no pupils.

Enter Joanne.

Congratulations on your revolution.

Joanne seizes the hockey stick.

Joanne Total annihilation.

Ann Very well.

They take up their stances but:

Joanne Enough.

They both immediately relax.

The experiment must be counted a flop. The fight began on a real pretext – we wanted the hearts and minds of our pupils. I was to set up a feminist community. The result is the first feminist birth.

Ann That's not the way I saw it.

Joanne The wrists I cut in summer several times. We have credentials of our suffering – all of us.

Elise My baby.

*Ann drops to her knees and puts her ear on Elise's
stomach.*

Ann Is that the little baby? Ooh. Diddums. Can I come
out now, Auntie? No you can't – not for a month or two.
Oh he's crying.

Elise He wants a little peace. Joanne, lock the doors.

Exit Joanne.

Ann Is he crying? Ooh. Are you sad?

Elise It wasn't worth waiting through the vac.

Ann We held on.

Elise Really it was just delay.

Ann What do you do now?

Elise Find a father.

Ann Elise.

Elise It's well enough for you. You have a man.

Ann I never knew Haskins. I pretended.

Elise But you said.

Ann Think I'd sleep with a tradesman? I've got some
pride left.

Elise Virility attracted you.

Ann I just wanted to annoy her.

Elise While you were poisoning her.

Ann Yes.

Elise This is not the way women speak together, it's not
the way they live. It doesn't ring true.

Ann The slow sprinkling of arsenic seemed as humane a way as possible. I've not thought Joanne evil or depraved. Wayward more like and needing me.

Enter Joanne.

Joanne So I can go now?

Elise (*with real, unparalleled enthusiasm*) I just wanted to say to you, Joanne, I think you're bloody marvellous and your generation is more bloody marvellous than any before it. And if ever I want a friend for life, I'll want you.

Joanne Women are going to be free one day to behave as they choose. We're only so far fledglings on this earth.

Ann Break it up.

Elise There was no virgin birth. There are simply declining standards in private education and that is all.

Exit Elise.

Joanne Private schools were always like this. We're not unusual.

Ann I know what you feel. We've all been brought up to be sold out and pitied and scorned and screwed and abused. She's right. So what?

Joanne So?

Ann Well, exactly.

Joanne Why are the workers silent, Ann? Why does the revolution land with such a sigh? Twenty-five years the war is over, and everyone trying to get the workers to respond. And they won't. Where are the working women? Lulled by romantic love and getting home to cook the dinner.

Ann I was weaned on R. A. Butler and the Beveridge report, so I don't know what you're talking about.

Joanne Why have half the world, the women, vowed never to fight, to be slow to anger, not to destroy the world?

Joanne starts moving the furniture.

Ann If you'd ever had anything but some generalized complaint I could sympathize. But you don't even know what you want. Some unstated alternative that evaporates like your breath on the air.

Joanne Help pack these away.

Ann Those are good chairs you're manhandling. What are you doing?

Joanne Historic evolution. The end of Brackenhurst. *Citizen Kane*. Orson Welles. 1942.

Ann I've no intention.

Joanne This is the end of it.

Joanne takes a machine-gun out of the furniture at the back. Ann is facing downstage and can't see Joanne, who has put on a Negro mask.

Ann Please don't leave me. Please.

Ann turns and sees the pointed machine-gun.

Joanne After the revolution, retribution.

Enter Elise with her bike.

Elise Look what I've been hiding in the wine cellar.

Joanne Get out the way.

Elise, excited, throws down the bike, runs to cower behind Joanne.

(*to Ann*) Don't move.

Elise See my bike. I'll be in Gloucestershire by dawn.

Joanne Shut up.

Elise Down the M1, pausing only for childbirth at an all-night caff.

Joanne Shut up. This is my revolution.

Joanne starts walking downstage to Ann.

Ann Don't think I can't take a joke, Joanne.

Elise Give it to her, give it to her, Joanne.

Ann I just –

Elise Let her have it.

Joanne Shall I?

Elise Yes.

Joanne Yes?

Elise Yes.

Joanne fires the gun, which is a toy; it goes phut-phut-phut.

You're joking.

Joanne No. (*Embraces Ann.*)

Elise Some gladiators you turned out to be. I've spent the last year watching you two throw each other round like Indian clubs.

Joanne We're all just sorry school is closing down.

Elise Why?

Joanne We're all just sorry.

Elise There's nothing in our lives that's worth redeeming, take my word for it. We're teachers and that's all, and you two are good teachers because there's nothing in your lives that doesn't constitute a lesson. And while you've been talking the children have left. You've lived so long on other people's behalf you've ceased to recognize yourselves. There's nothing here worth keeping and certainly nothing holds us together. My bike. (*Exit.*)

Ann Elise.

Joanne Let her be.

Ann Your fault.

Joanne Yours.

Ann Look what you've done to her.

Joanne If women are ever to be strong, they've got to be strong . . .

Ann Jo-jo.

Joanne And lighthearted. She is right.

Ann This school worked for a long time before you came and it can work again.

Joanne Sure.

Ann We can make it work. Circulate Burke's Peerage for new pupils. Build up towards next term.

Joanne She is right.

Re-enter Elise. Her stomach is quite flat.

Elise It's gone. There was a great wet fart and it had gone.

They shift from foot to foot, half-gesture, walk in small circles about the stage. Chronic unease, suspension, restlessness. Half a minute passes in silence.

Joanne (*raising her arms*) Well then –

Instant blackout.

TEETH 'N' SMILES

For Joe

Characters

Inch
Arthur
Laura
Wilson
Nash
Peyote
Snead
Maggie
Smegs
Anson
Saraffian
Randolph

The play is set during the night of 9 June 1969.

The playing area is mostly bare. Design is minimal. The band's equipment is on a stage which, for the musical numbers, trucks down to the front. In the first act the band are housed in a college room; in the second they are on a lawn behind their stage.

Note: When **Teeth 'n' Smiles** was first played it ran just under three hours. It was then cut during previews. This text accommodates most of those cuts, but not all of them. The text was further rewritten for a West End production.

Teeth 'n' Smiles, with music by Nick Bicât and lyrics by Tony Bicât, was first performed on 2 September 1975 at the Royal Court Theatre, London. The cast was as follows:

Arthur Jack Shepherd
Inch Karl Howman
Laura Cherie Lunghi
Nash Rene Augustus
Wilson Mick Ford
Snead Roger Hume
Peyote Hugh Fraser
Smegs Andrew Dickson
Anson Antony Sher
Maggie Helen Mirren
Saraffian Dave King
Randolph Heinz

Directed by David Hare
Designed by Jocelyn Herbert

Revived at the Wyndham's Theatre, London, on 26 May 1976 with Martin Shaw as Arthur, Gay Hamilton as Laura, Charlie Grima as Nash and Ronald MacLeod as Snead.

Of Mr Blake's company I have very little.
He is always in Paradise.

Mrs William Blake

SCENE ONE

As the audience come in **Inch** *is building the amplifiers into a bank of equipment on the band's platform. He is twenty, in leather and jewellery. Downstage there are a couple of benches, representing an undergraduate's room that has been specially emptied.* **Arthur** *is lying on one bench, staring. He is wearing a silver top hat and a silk suit but the effect is oddly discreet. He is tall, thin and twenty-six.*

Inch disappears.

The play begins.

Inch comes in carrying two suitcases which he puts down in the middle of the room.

Inch Right. Let's smash the place up.

He turns and sees Arthur.

'Allo, Arfer, din know you was comin'.

Arthur Motorbike. How is she?

Inch All right. They're liftin' 'er out the van now.

Inch goes out.

Arthur
You're the top, you're the Coliseum
You're the top, you're the Louvre Museum
You're a melody from a symphony by Strauss . . .

Inch returns with a Samuelsons box from which he takes a plug. Then **Laura** *appears, a small dark girl with lovely skin.*

Laura Are you set up, Inch, it's very late?

Inch Got Maggie out?

Laura They're getting her down the drive.

Arthur And hello, Laura.

Laura And hello, Arthur. Some bastard put sugar in the petrol tank, that's why we're late.

Arthur It's good to see you.

Laura How long can you stay?

Arthur How long do you want?

Laura Well . . .

> **Wilson**, *a small, bearded cockney, and* **Nash**, *a spaced-out black drummer, appear, look round the room and sit down. Wilson gets out a bottle of green lemonade. Laura begins to unpack the bags she has brought in.*

Arthur Saraffian said he thought she might be on the way down.

Laura How Saraffian's meant to know, sitting in that office all day . . .

Arthur He has a manager's nose. He's like a truffle pig, he can smell heroin at fifty paces.

Laura Don't be absurd, dumbo. It's not smack, it's booze. Liquid boredom. Twice a day she flips out.

Wilson Game.

Nash Wot's it to be?

Wilson Pope's balls. The game is the most borin' and useless piece of information you can think of. Thus the Pope 'as balls.

Nash Right.

Wilson Away you go.

> *Laura arranges a series of dresses on the back of the bench. Then starts sewing one of her choice.*

Nash The town of Nottingham was once called Snottingham.

Wilson Yeah, that's borin'.

Nash Thank you, pal, your go.

Inch returns with eight bottles of Scotch, which he sets out on a bench.

Wilson Efrem Zimbalist's first wife's name was Alma Gluck.

Nash Well done, Wilson, that's really dull.

Inch Diana Dors' real name was Diana Fluck.

Nash Hello, Arthur.

Arthur Nashy. How are you?

Inch Or Diana Clunt, I can't remember which.

Wilson The capital of Burundi is Bujumbura.

Inch Or possibly Diana Clocksucker, but I think I would've remembered that.

Inch goes.

Laura She starts drinking at breakfast, she passes out after lunch, then she's up for supper, ready for the show. Then after the show she starts drinking. At two-thirty she's out again. Morning she gets up. And drinks. She's a great professional. Never misses a show.

Arthur Pills?

Laura No.

Arthur Reds?

Laura No. Blue heavens, no. Yellow jackets, no. Bennies, no. No goofballs, no dexies, no dollies.

Arthur Still no acid?

Laura No.

Arthur And the heroin?

Laura No. She just drinks.

Arthur What is she, some kind of pervert?

Peyote enters with an electric kettle and sits down. A moment later Inch appears with an extension cable from the stage, and they plug the kettle in.

Laura No aeroplane glue, no household cement, no banana peel, no fingernail polish remover, no nutmeg, no paintstripper. No one in the world but her and Johnny Walker.

Arthur And the singing?

Laura The singing's OK.

*Laura goes out. Inch hails **Snead** who is carrying **Maggie** into the room over his shoulder. Snead is forty-five, in top hat and black tails, this side of his first coronary. We do not see her.*

Inch Waiter, can you take 'er up to a bathroom?

Snead Sir.

Arthur
You're the Nile
You're the Tower of Pisa
You're the smile
On the Mona Lisa . . .

Snead has taken Maggie away. Peyote arranges a plastic funnel and two glass tubes, which he then sets out with care on the bench. Nash gets up.

Nash And where the 'ell are we?

Pause. Then he starts changing his shirt. Inch begins mending a plug.

Wilson At this moment in time on planet earth the dead outnumber the living by thirty to one.

Laura returns, distributing pork pies.

Laura She doesn't speak very warmly of you.

Arthur I'm not meant to drag round the country, am I?

Laura (*smiles*) Or of me.

Arthur Still sings my songs.

Laura She'd prefer not to.

Arthur I'm sure.

Laura She'd prefer to get up there and scream.

Arthur
You're a Moscow view
You're oh so cool
You're Lester Young . . .

Smegs appears. He is dressed like a very baggy matelot. He never raises his voice.

Smegs Couple of slags here say anyone fancy a blow-job?

Arthur gets up as if to consider.

Arthur A blow-job. Do I want a blow-job?

Laura How did they get in here?

Smegs Inch? Blow-job?

Arthur Bound to turn out like a Chinese meal. Half an hour later and you need another.

Inch Butterfly flicks, do they do butterfly flicks?

Smegs Ask them.

Inch Sure.

Laura (*to Peyote*) Do you have to do that in here?

Peyote Fuck off.

Inch (*laughs*) But will they do butterfly flicks with a roadie?

He goes to find out.

Smegs Not a chance.

Arthur Isn't he meant to be . . .

Smegs What?

Arthur Setting up. You're an hour late.

Laura (*holding a dress up*) Does this look all right?

Smegs It's up to him.

Arthur Why don't you go and help him?

Smegs Because we're artists.

Arthur All right.

Smegs See?

Laura Artists don't set up.

Smegs You don't ask Oistrakh to go out and strangle the cat.

Inch reappears, picks up the plug.

Inch They do blow-jobs wiv singers, but nothin' below bass guitar.

Arthur That's right, love, keep your standards up.

Peyote I play fuckin' bass guitar.

He hurries out.

Smegs Artists. I mean. Keith Moon's chauffeur got run over, he said chauffeurs are two a penny, it's blokes like me what are irreplaceable.

Wilson There is no word in the English language as rhymes with 'orange'.

Nash Hey, these valiums, do they go with my shirt?

He tosses one in. Snead reappears.

Snead Is that to be everything, sir?

Inch No, you gotta get 'er clothes off and get 'er into the bath.

Snead Sir?

Inch You think I'm jokin'?

He heads out, his arm round Snead.

I'm doin' you a favour. You should be a member of the stevedores' union.

Snead Sir?

Inch We're gonna 'ave to wash 'er. Do you wanna know wot that's like?

Snead Sir?

Inch Well, 'ave you ever seen 'em cleanin' St Paul's?

They go out.

Arthur Is that what happens every day?

Laura just looks at him.

What does everyone do?

Laura Pretend not to notice, what would you do?

Arthur What . . .

Laura There's no choice. Stoke tomorrow. Then Keele. Bradford. Southampton. Quick one in Amsterdam. Back to Glasgow. Then they claim California, but nobody believes it.

Arthur Saraffian's mad.

Laura Not Saraffian's idea. It's her. She wants to hit San Francisco on her knees.

Arthur What's the money?

Laura A hundred and twenty, no more. It won't cover overheads, whatever it is. But she . . . likes to keep busy.

Smegs All this jumping on the spot makes you feel famous. But it's no real substitute for people knowing your name.

Smegs goes out.

Wilson Arfer.

Arthur Yes.

Wilson Your contribution.

Pause.

Arthur H. G. Wells was attractive to women because his breath smelt of honey.

Pause.

Wilson Very nice.

Nash I enjoyed that.

Wilson Very nice.

Anson appears. He is nineteen, unusually short with long frizzy black hair. He carries a clipboard and wears evening dress with a velvet bow tie.

Anson Are we nearly . . .

Arthur There's a plug.

Anson What?

Arthur We're waiting to mend a plug. Look. Over there.

They look at the plug.

And then we'll be ready.

Anson I'm the organizer. The booking. You are . . . ninety minutes late you know. Couldn't someone . . . one of you mend it yourselves.

Arthur Arms like penguins I'm afraid.

Anson I see.

He goes out. Peyote reappears with a piece of gauze. Inch and Snead appear.

Nash Three-quarters of all children are born before breakfast.

Inch 'Ave you got 'er dress?

Laura Here. Tonight Miss Frisby is in peach.

Snead Will that be everything, sir?

Inch Why not lie down there and I'll walk all over yer?

Snead Sir.

Inch Jus' can't get any decent room service round 'ere.

He goes out. Laura cuts a pork pie neatly in four.

Nash Every time we breathe we inhale several million molecules that was exhaled by Leonardo da Vinci . . .

Wilson No, no, Nashy.

Nash Wot?

Wilson You don' understand, that's really quite interestin', Leonardo, I mean, it's far too interestin' . . .

Arthur I'm thinking of marketing a pork pie, a new kind of pork pie, which when you put the knife through the pastry will let out an agonized honk, as of a pig being slaughtered. It would do well.

He looks at the hovering Snead.

Arthur A tip is it Mr Snead, is that what you're after?

Snead Sir?

Arthur Don't look at us, pal, we're too famous, we're like the Queen, we don't carry actual money.

Snead Sir?

Wilson An' you're playin' it far too fast.

Inch calls from offstage.

Inch She says will Arfer 'elp 'er out the bath?

Peyote Waiter.

Snead Sir?

Peyote Fuck off.

Arthur pulls at an imaginary dog on a lead.

Arthur Come on, Arthur, come on boy, come and meet Maggie. Come on, come on boy.

Arthur and Snead go out different ways. Peyote sterilizes the tubes with boiling water which he then throws on the floor.

Peyote Wot's that creep doin' 'ere?

Laura If . . .

Peyote Never said it.

Pause.

Laura Where the others?

Peyote I 'ate Canterbury. Every time we come to Canterbury I swear never to come again.

Laura So do I. Except this is Cambridge.

Peyote Yeah. Look.

Peyote holds up a fresh hypodermic in a sterilized packet.

The cleanest needle in showbiz.

Laura T'rific.

Wilson It should be *dull*.

Peyote The bag.

Laura What?

Peyote The bag. Pass me the bag.

Laura This is Maggie's.

Peyote Pass me the fuckin' bag.

Laura hands the carpetbag to Peyote. He lightly tears the lining. Takes out an envelope.

Jus' borrowed 'er bag.

Laura That . . .

Peyote Uh. Jus' borrowed 'er bag.

Anson returns.

Anson Has there been any . . .

Laura Progress? No.

Peyote She en't bin busted as often as me.

Laura That would be quite hard, Peyote. I mean, you would have to stand on street corners stuffing tabs up traffic wardens' nostrils to get yourself busted quite as often as you.

Peyote Fuck off.

Anson Is Miss Frisby with you?

Laura She's just being sandblasted next door. Why don't you sit down?

Anson Thank you.

Arthur wanders back.

Laura Did you see her?

Arthur What is she on?

Laura Huh, did she recognize you?

Arthur She said, who let this pieca shit in here?

Laura She recognized you.

Arthur Yes.

Laura I must call Saraffian. Do you know where there's a phone?

Anson In the porter's . . .

Laura Lodge? Thank you.

Arthur He doesn't care. As long as they stagger on to the stage. Get their hands somewhere near the guitar. Yes, Peyote?

Peyote Fuck off.

Arthur I don't care either. Butcher my tunes. Forget my lyrics. Steal my royalties. I expect it.

Pause.

Thought she . . . thought she wanted to see me.

Laura Sure.

Arthur Just tell me what she's on.

Laura Arthur, you lived with her . . .

Arthur Have you let her get hooked? Well? Have you let her get hooked again?

Laura Have I?

Arthur Well?

Laura storms out, furious. Arthur turns away. Peyote has melted twenty pills in boiling water and is now pouring them through the funnel and gauze into the other tube. Wilson and Nash are flat out, probably asleep, possibly concentrating.

Anson Have you had a look where you're . . .

Pause.

Arthur Peyote, do you know what she's on?

Peyote She's mainlinin' string. Pullin' it through 'er veins.

Anson Do you want to have a look at . . .

Arthur Little fella, why don't you ever get through a . . .

Anson Sentence. I know. It's . . . I just hear what I'm saying and it always sounds so dreary and second-hand I just am . . . too fastidious to . . .

Arthur Finish.

Anson Right.

Pause.

I'm hoping to interview Miss Frisby.

Arthur She's in the bathroom, walk right up.

Anson Does she have any clothes on?

Arthur It's never stopped her before.

Anson Ah.

Arthur What you going to ask her?

Anson Oh . . . general things. About the role of popular music in society.

Pause.

Arthur Yes, well, that's a very good subject. Very good subject. You could even ask Peyote here about that. He has a lot of words to say on that. Well, not a lot. Actually he has two. Off and fuck. Only usually he contrives to put them the other way round.

Arthur goes out. Peyote and Anson are now as if alone. Peyote ties a rubber tube round his upper arm, teases the liquid in the hypodermic. Anson is embarrassed.

Anson Hmph.

Peyote Ah.

Anson gets up and moves away. Peyote shoots up.

Anson Squeamish. Grotesquely squeamish for a medical student. It's a problem. Really. You call that shooting up?

Peyote Uh-huh.

Anson Is that heroin?

Peyote Preludin.

Anson Ah. Preludin is a fuck-pump, I think I'm right. I know that much. It enlarges your sexual capacity. You're meant to stay hard for twenty-four hours, is that not . . . I believe that's right.

Pause.

It's none of my business but I think you may be taking rather a chance. I mean in Cambridge. Knowing the overall standard of skirt in this town I'd say twenty minutes would be pushing your luck.

Pause.

I had a guitar once. When I was young. Had a guitar. And a drum.

Pause.

You make conversation seem a little unreal. I suppose the silence is what . . . turns you on.

Pause.

Yes. I know. Fuck off. Certainly. By all means.

He moves towards the plug.

Peyote Don't touch it.

Inch returns.

Inch Right.

Anson Are you nearly . . .

Inch Jus' gotta change this plug.

Anson Will it take very long?

Inch Don't know, it's a technical thing.

Anson Is it going to be good tonight?

Pause.

Inch It's gettin' really nasty out there.

Anson What?

Inch The audience. They're stamping all over the lawn.

Fuck.

Anson What?

Inch Forgotten the flowers.

Inch goes out again, putting the plug down. Snead appears at the same time.

Anson Are you . . .

Snead Everyone's now ready for the orchestra, sir.

Inch Tell 'em they're jus' gettin' inta their dickies.

Inch gone.

Snead I think you'll have to make some announcement, sir. They're getting very restless having to wait.

Anson Tell them . . . er . . . tell them they're coming just as fast as they can.

Arthur comes on, goosing Laura who is wearing his top hat and laughing.

Ah . . . do you think they're almost . . .

Arthur Listen, they got the place right, didn't they? That's three-quarters of the battle. The time, the time is a sophisticated detail.

Anson I don't know, Mr Snead.

Peyote Wot is this place, anyway?

Arthur You are in what scientists now know to be a black hole, Peyote. Floating free, an airless, lightless, dayless, nightless time-lock, a cosmic accident called Jesus College Ball.

Peyote Jesus.

Arthur College Ball.

Peyote What does it mean?

Arthur It means the college at which I was educated. Yes, Mr Snead?

Laura It means undergraduates.

Arthur Narcissists.

Laura Yahoos.

Arthur Intellectuals.

Arthur embraces Laura from behind, his hands on her breasts.

Rich complacent self-loving self-regarding self-righteous phoney half-baked politically immature neurotic evil-minded little shits.

He stares at Snead.

Expect nothing and you will not be disappointed.

Silence. Snead turns and goes out. Anson looks at his hands. Arthur turns his back to us.

Wilson Internal memorandum. Rhyl Town Hall. The life expectancy of a civic deckchair is now a season and a half.

Laura He used to clip tickets.

Arthur I was at this college. I know Mr Snead of old. Give me that.

Laura gives him her current cigarette.

Where I first met Maggie. She was singing in the Red Lion. She was sixteen, seventeen, a folk singer. Let us go a pickin' nuts, fol de ray, to Glastonbury fair, a tiddle dum ay. I had to carry her over the wall, can you imagine, to get her to my rooms. They build walls here to stop undergraduates making love. Well, we got caught, of course, by this very Mr Snead coming in satirical German manner, even shining a torch, an English suburban stormfuhrer. He hauled me up to my tutor, who said, do you intend to marry the girl? I said, not entirely. He said, as this is a first offence you will not be sent down, instead I fine you ten pounds for having a girl on the premises. I said what you mean like a brothel charge? I was furious, I was out of my mind. Do you have another?

Laura lights him another.

Thanks. And everyone told me: don't waste your energy. Because that's what they want. They invent a few rules that don't mean anything so that you can ruin your health trying to change them. Then overnight they re-draft them because they didn't really matter in the first place. One day it's a revolution to say fuck on the bus. Next day it's the only way to get a ticket. That's how the system works. An obstacle course. Unimportant. Well, perhaps.

Pause. He stands a moment.

Nash The word Cicero literally means chick-pea.

Anson Oh God. I think I'd better . . . go and . . .

Laura Don't. Don't go away.

Arthur Sit down, tell us something about yourself.

Anson I'm sorry. It's just so late. I . . .

Arthur People appreciate things more when they've had to wait.

Anson That's not how we advertised . . .

Arthur Let them suffer.

Anson We didn't sell the tickets on the quality of the suffering we could offer.

Arthur Well done. Whole sentence. This band has converted more people to classical music than any other human form of torture.

Anson I don't understand why . . .

Arthur They come out saying, please, please, give me a drip in a bucket.

Inch returns.

Inch She says she's not going on tonight.

Anson On no.

Arthur Uh, it's fine. Don't panic.

Inch It's quite all right, it's fine.

Arthur The nights she's not going on are fine. It's the nights she can't wait to get on, they're the ones to watch for.

Wilson Right.

Inch goes. Smegs wanders back on.

Smegs How we doing?

Laura Fine.

Arthur Fine.

Wilson Fine.

Smegs (*sits*) Must be almost time.

Anson Yes.

Wilson Only one man 'as actually died on television. In a television studio. 'E was on a stool, talkin' about 'ealth food, about honey, an' 'e jus' fell over an' died.

Nash Fantastic.

Wilson Yeah.

Peyote stretches out.

Peyote It's so good, it's so very good . . .

Smegs I wouldn't have minded a sound check.

Arthur When did you last have one of those?

Smegs Barnsley, Halifax. I don't know. They carry me about in a sealed container. And sometimes the seasons change. Or we run over a dog. Or they change the design on my cigarette pack.

Arthur Well . . .

Smegs I don't know.

Arthur It seems to be what she wants.

Smegs It's needless you know. It just makes her feel good.

Arthur How is she to you?

Laura Unspeakable.

Arthur Ah.

Laura She treats me barely human.

Arthur Still?

Laura More than ever. She is jealous.

Arthur I don't see . . .

Peyote sits up suddenly. Panic.

Peyote There's a wheel comin' off the van.

Arthur It's all right, Peyote, it's just a brain cell dying.

Peyote It's comin' off.

Smegs It'll be horses in a minute, on sweeties he always has horses.

126

Anson I'm sorry but I really do have to insist . . .

Wilson What is wrong with you?

Anson I . . .

Wilson I don't think I've ever met a man wiv so little karma.

Anson How can I . . .

Wilson You should leave your brain to a Buddhist 'ospital, they'd be very interested in you.

Anson We are waiting for one plug to be connected.

Wilson Correct.

Anson It's ridiculous.

Wilson Don't touch it.

Anson It's absurd.

Pause.

I'm sorry, I just can't . . .

Anson moves towards the plug.

Wilson Don't fuckin' touch it, you miserable little turd.

Pause.

Arthur Just leave it to Inch.

Laura Inch changes a mean plug.

Wilson Right.

Arthur Inch is a great roadie. Inch is the Panama Red of roadies.

Anson I'm . . .

Arthur Just . . .

He holds up his hands. Pause.

It's just best. OK?

Inch returns.

Inch She says she's goin' on.

Arthur Ah.

Inch She says she can't wait to get out there.

Arthur Fine.

Inch Now. What? I'm almost ready. There was somethin'.

Anson Plug.

Inch I jus' gotta change this plug.

Arthur Fine. No hurry. Enjoy it.

Inch sets to. Then stops.

Inch I can't work if I'm watched.

Anson turns away.

Wilson A pullet is a pullet till the first time it moults. Then it's a hen.

Smegs Sussex have never won the County Championship.

Nash Marilyn Monroe was colour blind.

Arthur Oscar Wilde died Sebastian Melmoth.

Wilson Two gallons to one peck. Four pecks to one bushel. Eight bushels to one quarter. Four and a half quarters to a chaldron. One hectolitre per hectare equals one point one bushels per acre.

Inch Right. Ready when you are.

Anson I think we're ready.

Inch OK, band?

Wilson You might plug it in first, then we'll join yer.

Inch Fine.

Inch goes.

Wilson Not gonna walk across there if the plug's not gonna work.

Nash Get yer sneakers dirty.

Wilson Quite.

Anson Well, everyone . . . let me say . . . go out there and break a leg.

Anson goes.

Wilson Wot an 'orrible little man.

Nash 'E's very *short*, in' 'e?

Wilson Yeah, an' that 'orrible black 'air. Makes 'im look like a lavatory brush.

Smegs Are we playing outside?

Laura Yes. On the lawn.

Wilson Wot if it rains?

Arthur Somebody had better . . .

Smegs Yes.

Arthur Peyote.

Arthur wakes him.

Peyote Horses.

Smegs Told you.

Wilson Come on, Peyote, once through the Christmas oratorio.

Nash You take one arm.

Wilson Yeah, come in loud, eh Nashy? Drum all over 'im if you find 'e's on the floor.

Nash Will do.

Peyote Horses poundin' down the Mall.

Wilson Right, right, Peyote.

Smegs Off we go.

Peyote is guided towards the stage. The rest drift with him. They disappear behind the equipment.

Wilson (*as he goes*) I wish we'd found somethin' more, well, more kinda staggeringly borin'.

Arthur and Laura left on their own.

Laura Are you going to watch?

Arthur What?

Laura Arthur.

Arthur Yes, of course.

Laura I'll see you later.

Arthur Good.

Laura Arthur. Don't drift away from me.

She goes. Arthur alone at the front. Then at the back you see Inch raise his arm. He is holding the mended plug.

Arthur Paganini played the violin so well . . . people said he was in league with the devil.

The plug goes in. The music crashes on.

THE FIRST SET
*The band's truck rolls downstage, the music already on
the way. The band is Peyote (bass), Wilson (keyboard),
Smegs (lead), Nash (drums).*

*Standing about watching and talking are Inch, Laura
and Arthur.*

The band sing by themselves.

Close To Me

In a cafe called Disaster
Photos of the movie stars
Looked down upon the customers
As if they came from Mars
In a cafe called Disaster
Shelter from the rain
You said you couldn't love me
That we should never meet again

*Will you always be this close to me
When you're far
When you're far
When you're far away from me
And will you always
Will you always be this close to me
When you're far
When you're far
When you're far away from me
And will it always be the same*

In an age of miracles
In the heat of the afternoon
Falling on your funny face
The shadow of the moon
In an age of miracles
As sharp as any knife
I felt a touch of winter
In the summer of my life

And will you always etc.

>*Then without a break the band go straight into the next number. Dazzling light. Maggie joins them, singing, burning off the fat as she goes.*

Passing Through

Mamma said I had the morals
Of an alley cat
Just because I wanted more
Sister fuckin' Rita
Was a mean child beater
But she said I was a high street whore

Burning down the freeway
Like a shootin' star
Bitching how my life is run
Learning how to shake it
In the back of a Bedford
Taking it from every mother-fucker's son

Shut your mouth honey
I don't wanna know your name
Shut your mouth honey
I don't care why you came
Pass me the bottle
Roll over let's do it again

Say you gotta save it
For someone special
And you know that that's a lie
If you don't holler
When the lights go out
Life is gonna pass you by
Gotta reputation as a
One night stand
Kinda precious too
If you let a greaser
Stay another night
They're gonna get a lease on you

Shut your mouth etc.

I'm a sunflower lady
With a sweet electric band
I'm a sunflower lady
With a bottle and a man
Don't want quiet
I don't want care
When the sun comes up
And the lights blaze out
If you don't scream honey
How do they know you're there

The truck goes back almost before the song ends.
Arthur wanders down and sits quietly at the front.

PASSING THROUGH

♩ = 76

Em / Am / G
Mam-ma said I had the mor – als of an al-ley cat Just because I wan-ted more

F#m⁷ sus 4 / Em / Am
Instr. Sis-ter fuck-ing Ri-ta was a mean child bea-ter But she

G / F#m sus 4 / E
said I was a high street whore Burning down the free-way like a

Am / G / F#m⁷ sus 4
shoot-ing star Bitch-ing how my life is run

Em / A / G
Learning how to shake it in the back of a Bed – ford Tak-ing it from ev – ery

F#m / B⁷ / E / A
mo-ther-fucker's son. Shut your mouth honey I don't wan-na know your name

B⁷ / E
Instr. Shut your mouth hon-ey I don't

A / B
care why you came

Unison
Pass me the bot-tle Roll o-ver let's do it a-gain.

2nd time to Coda
𝄋 Em

Em / Am / G
Say you got-ta save it for some – one special And you know that that's a lie

F#m⁷ sus 4 / Em / Am
If you don't hol-ler when the lights go out

G / F#m⁷ sus 4 / E
Life is gon-na pass you by Got a re-pu-ta-tion as a

135

SCENE TWO

Arthur sits staring out front. Then Wilson and Nash come in, both fuming to a standstill.

Arthur Sorry about that.

Wilson Necrophilia. Like fuckin' the dead.

Nash Amateur night at 'Arrods staff canteen.

Wilson Like floggin' a corpse.

Nash The bastards.

Wilson Fuck 'em.

Nash Bastards.

  Smegs comes in.

Smegs What bastards.

Wilson Do you know, some woofter comes up to me after the set, says I expectin' somethin' altogether more Dionysiac, I says Thursdays we're Dionysiac, Fridays we're jus' fuckin' awful.

Arthur Right.

Wilson Not that I care.

Nash Right.

Wilson Fuckin' penguins.

Arthur Right.

Wilson I'm sitting there, I'm thinking the Marshall Stack's up the spout an' the Vox AC30 'as gone on the blink, an' not even the cloth-ears of Cambridge are fooled.

Arthur And that's just the first set.

Nash Right.

Wilson 'Ow long till the next one?

Arthur One o'clock. And the last at three-thirty. Then you can go to bed.

Nash hands out joints. Inch comes in carrying a guitar which he sets about mending.

Nash And you . . .

Inch Sorry lads, bit o' wobble on the Vox.

Nash Wobble?

Inch I've smeared it with pork fat, usually does the trick.

Anson appears.

Anson I've come to interview Maggie. She told me . . .

Wilson Last month in Miami, Florida . . .

Nash Again.

Anson . . . to wait here.

Wilson Jim Morrison of the Doors got it out. Not the only occasion this 'as 'appened. By no means. There is the example of our own P. J. Proby in the Croydon Odeon splittin' 'is velvets from knee to crotch.

Smegs A great moment.

Wilson The. Great. Moment.

Arthur Yes.

Wilson Slightly spoilt, it must be said, by the fact 'e then spontaneously split 'em every night till 'e was thrown off the tour.

Arthur A mistake.

Wilson Certainly. That bit. A mistake.

Nash That's right.

Pause. Wilson inhales deeply.

Wilson Fuck 'em. An' I know 'ow 'e feels.

Anson How do you think it went?

Silence. They all smoke. Maggie appears talking from a long way off. Laura dancing attendance.

Maggie Mother born in Hitchin, father born in Hatfield, so they met halfway and lived all their life in Stevenage. That's how my interview begins.

Arthur Oh, Jesus.

Nash, Wilson, Smegs and Inch rise as a man, and leave as quickly as they can.

Maggie Guess I must have been unhappy as a child . . .

Arthur Oh, my God.

Maggie Laura, I would love something to eat.

Laura Sure.

Laura goes off.

Maggie Well, hello, Candy Peel, I thought it was you.

Arthur Hallo, Maggie.

Maggie Do you know why I call him Candy Peel? Because he has a small scrap of that substance hanging where real men . . .

Arthur Thank you, Maggie, do the same for you.

Maggie Do you know how you survive in Stevenage? You say this isn't happening to me. That's what you say. You say I may appear to be stifling to death in this crabby over-heated mausoleum with these cringing waxworks who claim to be my parents. But it's not true. I'm not here. I'm really some way away. And fifty foot up.

Arthur Right.

Maggie In fact I'm a Viking.

Arthur Have you got this?

Anson I . . .

Arthur I would write it down if I were you.

Maggie In another age. I was a Viking. Reincarnation. I had a dream last night, I was called Thor, and I was wrapped in furs and I had strips of dried meat tied round my waist.

Arthur Well, I think we can guess what the dried meat means, honey.

Maggie No nourishment in Stevenage. You draw no strength. It's like living on the moon.

Anson I have heard you saying that before.

Maggie Listen, kid, you ask for an interview, I give you an interview. If you wanna *new* interview you gotta pay more, understand?

Anson Yes. Sorry.

Maggie Like to rub my back, Arthur?

Arthur Give me the bottle.

Maggie I won't drink before the show, Arthur. I just like to hold it, OK?

   Pause.

Ask us another question.

Anson Would you say . . .

Maggie Yes?

Anson Would you say the ideas expressed in popular music . . . have had the desired effect of changing . . . society in any way?

Pause.

Maggie Hamburger. Dill pickle. That's what I want.

Laura returns with Snead.

Laura I got the gay boy back.

Arthur Ah, come in, waiter.

Maggie Hallo, ringer, must have been you in the tub just now.

Snead Sir?

Arthur Did you say sir?

Maggie That's all right, I'm just one of the boys.

Arthur Hamburger, please, Mr Snead. With dill pickle.

Maggie And relish and French fries. Coca-cola. And a banana pretty. And a vanilla ice with hot chocolate sauce. Chopped nuts. And some tinned peaches. And tomato sauce for the hamburger. With onion rings. And mayonnaise. And frankfurters. Frankfurters for everyone, OK? With French mustard. And some toasted cheese and tomato sandwiches. With chutney. On brown bread, by the way, I'm a health freak.

Arthur Got that, Mr Snead?

Snead I'm afraid I'll have to send out for this. Do you think you could give me some money?

Laura Money?

Maggie Don't make with the jokes, ringer, they don't go with the grovelling.

Snead I can get you something from the college kitchen.

Arthur OK, just get us whatever's nice and greasy and answers to the name of Rover, OK?

Snead Sir?

Maggie Then the first time I heard Bessie Smith, that was somethin'.

Arthur Off you go.

Snead Sir.

Snead goes out.

Maggie That was really somethin'. In a record shop, I was fourteen. Did you know that as well?

Anson Actually I . . . read your press release.

Maggie Did you?

Pause.

Laura I reckoned he should . . .

Maggie Yes, well I do have some sort of life outside my press release. I can't remember where I put it, but I do know I have it.

Maggie gets up and slips the Scotch bottle back in the rank of eight.

Laura Do you want to change for the next set?

Maggie What you gawpin' at?

Anson Looking at you.

Maggie points to where she had been sitting.

Maggie Still looking at the tragedy? That was over there. The girl with no life of her own. I left her over there.

Anson That easy?

Maggie Tragedy's easy. I pick it up, I sling it off. Like an overcoat.

Pause.

Arthur What is she on?

Laura Arthur.

Arthur Will somebody please tell me what this girl is on?

Pause.

Maggie So I tell you the story of my life. Everyone in Stevenage hated me, they hated me when I was a child. Cos I was big and fat and rich and took no shit from anyone. What's this for?

Anson A university paper.

Maggie So they sent me to a convent. Anything you heard about randy nuns, forget it. They have tits like walnuts and leathery little minds. But me, I'm like a great slurpy bag of wet cement waiting to be knocked into shape. Everybody at the convent, they hate me too.

Anson You . . .

Maggie How did I lose it, is that what you want to know?

Anson I didn't . . . get . . .

Maggie I lost it to an American airman on top of a tombstone in Worthing cemetery. He was very scared. I was only thirteen and he didn't want to lose his pilot's licence. Write this down for Chrissake, it's good.

Anson's pencil obeys.

So then even the American gets to hate me, yes, Laura?

Laura Oh, yes.

Maggie She was at school with me, you see. We both had it, this English education. Takes a long time to wipe that particular dogshit off your shoe.

Anson And Arthur?

Maggie Arthur I meet when I'm seventeen. A case of Trilby. Which is Trilby? I never know.

Arthur The woman is Trilby.

Maggie And the monster is Frankenstein.

Arthur No.

Maggie The doctor is Frankenstein.

Anson The monster doesn't have a name.

Laura The man is Svengali.

Maggie Anyway. He invents me.

Arthur smiles and shrugs.

Laura Do you want to change?

Maggie Yeah, I'll change.

Laura organizes a new dress from the bags.

Anson Are there . . . any other singers you greatly admire?

Maggie Well, it's a funny thing you'll find . . . singers mostly admire Billie Holliday, same as jazzmen admire Charlie Parker. Conductors say they admire Toscanini. It's something to do with how they're all dead.

Arthur No competition.

Maggie (*smiles*) Yes.

Anson Among the living?

Maggie stands behind Anson and puts her hands on his shoulders.

Maggie This is all real you know, kid. None of the others can say that. Never had a nose-job. Or a face-lift. Or my chin pushed in. Or my jaw straightened. No paraffin wax, no mud-packs. All my own teeth. This is it. The real thing. I am the only girl singer in England not to have been spun out of soya bean.

Anson You never seem very happy to have been English. What would you rather have been?

Maggie American.

Anson Why?

Maggie smiles at Arthur.

Maggie America is a crippled giant, England is a sick gnome.

Arthur makes an O with his fingers.

I sing of the pain. Do you understand?

Anson No.

Maggie The words and music are Arthur's but the pain is mine. The pain is real. The quality of the singing depends on the quality of the pain.

Pause. She smiles.

Yeah. What you study?

Anson Oh . . . medicine.

Maggie Great.

Anson Well, yes, in a way except I don't seem very suited. It's not my . . . anyway . . . I don't want to bore you with my problems.

Maggie What would you like to be?

Anson Well . . . I don't know. If I was free . . .

Maggie stares at him.

Maggie Round the back of the Odeon? Yes? After the show? Would you like that?

Anson Odeon?

Maggie It's a figure of speech. Kid.

Arthur You could stand on a beerbox, reach up to her.

Laura Shake hands with Saigon Charlie.

Maggie smiles at them. Then cuffs lightly the top of Anson's hair.

Maggie First man I knew played rock music, he was nobody, a real nothing. I say rock music, but really it was all that hoopla and fag dancing the groups used to do. This boy got his big break, bottom of the bill with The Who, national tour. At the end of the tour he came back to Stevenage, he threw it in. I said, you got depressed because they're so good? He said, I got depressed because they're so very good and yet even they ask the same questions I do every night: where is the money and where are the girls?

Pause.

And that is it. Where indeed is the money? And where are the girls?

Silence. Peyote walks into the room and lies down, says nothing.

You know Jimi Hendrix gets depressed, he gets livid, because he says people don't come to hear his music, not really to listen, but simply because they've all heard he's got a big cock and plays the guitar with his teeth.

146

Arthur Yar.

Maggie And I say, sure Jimi, you're right to complain, people are cunts, but wouldn't it be a better idea to stop wearing tight trousers and give up clamping your mouth round the strings?

Laura I think I'd better keep an eye on Peyote tonight.

Maggie He'll be OK.

Laura He may need looking after.

Maggie If it makes you feel good.

Pause.

The hat.

Laura What?

Maggie I'd like that hat, Laura. Gonna wear that hat tonight.

Laura hands it to her.

Does Peyote have any chicks lined up?

Arthur He didn't say so.

Maggie Well, where's he gonna put it then?

Arthur Can't guess.

Maggie Can't go around with blue balls all night, Laura.

Laura I get sentimental about my body, Maggie. Everything else I give to the band, but the body . . . you know . . . I still like to choose.

Maggie laughs, turns to Anson.

Maggie You couldn't make her with a monkey wrench. Arthur will tell you all about . . .

147

Laura End of interview.

Maggie Laura here is my press secretary.

Laura End of interview. Anything else you need to know . . .

Maggie rides in over her, definitive.

Maggie I only sleep with very stupid men. Write this down. The reason I sleep with stupid men is: they never understand a word I say. That makes me trust them.

Arthur gets up, moves away, turns his back.

So each one gets told a different secret, some terrible piece of my life that only they will know. Some separate . . . awfulness. But they don't know the rest, so they can't understand. Then the day I die, every man I've known will make for Wembley Stadium. And each in turn will recount his special bit. And when they are joined, they will lighten up the sky.

She picks up the dress Laura has laid out.

Come on, kid, I'll change after. No point in getting another dress dirty.

Anson No.

She leads Anson out. On the way they pass Snead wheeling in a huge trolley of steaming food. Salvers, tureens, etc.

Laura Hey, Maggie, the food.

Maggie Not hungry.

She and Anson go out.

Laura Just . . . leave it there will you, Mr Snead?

Snead Madam.

Laura And thank you.

Snead goes.

Arthur She knows exactly what she's doing. Always. That's what I learnt.

Laura Yes.

Arthur She knows the effect she's having. Even when she's smashed, when she's flat out on the floor, there is still one circuit in her brain thinking, 'I am lying here, upsetting people.'

Laura Yes.

Arthur (*smiles*) There you are.

Laura Arthur.

Inch reappears with Nash, then Wilson. They check the place.

Inch 'As she gone?

Arthur Yes.

Inch All right everyone, you can come out now.

Laura The little fellow with her.

Arthur She swallowed him up like a vacuum cleaner.

Laura dips a plastic cup in the tureen, drips green lumps of soup on the floor.

Inch Did she tell the Jimi Hendrix gag?

Laura Of course.

Inch Did she say . . .

Laura Yes, she said it.

Inch You 'aven't 'eard it yet.

149

Laura I haven't heard it but she said it. Just terrible.

Nash 'I sing of the pain.'

Laura She said that.

Inch 'The pain is real.'

Nash The pain is bloody real.

Inch Mostly in the arse.

Arthur All right.

Peyote gets up from the bench and leaps into the air. At the last moment he catches hold of an iron bar across the roof. He hangs there swinging slightly, eight feet above the ground, joint between his teeth. Wilson appears and opens a large book.

Wilson Readings from the London telephone directory.

Inch Oh no.

Wilson The game is:

Inch No.

Wilson The game is: I read from the London telephone directory. You lot remain completely silent. The first person to make a sound is disqualified. The winner is the person who can stand it longest.

Arthur Oh, my God.

Wilson Arfer, you'll get yerself disqualified before we begin.

Arthur Is that a . . .

Wilson Now, where shall I begin? I think I was jus' gettin' inta the Smiths . . .

Saraffian *enters. He is in his early fifties with a paper* *hat, camel hair coat and streamers round his neck.*

Saraffian Saraffian comes.

He releases a balloon full of water which squirts away into the air.

And at once we have a party.

Arthur Saraffian. My God.

Randolph *follows on. He is heavily made up, you cannot tell his age. He is carrying a crate of champagne. Saraffian takes a chicken from inside his coat.*

Wilson 'Ello, Boss.

Saraffian *Poulet farci aux champignons.* Loot from the ball, my dears. And twelve bottles of a bleak little non-vintage Dom Perignon. Za za.

Inch Fantastic.

Nash Za za.

Saraffian Just in case we don't get paid. Wilson, you old dog, I've come to show you this . . . thing.

He gestures at Randolph.

Put the crate down. Come here. Look. Look at my glittering pigeon-chested youth. How do you like it? My future star.

They all look at Randolph.

Nash Great.

Saraffian Beautiful, isn't it? I'm really proud. He's going to wipe up the queer market, no question.

Randolph I . . .

Saraffian Uh, don't risk it, just don't spoil it, lad. Don't mess with the words, OK? Don't risk them, they only get you into trouble.

Randolph Pl . . .

Saraffian He wants to protest his heterosexuality. Just don't mention it, underplay it and we might believe in it. Might.

Pause.

Much better. So. Hallo, Peyote, don't bother to come down, just stay up there if you want. So. I'm a fine surprise.

Laura Saraffian.

Saraffian My dear.

Laura What are you up to?

Saraffian Come to hear the band.

Laura I've been trying to ring you these last few days.

Saraffian Ah.

Laura Have you seen her?

Peyote The sun goin' da'an. A tha'asand golden chariots. Leather. Metal. Horseflesh. Careerin' da'an through the sky.

He drops from the beam simply to the floor.

Ten tha'asand angels in a single file.

Laura Have you seen her?

Saraffian Well . . .

Wilson Did you 'ear the first set?

Saraffian Certainly I heard it. I heard it all. From beginning to end. And I'm hoping it will have earned me some small remission in hell. (*to Randolph*) Look lively, open the bottles, son.

Laura When are you going to talk to her?

Saraffian Well, this is nice. Peyote, I saw your old woman last night. Would you believe it, she has another husband, she's still only nineteen.

Wilson Wot's 'e like?

Saraffian Very charming. Easy-going bloke. Nose-flute player in a monastery band.

Laura She's not very well, Saraffian.

Nash Let's 'avva game.

Saraffian Snap.

Wilson Poker.

Nash Monopoly.

Wilson Lost the board.

Laura Saraffian.

Wilson And Peyote swallowed the boot.

Saraffian Poker.

Laura And she's drinking again.

Saraffian Yes.

Laura Arthur, will you tell him?

Arthur I . . .

Laura Why do you think she drinks?

Saraffian I never ask, in my profession you expect to spend a portion of your time sitting by a hospital bed . . .

Laura Listen . . .

Saraffian I've got very good at it. I think the ultimate accolade of my profession should not be a disc, it should be a golden hypodermic.

Laura Saraffian.

Saraffian What is this? I pay a courtesy call on one of my bands . . .

Laura Don't be stupid. Courtesy call. When did you last see a band on the road?

Saraffian Glenn Miller, I think.

Laura Saraffian, why does she drink?

Saraffian Why do we discuss her all the time? That's why she drinks. So we'll discuss her. You know, so we won't have time to do things like cut our fingernails or make love to our wives. That's why she drinks. So as to stop any nasty little outbreaks of happiness among her acquaintances. Are there any glasses for this stuff?

Inch goes to get some.

Laura So tell me why you thought Arthur should come.

Saraffian Kid.

Arthur Please.

Laura Why does he have to come and see her again, it only screws her up.

Saraffian Please leave it, Laura, there are no answers and there is absolutely no point in the questions.

Laura I see. Can I say anything at all?

Saraffian No.

Laura Can anyone say anything?

Saraffian No.

A long pause.

I'm very grateful, Laura, for all the work you've done.

Laura Don't crawl up my arse, Saraffian, what is Arthur doing here?

Saraffian He . . .

Arthur I wanted to come.

Laura What?

Saraffian He wanted to see her.

Laura Arthur?

Saraffian His own idea.

Arthur Yes. Just to see her for Chrissake. I wanted to see her. Is that . . . just to see her.

Arthur goes out. A pause.

Saraffian Everyone should love everyone. Take the global view, Laura, please. Champagne.

Inch back with beer mugs. Saraffian pours out. Laura as if about to cry.

Ease up will you, Laura, you're doing Joan Crawford out of a job.

Laura Listen . . .

Saraffian Shit, Laura, a man can love two women at once. I've seen it done. The human heart. Shall we ever understand it, Tone?

Randolph I . . .

Saraffian The answer is no. The boy adored her. Now he feels responsible. So.

Laura gets up. Moves. Stops dead. The rest are sitting,

staring into their mugs. Almost all comprehensively stoned now.

Wilson And . . .

Laura Well . . .

Inch There.

Pause.

Saraffian Look at it this way, Laura. I knew a Viennese teacher who said that desperate people who try to kill themselves but only succeed in shooting their eyes out, never, ever attempt suicide again. It's the sense of challenge you see. Once you've lost your eyes, it gives you something to live for.

He laughs.

Peyote Dubbin. Brass. Bells.

Nash Wot's up wi' 'im?

Peyote Streakin' through the sky. The 'ouse'old cavalry itself.

Wilson 'E's on 'orses again.

Peyote Pomades. The royal 'orses.

Wilson Said in the paper seventy per cent of adult males dream regularly of fuckin' Princess Anne.

Inch Quite right. I mean, what's a royal family for if not to . . .

Wilson . . . dream.

They smile. Pause.

Peyote An' a cry of 'allelujah.

Saraffian sits back. They all drowse.

Laura It's just possible anywhere, any time to decide to be a tragic figure. It's just an absolute determination to go down. The reasons are arbitrary, it may almost be pride, just not wanting to be like everyone else. I think you can die to avoid cliché. And you can let people die to avoid cliché.

Saraffian Quite.

Pause.

Wilson Shall we play the telephone game?

Saraffian I can't tell you the beauty of this profession. Years ago when I was young. It was full of people called Nat and Harry and Dick in brown suits and two-tone shoes. With thick chunky jewellery as if someone had splattered hot melting gold over their bodies with a watering can, and it had set in great thick blobs. And golden discs on the walls. And heavy presentation ballpoint sets, on their desks. Would sell you their grandmother's wooden leg. Nat did sell his grandmother's wooden leg, after she died, admittedly. And they muttered the totem phrases of the trade like, 'Tell him I'll get back to him.' There was no higher compliment an initiate could be paid than to be taken out for pickled brisket and beetroot borscht and be told in perfect confidence, 'The real dough's in sheet music. My son.' And they snapped great white fingers round the piano and used words like 'catchy' and 'wild'. And the artists . . . the artists bore no connection to the world I knew. When Nat travelled he carried them in the back of the van with a sliding glass compartment between him and them so he wouldn't have to listen to their conversation. He talked about installing sprinklers, as in Buchenwald. It was organized crime. Really. Those days. That's what interested me. The blatancy of it. The damnfool screaming stupidity of popular music. I loved it.

Pause. His eyes are closed.

You want me to sack her, you all want her to go.

Pause. He opens his eyes.

You are making the Mafia sign.

Pause. Nobody moves a muscle. Laura looks furious.

OK.

The band's equipment comes down silently and Scene Two scatters.

SCENE THREE

The abandoned stage. Just Laura. She walks behind the bank of speakers. She gets out a packet of fags. Lights two. Hands one down behind the amplifiers where it disappears. She moves away.

Laura Where the people?

Maggie's voice In the dinner tent.

Laura Ah.

Maggie's voice They're having dinner. In the dinner tent.

Laura goes behind the organ, picks up the clean dress and throws it behind the speakers.

Laura You ought to . . . put this on. The other's got dirty.

Maggie's voice Laura.

Laura Yeah.

Maggie's voice The boy, the student . . .

Laura Yes, I can imagine.

158

Pause.

Maggie's voice The journalist.

Laura Yes, yes, I know who you mean.

Maggie's voice He was in a bit of a state, I couldn't believe it. I think he must have juiced himself up.

Laura Yes.

Maggie sits up behind the amplifiers.

Maggie He said your thighs are so beautiful, your thighs are so beautiful, well, Laura, you seen my thighs . . .

Laura Yes.

Maggie I said please let's not . . . I'd rather you just . . .

Pause.

Laura You better go on.

Maggie He said your body is like a book in which men may read strange things, a foreign country in which they may travel with delight. Your cheeks like damask, the soft white loveliness of your breasts, leading to the firm dark mountain peaks of your, Laura, now I am dreading which part of my body he will choose next on which to turn the great white beam of his fucking sincerity. Between your legs the silver comets spiral through the night, I lose myself, he says . . . he says . . . how beautiful you are Maggie and how beautiful life ought to be with you.

Pause. She cries.

Laura Don't.

Maggie So. I don't want to know.

Laura No.

Pause. She begins to recover.

Maggie Then eventually . . . I say please, faking. He says yes of course, he stops talking. We wait. For thirty minutes. For thirty minutes it is like trying to push a marshmallow into a coinbox.

Pause.

Then he manages. In his way. Afterwards he says it's his fault. I say no mine, perhaps the choice of location . . . he says it can't be your fault, you have made love to the most brilliant and beautiful men of your generation, you have slept with the great. I say, there are no great, there is no beautiful, there is only the thin filth of getting old, the thin layer of filth that gets to cover everything. So. Off he goes. Za za.

Pause. Then a complete change.

Maggie Where's Arthur? God, how I used to love that man.

Laura Yeah.

Maggie He used to make me feel good, you know, he made me want to curl up foetal.

Laura Across the way they . . . talking about you.

Maggie I'm a Zeppelin. I'm fifty foot up.

Laura Saraffian's here.

Maggie No kid.

Laura That's right.

Maggie Why'd he come tonight?

Laura I don't know.

Laura reaches down for a near-empty Johnny Walker from behind the speakers.

Maggie Bum set. Bum gig. Think he noticed?

They look at each other.

Gimme the bottle will you, Laura?

Laura Arthur has travelled quite a long way.

Maggie Yeah.

Laura Say seventy miles. I think he's entitled to a little of your time. If you can fit him in between . . .

Maggie Do you know Arthur was a good man? When we first met? Really good man. He used to leave half-finished joints in telephone booths just so passers-by could have a good time.

Laura Listen . . .

Maggie But he's become a little over-earnest for me, don't you think? I mean, if there was going to be a revolution it would have happened by now. I don't think 1970'll be the big year. I mean the real revolution will have to be . . .

Laura Inside?

Maggie Gimme the bottle.

Laura Why do you talk like that, Maggie?

Maggie Gimme the bottle.

Laura Where does that stupid half-baked bullshit come from?

Laura holds on to the bottle.

Maggie Well . . .

Laura If you really wanted rid of him you wouldn't sing his songs. And you wouldn't be afraid to tell him to his face.

Pause.

Maggie All my life I've noticed people in telephone booths, in restaurants, heads down, saying things like, 'I don't want to see you again.' Once you start looking, they're everywhere. People rushing out of rooms, asking each other to lower their voices, while they say, 'You've got to choose between her and me.' Or, 'Don't write me, don't phone me, I just don't want to see you again.' People bent over crawling into corners at parties, sweating away to have weasely tearful little chats about human relationships. God how I hate all that. It seems so clear. I've finished with Arthur. And I'm fed up with his songs. I'm resentful and jealous and I want to be left alone. And I don't want to look in his lame doggy eyes.

Pause.

God, the singing is easy. It's the bits in between I can't do.

They look out from the stage into the void. At the back Inch comes on and starts preparing the equipment.

Laura They're coming back.

Maggie Look at carrot-top over there.

Laura Must be almost time.

Maggie Look, he's laughing.

Laura And his hand's coming up. Look . . .

Maggie Yes.

Laura No, she's wriggled out of it.

Maggie She's saying something.

Laura I think his name's Rodney.

Maggie What did she say?

Laura Dunno. Something like don't touch me, Rodney.

Maggie Christ, look at him.

Laura He's taking it badly.

Maggie They're funny the rich . . .

Laura He's standing there gasping.

Maggie They do it all so slowly.

Laura Like someone hit him with a cricket bat. He's . . .

Pause. Appalled.

Jesus.

Pause. Relief.

Ah no, he's seen a friend. Look, he's all right. He's trotting away into the paddock. Hallo, Roger, hallo, Rodney. He's quite frisky now. Lifting his fetlocks. Ha, ha, ha. All well.

Inch You can't 'elp wonderin' . . . wot a bomb would do.

Saraffian Hallo, my dear.

Saraffian has crept in silently and is staring at Maggie. Towards the back of the stage a conga of Wilson, Nash, Peyote, Arthur and Randolph snakes down; then the band begin to set up.

Conga
'Ow do yer do what yer do to me
'Ow I wish I knew . . .

Maggie Saraffian. Come to check on your investment?

Saraffian That's right.

Maggie Just merchandise to you.

Saraffian Sure are.

Maggie We could be anything. Soapflakes we could be. Well, that's fine. Yes. That's fine by all of us. Yes, Arthur?

She looks at him for the first time.

Arthur I don't know. It's not so easy of course. I believe the acid dream is over, it said in the *Daily Express*. But you and I, Maggie . . . we still want to say something. Yes?

Maggie smiles and leans over him.

Maggie Love you. Where my shoes?

She moves away. Laura goes to get her shoes.

Saraffian At the present rate if you lot go on working for another three years, you'll just about cover the advance I gave you.

*Arthur plays a few chords of 'My Funny Valentine'.
Maggie turns and stares.*

Arthur Leonardo da Vinci drew submarines. Five hundred years ago. They looked pretty silly. Today we are drawing a new man. He may look pretty silly.

Maggie (*to Arthur*) You still want it to mean something, don't you? You can't get over that, can you? It's all gotta mean something . . . that's childish, Arthur. It don't mean anything.

Laura Do you want the flowers?

Maggie Fuck the flowers.

Maggie disappears.

Arthur Haven't I seen Randolph before?

Saraffian Used to be a drummer. Year or two ago. Used to lay down a beat for Eve Boswell.

Arthur Eve Boswell?

Saraffian (*beaming*) Well, he is nearly thirty-five you know. They all come round. It all comes round again.

Maggie goes to collect her Scotch. The band quiet and almost ready.

I first knew Randolph in the fifties. My generation. The golden days of British rock. Crêpe soles, a tonic solfa and a change of name. That was all you needed. He was . . .

Randolph Tony Torrent.

Saraffian Right. It never got better you know. It'll never get better than 1956. Tat. Utter tat. But inspired. The obvious repeated many times. Simple things said well. Then along came those boys who could really play. They spoilt it of course. Ruined it. They were far too good. Before that . . . very fine my dears.

Maggie Saraffian.

Saraffian Yes.

Maggie Shut up.

Maggie walks to the back of the stage. Silence. Smegs comes in and picks up his guitar. She lifts her bottle, drinks. Turns. The band look one to another.

Saraffian Rock me baby till my back ain't got no bone.

He gets up.

After that the rest was downhill.

He walks away. She comes down.

THE SECOND SET
Arthur, Randolph, Laura and Saraffian all wander out of

sight during the first song. The band start an aggressive rock number; at the point Maggie should come in, they stop. Nothing. Then Maggie speaks.

Maggie Just try and forget, eh? Forget who you are. Don't think about it. Pack your personality under your arm an' have a good time. I really mean it.

Mama, take yer teeth out cos Daddy wanna suck yer gums.

Pause. Then the band begin again. At the moment of entry Maggie wanders away from the microphone and picks up her bottle. Pause.

It's enough to make a haggis grow legs, man.

An abrupt drum solo from Nash and a couple of chords from Wilson. Then silence.

Now listen, kids, call you kids, so far you're schlebs and secret assholes. What you say, sir?

She listens.

Yeah, well, what you do with it is your business. Just don't ask me to hang it in my larder. Now this is meant to be a freak-out not a Jewish funeral. Let me make this plain. I don't play to dead yids. What you say, what are you saying, madam?

She leans forward, her hand in front of her eyes.

Sure. If that's what you want. Meet you in the library in half an hour. Bring your knickers in your handbag.

She leans forward again.

I am what? What is that word? I have not heard it before. What is stoned? (*She holds up the whisky bottle.*) This is a depressant, I take it to get depressed. Now I have some very interesting stuff to say. First we're gonna talk about

me. Then we're gonna talk about me. Then we'll change
the subject. Give you a chance to talk . . . about what you
think about me.

Right. So. It's mother born in Hitchin, father born in
Hatfield. So they met half way and lived all their life in . . .

Wilson Get on with it.

*Long pause. The band look bored and regretful at her
behaviour. She turns to Wilson.*

Maggie Wilson here . . . this is Wilson . . . on keyboard.
Wilson has always entertained the notion of taking his
trousers down. On account of the pain. So let's have them,
Wilson.

*Maggie lurches at the organ. Wilson's seat crashes over.
She climbs on top of him and tries to rip his jeans off.
Inch pulls her off, the others stand on one leg, play the
odd note.*

Right, let's have it, that's it, that's it, that's it, that's it, let's
have it, that's it, that's it, that's it, that's it.

Inch Come on, come on now.

*Wilson stands well away. Inch has his arms round
Maggie. Then Wilson slips nervously back to the organ.
Inch slowly lets go of Maggie then stands behind her
like a puppet master. Pause. Then superb coherence.*

Maggie Ladies an' genel'men . . .

Brief drum from Nash.

The acid dream is over lezzava good time.

*The next number begins shatteringly loud. Where the
words should be Maggie sings tuneful but emphatic.*

Yeah yeah yeah yeah yeah yeah yeah yeah yeah . . .

The truck pulls back upstage. The music fades and falters as it goes.

YEAH YEAH YEAH

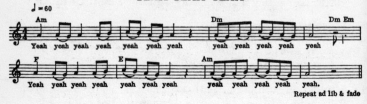

Yeah yeah yeah yeah yeah yeah yeah yeah yeah yeah yeah yeah

Yeah yeah yeah yeah yeah yeah yeah yeah yeah yeah yeah yeah.

Repeat ad lib & fade

SCENE FOUR

Saraffian and Arthur straight in at pace. The music stops.

Arthur Great stuff.

Saraffian Really terrific.

Arthur Where is she?

Laura comes in.

Saraffian Getting her head kicked in.

Laura Didn't get us very far.

Wilson comes in.

Wilson My jeans.

Laura Where did she get to?

Wilson My beautiful jeans.

Saraffian Winner of the 1969 Judy Garland award for boring boring boring . . .

Inch comes in.

Inch Wot the fuck was that about?

Wilson Somethin' to do with the pain.

Inch Wot pain?

Laura Go and get a shower ready.

Inch Wot fuckin' pain?

Saraffian The pain, you know, the pain that makes her such a great artist.

Nash comes in carrying Maggie over his shoulder.

Inch I'm not washin' 'er again.

Laura Put her down.

Nash (*swivelling Maggie round*) Anyone want 'er?

Inch (*stands on the table*) Will somebody tell me wot fuckin' pain?

Wilson The pain.

Nash puts her down. Inch stands belligerently above them.

Inch It's meant to be somethin' ta do with the pain. But wot pain? She can't even remember wot it was 'erself. Somethin' ta do with 'er upbringin'. Well, my upbringin' was three in bed and jam if yer lucky on Sundays, but I rub along. Somethin' ta do with bein' unloved, but she don' wanta be loved, she wants to be flattened by a Sherman tank.

Arthur Leave it alone.

Inch Of course, bloody Arthur thinks it's wonderful.

Laura Tell her now.

Saraffian What?

169

Laura Tell her, for God's sake, get it over with. It can't get worse. She'll understand, she'll pretend not to, but get it over with.

Inch Wot a cow.

Saraffian Shut up.

Saraffian goes over to Maggie who is propped up, lolling. You don't know if she's faking.

Maggie?

Pause.

Maggie . . .

He slaps her face.

Laura She's listening.

Saraffian Some pressure building up, my dear, amongst us all. The boy . . .

Arthur I . . .

Saraffian Shut up. In his stumbling way. I, in mine. The band, all in theirs. Arthur would like to be free of you. He would like to set up a home with Laura. Yes. And you're sacked.

He puts his hand under her chin.

All right?

Snead appears with an Alsatian and a **Policeman.**

Snead This is a raid. You're all busted.

Blackout.

Interval

The equipment stands deserted on its rostrum at the back of the stage. The speakers now have their backs to us.
    Arthur speaks from the absolute dark.

Arthur
What matter? Out of cavern comes a voice
And all it knows is that one word: rejoice.

SCENE FIVE

The light comes up on Arthur who is sitting at the front of the stage on a pile of champagne crates, staring at a small white box of potato salad in his hands.
    The stage merges into darkness at the sides so that the characters come and go in the night. First Anson approaches, jacket over arm.

Anson I saw the second set. She rather . . . pushed the boat out, I thought.

Arthur Yes.

Anson I saw the police about.

Arthur We were busted.

Anson Gosh, I'm sorry.

Arthur Mmm.

Anson That's terrible. Vicious.

Arthur Vicious.

Anson Terrible.

    Pause.

Arthur What's everyone doing?

Anson Who?

Arthur Everyone.

Anson Oh, you mean the revellers.

Arthur Yes.

Anson They've scattered. It rather loses its focus, you know. Till the champagne breakfast. It's . . . all over the place. The dinner tent's a disco and . . . they've got a Deanna Durbin in the buttery.

Arthur Of course.

Pause.

Anson I did have a partner, you know.

Arthur Yes.

Anson I rather lost track of her, I'm sure she's . . .

Arthur Yes.

Anson You were at this college?

Arthur I read music.

Anson What happened?

Arthur I met Maggie. It seemed academic just to go on reading it.

Anson Yes.

Arthur At the time troubadour was the fashionable profession. It was also very good fun.

Pause. Arthur sets the salad aside.

Still the same shit-hole, eh?

Anson I don't like it very much.

Arthur The people don't seem to have changed.

Anson Oh, I don't know. There are a few more totallys,

you know. I should think. I share digs with a totally. I mean, I call him a totally, what happens is he has his friends to tea, I never stay, I just occasionally have to let them in the door and I overhear them, they're always sitting there saying, 'The whole system's totally corrupt an's gotta be totally replaced by a totally new system', so I just stand at the door and say, 'Couple more totallys for you, Tom.'

A Dietrich figure goes by in a long silver evening dress. It is Peyote. He is radiant.

Arthur Hallo, Peyote.

Peyote If ya 'appen to see a chick wiv jus' a pair o' jeans an' a leather waistcoat, say 'ello from Peyote, will ya?

Arthur Sure thing.

Peyote passes.

Anson I'm hoping to drop out, you know. When I get my degree. I just want to groove.

Arthur Course you do. But it's not so easy is it? I mean, the rules are so complicated, it's like three-dimensional chess.

Anson Yes.

Arthur Just . . . work at it, eh?

Inch passes through heading for the tent. Arthur tries to get away.

Inch 'Allo, Arfer.

Arthur How they doing?

Inch Still doin' the interviews.

Arthur What have they found?

Inch I don't know. I think Peyote swallowed a certain amount of the evidence. 'E's very quick.

Anson I wonder . . .

Arthur Where you off to?

Inch Look for some crumpet.

Arthur Can I come with you?

Inch You'd cramp me, Arfer. Somewhere in that tent is my ideal.

Arthur What's that?

Inch A short dirty-minded blonde.

He goes out.

Anson I've got a finger in my pocket.

Arthur Ah.

Anson You know I'm a medical student?

Arthur Yes.

Anson Can I show it to you? I think it's rather a good joke. Handshake, you know, and one drops off.

He shows Arthur the severed finger. Arthur takes it and looks at it seriously.

I cut it off a corpse in the lab. Here. It's quite a good joke.

Arthur Yes. Yes.

Saraffian comes in with a silver candlestick which he tucks away in the crates. Randolph follows.

Saraffian Here we are, lads. Za za. Small advance. In lieu of. It's ten grand to a spent rubber we don't get paid.

Arthur You must be mad, the police are everywhere.

Arthur hands over some silver spoons. Smegs on from the other direction.

Saraffian Well?

Arthur Here, you can guard your own loot now.

Saraffian What did they say to you?

Smegs Same as everyone. Name and address and not to leave the area.

Saraffian Do you know what they found?

Smegs Apparently the Alsatian went berserk. It found so much stuff its eyes kept crossing and its knees caved in.

Saraffian Where's Nash?

Smegs Gone for a smoke in the bog. Said he needed a joint to calm himself down.

Smegs takes loot from his pocket.

Pepperpot.

Saraffian Ta.

Arthur And Maggie?

Saraffian looks at Smegs.

Saraffian They can't find her. Disappeared. Don't say 'oh God', that's what she wants you to say. That's what you're programmed to say, Arthur.

Saraffian holds up a hand to interrupt.

Arthur Where is she?

Saraffian After the bust she just slipped off . . .

Arthur Saraffian.

Saraffian Listen. She is sacked. Keep your nerve. Arthur.

Pause. Arthur glares at him.

Randolph Guv, can I . . .

Saraffian Here's something. Look. You have to get the little ball in the hole.

> *Saraffian has taken a toy from his pocket. Randolph sits down and tries to get the ball in the hole. Arthur watches, then turns to Anson.*

Randolph Right.

Arthur Do you know how Saraffian made his money?

Smegs Not us.

Arthur No, real money.

Saraffian Go on.

Arthur He used to wait for some black group to do well in the States, you know like the Temptations, then he says he's bringing them over. Sell out, of course. Except when they arrive they aren't quite the same people they are in the States. They're just five guys he's met in a bar.

Saraffian (*smiles*) This is true.

Arthur Who he calls the Fabulous Temptations, then teaches them the songs the real group plays.

Saraffian I've brought over some great sounds this way.

Arthur And in England nobody knows the difference.

Saraffian Seeing how they're black.

> *He laughs.*

Arthur Yeah, you wouldn't try it with the Beach Boys, would you?

Saraffian Well, one or two cheap tricks it's true. People expect it. The odd artist hung upside down from a third-floor window. It's part of the show.

Arthur No doubt.

Saraffian And Arthur feels strongly that . . .

Arthur All right.

Saraffian No, come on, you feel strongly that . . .

Arthur It's not worth saying. Nothing's worth saying. It's all so obvious.

Smegs Anyone got a fag?

Pause.

Anson Gertrude Stein never put her car in reverse.

Pause.

Arthur Yes, there is the inkling of an objection, just a smudge, perhaps the feeling Al Capone might greet you in the street.

Saraffian I told you.

Arthur Of course, it's a big organization, fair number of clients, so if some junior oddball wants to drive her band until they're catatonic with fatigue, with pills, with petrol fumes, well, at least that is her taken care of, until you choose to flick her off your balance sheet.

Wilson comes in.

And if the damage is in the head and irreversible, well at least you were many miles away.

Wilson Wot's 'appenin'?

Smegs Cambridge Union Debate.

Wilson Oh. Wot's the subject?

Arthur Ethics.

Wilson County Championship?

Smegs No, no, not Ethex like Thuthex, ethics like – what you're meant to do.

Arthur I'm going to go and find her. Take this.

Arthur hands Saraffian the finger. Goes out.

Anson It's my finger.

Saraffian Course it is, lad.

Anson I get screwed up you know. If you can imagine my life.

Saraffian Mmm.

He smiles at him and wanders away.

Anson I just long to get away. Join a band. On the road. Eh? I wouldn't mind how menial . . . anything. It's just every day here I know what the next day will be like. Isn't that dreadful? Going to lectures. Work in the lab. And all the time I want my mind to float free. I want it above me like a kite, and instead it's . . . why have I no friends? And why does nobody talk to me?

Pause. He looks round.

And, of course, I'm being boring.

He turns and goes out.

Wilson Bloody 'ellfire.

Saraffian Well.

Wilson Never go to the piss'ouse wiv that one, 'e'd chop it off soon as look at yer.

Saraffian He's just lonely.

Wilson Wot else 'as 'e got in 'is pocket, bits of old toe 'n' little chunks of earlobe?

Saraffian He's trying to be interesting, you know. Have some character. The man who goes round with a finger in his pocket. Very casual, very interesting. Rather dark. He just wants to be liked.

Wilson You know the real killers?

Saraffian Yes.

Wilson The ones who jus' wanna be liked.

Arthur reappears upstage.

Arthur Where is she? She's not in the tent.

Saraffian Nobody knows.

Wilson 'Where is she, wot is she on?'

Arthur Where is she?

Saraffian Look in the common room. Or the cricket pavilion. She might be there. But don't let her know you're looking.

Arthur goes out.

Nice boy.

Smegs Yeah.

Wilson Let's 'avva look at that.

Smegs How long till we play?

Wilson wanders upstage with the finger.

Saraffian The first day they met he drove her to the north of Scotland. The northern sky was wide and open so that strange Hebridean light came through white blinds on to their bed in a perfect square. A perfect white square in a

179

dark hotel room. And they felt that first night they were almost not in the world at all.

He smiles.

I can give you more. Much more. Many more moments of . . . one thing or another. Arthur is obsessed. What happened in rooms. On trains. The telegram she sent. Some pair of shoes. Everything.

Smegs How do you know?

Saraffian Oh, she used to tell you.

Smegs Why?

Saraffian To make you think it didn't matter to her. That's why she told you. As a hedge against disaster. Like her whole life.

Smegs What gets me is, it's her we talk about all the time, but it's Peyote'll actually kill himself.

Laura appears.

Laura Has anyone seen Arthur?

Saraffian Oh jeepers.

Wilson Where is 'e? Wot is 'e on?

Laura I just wondered if anyone had seen him.

Smegs The footsteps go from left to right. Stop there briefly. Then we say . . .

Saraffian Try the common room.

Smegs Or the cricket pavilion.

Saraffian But don't let him know you're looking.

Smegs You look puzzled and depart.

Laura What?

Smegs Next.

Wilson Laura. Jus' let me show you somethin'.

Wilson turns round. The finger is now sticking through his fly.

You see doctor . .

Laura Wilson . . .

It drops from his fly to the ground.

Wilson Whoops, there it goes again.

Laura Very funny.

She goes out. Wilson calls after her.

Wilson Laura, I promise to concentrate next time.

Saraffian Where did you stash it?

Smegs What?

Saraffian The stuff.

Wilson Oh, we only 'ad some giggle-weed, it 'ad nearly all gone.

Smegs Shouldn't we talk about the future of the band?

Wilson Yeah.

Smegs Do something different, what do you think?

Wilson I'd like to do some songs about Jesus Christ.

Smegs Wilson, he's been done to death.

Wilson Ah – 'is own complaint exactly.

Saraffian And who carried the rest, the hard stuff, who carried that?

Pause.

Don't tell me.

Wilson Well . . .

Saraffian Did she know?

Wilson She 'ad a carpetbag. It's only Peyote. 'E used to . . .

Saraffian Did she know?

Pause.

She was the bagman and she didn't know.

Wilson Yes.

Saraffian You think the police are going to believe that?

Wilson It's true.

Saraffian Of course it's true, that's not the point. The point is, who gets to go to jail.

Peyote comes in.

Peyote I jus' bin propositioned by the rowing eight.

Wilson Wot did you tell them?

Peyote I told 'em I wasn't that sort of girl.

Saraffian Listen, Peyote, you're going to have to come with me to the police, you're going to have to tell them about this bag . . .

Peyote I said I'd smash a bottle in their face.

Peyote smashes the bottle he is holding against the crates. It shatters, leaving him with nothing but the smallest neck.

Wilson Never works that. I never believe it when they do it in the films . . .

Peyote Jus' who the hell do they think I am?

Pause. He is out of his mind and commands a sudden healthy respect.

Saraffian Yes, Peyote.

Peyote I'm not anybody's.

Pause.

Saraffian No, Peyote.

Peyote I'd rather busk, I'd rather play free gigs, I'd rather busk in the foyers of VD clinics than play to these cunts.

Saraffian Yes.

Wilson It's pointless.

Peyote throws his wig violently to the ground.

Peyote An' they've ruffled my fuckin' wig.

Pause.

Wilson It's pointless. You'll never get through to him now.

Saraffian All right everyone. Find the girl.

Blackout. At once Smegs plays acoustic guitar and sings amazingly fast in the complete dark.

Don't Let The Bastards Come Near You

I come from the rulers you come from the ruled
We were making the film of our lives
And the media dwarves were howling for masterpieces
People were dropping like flies
The crew were on librium I was on brandy
Struggling hard to get through
And the days and the nights were alive
With the hatred directed at you.

*Eight single spots come up on Smegs, Wilson, Nash,
Peyote, Randolph, Arthur, Laura, Inch as they join in
the chorus.*

Don't let the bastards come near you
They just want to prove you're sane
To eat up your magic and change you
So I'll help keep the bastards away

The spots fade and we are back in complete black.

It was in your dark night of disaster
We watched as you smashed up your room
And Spanish and I we decided
We just couldn't stay in your tomb
In the morning I drove for the border
And Spanish he stayed till the end
But he has resources of humour
To which I cannot pretend

The spots come up again on the eight suspended faces.

Don't let the bastards come near you
They just want to prove you're sane
To eat up your magic and change you
So I'll help keep the bastards away

The spots fade.

Now I don't like singing with sailors
And I don't like drinking with fools
But I'll do anything that I have to
Because I know those are the rules
I know that the pain is like concrete
And the road is lonely it's true
And the load that we carry is studded with nails
So this is my message to you

The spots return.

Don't let the bastards come near you
They just want to prove you're sane
To eat up your magic and change you
So I'll help keep the bastards away

SCENE SIX

The deserted equipment. At the front of the stage Maggie is sitting reading a book. Her lips are moving. A bottle stands by the chair.
  Then Saraffian finds her.

Saraffian Looking for you. Everyone. Everywhere.

Maggie In the library.

Saraffian Didn't think of that. There are some things you should be told.

  Maggie holds up the tiny book.

Maggie Thoughts of St Ignatius. Look. Pretty thin, eh?

Saraffian Yeah.

Maggie Poor value. Just whatever came off the top of his head.

  She throws it to him.

Saraffian Maggie . . . there's a problem with the bust . . .

Maggie And I got you a trinket.

  She tosses him a napkin ring.

Saraffian Thank you.

Maggie You can melt it down.

Saraffian I will.

Maggie And pour it down your throat.

Saraffian Maggie . . .

Maggie You really got me Saraffian.

Saraffian I know.

Maggie You did well.

Saraffian The timing . . .

Maggie I was going to quit.

Saraffian I'm sure. But I sacked you first.

Pause.

Are you hurt?

Maggie Not in my overself.

Saraffian What does your overself say?

Maggie My overself says: everything's OK.

Pause.

Saraffian Maggie about the bust . . .

Maggie Why are girls who fuck around said to be tragic whereas guys who sleep about are the leaders of the pack?

Saraffian Why do people drink?

Maggie Can't stand it?

Saraffian Wrong. Need an excuse.

Maggie Ah.

Saraffian They want to be addicted so's to have something to blame. It's not me speaking. It's the drink. The drugs. It's not me can't manage. They want to be invaded, so there's an excuse. So there's a bit intact.

Maggie I've never been addicted.

Saraffian No?

Maggie This goes through me like a gutter. Even on heroin I knew I could beat it. I did beat it. There's something in me that won't lie down.

Pause.

You know I've always pitied schizophrenics.

Saraffian Oh yes.

Maggie Struggling along on two personalities. I have seventeen, I have twenty-one.

Saraffian Like everyone else.

She doesn't hear.

Maggie Do you know the purpose of reincarnation?

Saraffian Not exactly.

Maggie You get sent back because you failed last time.

Saraffian I see.

Maggie I believe all we're doing here is trying to avoid coming back. I think you get sent back because you didn't get it right last time. Basically. You got sent back for having blown it the time before. Well, this time . . . I'm not coming back.

Pause.

I was a Viking, I was a Jew . . .

Saraffian Ah.

Maggie I could get you through the Sinai desert, no map, no compass. I'd know. Just like that.

Saraffian Really?

Maggie Why don't people take more care of their overselves? They just rub them in the mud.

Saraffian Yes.

Maggie Why is that?

Saraffian It's a failing people have.

Maggie You don't believe a single word I say.

Saraffian No. Nor do you.

Maggie *Con safos.*

   Pause.

Go to San Francisco, sing in a bar.

Saraffian You never would.

Maggie Well, what am I going to do tomorrow? Tonight?

Saraffian I thought you had the little fellow . . .

Maggie Don't patronize me, Saraffian.

Saraffian . . . the finger freak. What happened to him?

Maggie I don't know. I gave him some acid, told him to get high.

Saraffian How did you get it?

Maggie What?

Saraffian The acid.

Maggie Oh, some creep. Liked the way I sang.

Saraffian Have the police talked to you?

Maggie I'm OK. Don't worry. I'm cool. This is legal and it's all I've got.

   She shows him the bottle and smiles.

Saraffian Maggie.

Maggie You're not my manager now.

Saraffian No.

   They both smile.

DAVID HARE

Maggie Do you know why I liked you as my manager?

Saraffian I have a fairly shrewd idea.

Maggie Because you were such an unspeakable shit.

Saraffian That's right. I was aware of that. You'd say to people, I'd love to do your charity gig, play free in the streets of Glasgow, great but – er – that bastard Saraffian would just never let me. And everyone says, poor girl.

Maggie You're right.

Saraffian I know. That's why everyone likes to be handled by me. I'm an excuse. Any artist stands next to me looks like a saint. Canonization. Cheap at twenty per cent.

Maggie Then why did you like me?

Saraffian I don't know. Two-bit band, one of five hundred, fifteen hundred. Your tunes were better and the singer had balls. But where did I get you? One week in the *Melody Maker* at number eighty-four. And what's called a minor cult. I'd rather have leprosy than a minor cult. You know, some booking manager rings you, says what've you got? I say Maggie Frisby's lot, he says, no no, I never take minor cults. You have it round your neck in letters of stone.

Maggie So what happened?

Saraffian Well. What happens to everyone? Bands just break up. Travel too much. Drop too much acid. Fifty-seven varieties of clap. Become too successful – never your problem, my dear – they break up because they don't feel any need. I don't mean fame, that's boring, or money, that's a cliché, of course it goes without saying that money will separate you from the things you want to sing about, we all know that. I mean – need. Maggie. Where's the need?

Maggie I don't know. What do you think?

Saraffian I don't know. I don't sing.

Pause.

Maggie It's nothing to do with singing.

Saraffian No?

Maggie Oh, come on, it's nothing to do with being an artist, artists are just like everyone else . . .

Saraffian Then what . . .

Maggie I have this sense of arbitrariness you know. Like it was Arthur but it could have been one of ten thousand others.

Saraffian Just . . .

Maggie Where did we get this idea that one human being's more interesting than another?

Pause.

Saraffian. In Russia the peasants could not speak of the past without crying. What have we ever known?

Pause.

My aunt's garden led down to a river. It was the Thames, but so small and green and thick with reeds you wouldn't recognize it. It was little more than a spring. I was staying there, I was six, I think, I had a village there by the riverbank, doll village with village shop, selling jelly beans, little huts, little roads. I took the local priest down there, I wanted him to consecrate the little doll church. The sun was shining and he took my head in his hands. He said, inside this skull the most beautiful piece of machinery that God ever made. He said, a fair-haired English child, you will think and feel the finest things in the world. The sun blazed and his hands enclosed my whole skull.

She smiles, pours whisky over her head, down her front, and inside her trousers. Then goes over to Saraffian, takes hold of him. Puts her hands round his head. Then she lets go.

Saraffian. Thank you. Great relationship. Great creative control.

Saraffian Maggie.

Maggie Great help in career at time most needed. Never forgotten. Farewell.

Saraffian Maggie. The band didn't get around to telling you. They stashed all their stuff in your bag. That means the bust sort of settles on you.

Long pause. Maggie turns back and looks at him.

Maggie OK. Try prison for a while, why not?

She sits down where she is. Pause. Then she lies down.

Saraffian Ah. Is that all right?

Pause. You can see him thinking. Then he takes some fags out and goes over to her.

Cigarette?

Maggie No.

Saraffian You know . . .

Pause.

You know how people crap on about Hollywood in the thirties.

Maggie Yes.

Saraffian Long books about Thalberg and Louis B. Mayer. Who laid the ice cubes on Jean Harlow's nipples? But nobody notices they're living through something just as rich, just as lovely. And in thirty years' time they'll write books about the record business of the fifties or sixties. What it was like to have known Jerry Wexler. Or glimpse Chuck Berry at the other end of the room.

Maggie You think?

Saraffian I'm banking on it. If I'm to have had any life at all. It's going to look so special. Once it's over, of course.

Pause. Then Inch comes on holding up one hand.

Inch Upper-class cunt, it's in a world of its own. Smell my fingers.

Saraffian Thank you, no.

Inch Dab some be'ind yer ears.

Saraffian Inch . . .

Inch sits down with a vacuum flask and a Mars bar.

Inch Now I'm 'ungry.

Saraffian They should invent a machine.

Inch Wot?

Saraffian Gratify all your senses at once.

Inch Well, I did know someone used to eat Complan sittin' on the can. 'E was into 'is 'ead, you see, despised the body, so 'e reckoned it best to sit shovellin' it in at one end and pushin' it out at the other, an' that way get the 'ole job over with. Now I reckon if 'e coulda jus' spared 'is left 'and as well . .

Saraffian Quite.

Inch Do the lot in one go.

Saraffian Yes. The rest of us, well, we spread our pleasures so thin.

Laura comes in.

Laura What's happening?

Saraffian Did you find him?

Laura No. Is she all right?

Maggie is lying still on the ground.

Saraffian Yes. Get ready for the third set.

Laura It's cancelled. There are notices all over saying it's cancelled by popular demand.

Inch Great.

Saraffian I knew it. It's in the contract. Three sets or we don't get paid.

Laura So what do we do?

Saraffian Play it. Just play it, it's our only chance of the cash. I don't care if nobody's listening. Why don't you round up the band?

Laura It's not my job.

Inch I'm 'avin' me tea.

Saraffian Laura. Please.

She goes out to start looking.

Getting your hands on it. I mean, actually getting your hands on the cash. That is the only skill. Really. The only skill in music.

From offstage the sound of Peyote playing the piano with his feet. He is wheeled on by Wilson, Nash and Smegs as Saraffian goes out.

Peyote 'Ere we are.

Inch That's not ours.

Peyote Saraffian said nick somethin', I nicked somethin'.

Inch We can't nick that, we can't get it in the van.

Peyote Let's 'ave a ball of our own.

Wilson Did yer talk to the pigs?

Peyote Let's 'ave a party.

Laura returns.

Laura Right. Is everyone ready?

Wilson 'Ow yer feelin', Peyote?

Peyote Fantastic. Let's 'avva party.

Laura It's three-thirty, let's just play the . . .

Wilson 'E's right back up there, 'ow does 'e do it?

Peyote Listen, mate, if you'd dropped as much stuff as me . .

Smegs It always comes back to this.

Peyote You lot'll never understand . . .

Smegs If there's one thing I really despise it's psychedelic chauvinism . . .

Peyote I want some fun.

Smegs 'I've had more trips than you.'

Peyote Fun.

Inch If you like I can . . .

Wilson Wot?

Inch Set light to my fart.

Nash Oh no.

Wilson Not again.

Nash We've seen it.

Wilson Dozens of times.

Smegs One streak of blue flame and it's over.

Wilson Can't you do anything else?

Inch Yeah. I do bird impressions.

Smegs Really?

Inch Yeah. I eat worms.

Saraffian returns with a conductor's baton which he taps on the piano.

Saraffian Right. Look lively, everyone. Third set. Any ideas? Requests?

Wilson I would like to 'ear Richard Tauber sing 'Yew Are My 'eart's Desire'.

Nash Wot is this?

Smegs Get in a line.

Peyote Let's get on with it . . .

Saraffian This is the third set.

Peyote I'm gonna need a fuck in about forty-five seconds.

Nash Did you take sweeties again?

Randolph has appeared.

Randolph Guv, this little ball it just won't go in . .

Saraffian Keep trying.

Nash Who's the vocals?

Saraffian Just stay in a line.

Peyote I'm not gonna last.

Wilson Listen, we gotta 'ave real vocals.

Saraffian Tony. Sing with the band.

Randolph But I gotta try and . . .

Saraffian You may stop. You may sing with the band.

Randolph Wot key are we in?

> *A photographic moment. Held for a second, the new team with Randolph at the centre. Then the music begins with Smegs on Jew's harp, the rest come in one by one. An improvised jam, very inspired.*

Let's Have A Party

Peyote
Ball gown baby
Bubble gum queen
Left her body
In my new blue jeans
Said hello
That was that
Didn't have time to check my hat
So

Band
Let's have a party, let's paint the town
Let's have a party, chase away that frown
Let's have a party, let your hair down.

> *Instrumental verse, then:*

Let's have a party, etc.

Ball gown baby
Bubble gum queen
Saw her picture in a magazine
Said she'd go down
The butterfly flicks

All of them changes all of them licks
So

Let's have a party, etc.

> *They leap back, challenging Randolph to enter the song.*
> *He does, falteringly, inventing the words as he goes.*

Randolph
Ball gown baby
Bubble gum queen
Spread some sauce on my baked beans
Said hey I got you
Special treat
Be bop a lula
You eat meat
So

> *He is accepted. They all bash hell out of the piano.*

All
Let's have a party, etc.

> *Saraffian stops them.*

LET'S HAVE A PARTY

Saraffian All right. Hold it. There's no one to witness the third set took place. We need that little bloke. The one that booked us.

Wilson The one wiv the finger.

Saraffian Yes.

Wilson You won't find 'im. Some cretin gave 'im some acid. They took 'im to 'ospital. Stupid little shit.

A pause. Maggie sits up. She looks at the band. A silence. Only Saraffian doesn't see her. Maggie stands up and looks at them, then goes out. Sudden deflation.

Saraffian Oh dear.

Laura What happens next?

Saraffian Just let me think . . .

Laura What about . . .

Saraffian Tony, ring Mrs Saraffian, say I'm not going to get back tonight so she's to change the budgie's sandpaper, OK?

Randolph Will do.

He goes.

Peyote Are we gonna do this or are we not?

Nash I'm beginnin' to feel jus' a bit of a fool.

Wilson You think there'd be somebody. Wouldn't you? Don't you think? Jus' somebody to hear us? Wouldn't you think?

They stop and look out into the night. Then Arthur comes in.

Arthur What the hell is going on?

Saraffian Arthur . . .

Arthur I just talked to the police.

Saraffian Don't worry, everything's in hand . . .

Arthur They seem to think Maggie was pushing the stuff.

Saraffian That's right.

Arthur Well, who the hell put the stuff in her bag?

Peyote I think I'll jus' phase out, you know . . .

Arthur He knows bloody well what's going on.

Peyote Jus' go and get laid.

Arthur He's a bit fucking selective about what he blocks out.

Peyote shrugs and giggles.

Peyote Well.

Saraffian Arthur . . .

Arthur Did you tell Maggie?

Saraffian Yes.

Arthur Does she know she's going to get done?

Saraffian Oh yes.

Arthur Well, what does she say?

Pause.

Saraffian Well . . . to be honest . . . she doesn't seem to mind.

Randolph returns quickly.

Randolph You better come quick. She's burning down the tent.

Blackout. Pitch black. Silence.

SCENE SEVEN

Pitch dark. You can see nothing at all. You just hear their voices: Maggie is very cheerful.

Arthur Maggie. Maggie. Are you there?

Pause.

Are you there?

Maggie Arthur.

Arthur Ah.

Maggie I'm here. I'm naked and I'm covered in coconut oil.

Arthur Oh fuck, what was that?

Maggie It's a rugby post.

She laughs.

Arthur You've done pretty well.

Maggie Thank you very much.

Arthur Yip. Police. Ambulance. Fire brigade. You just got to score the air-sea rescue service and you got a full house.

Maggie Thank you. What's the damage?

Arthur Not bad.

Maggie (*complaining*) I can't see any *flames*.

Arthur No, no, they're all coping rather well. They all love it you know. Dashing about in the smoke. They're hoping to make it an annual event.

Maggie Really?

Arthur Bit of fun.

Pause.

How've you bin?

Maggie All right.

Arthur Haven't seen you for a long time. Must be six months. What have you been up to?

Maggie Nothing really. I had the flu.

Arthur What else?

Maggie Do you have some cigarettes?

Arthur Sure.

Maggie Can you give me the pack? It's just if I'm gonna be arrested I'm gonna need some.

Arthur Of course. Here.

Maggie Thank you.

A match flares. We see their faces as they light their fags.

Arthur What were you doing?

Maggie What?

Arthur The tent. Just making sure?

Maggie Oh yes. Just making sure.

The match out. Darkness again.

Arthur I can get you a lawyer.

Maggie Don't be stupid. What else?

Arthur Oh, you know. Larry says, come and see him

soon. Martha says will you cover the new Dusty
Springfield for the supermarket? Derek says . . . Derek
says . . .

Maggie Yeah, what does Derek say?

Arthur Derek says . . . I don't know what Derek says. Far
out. Out of sight. Wow man. Jeez. That's what Derek says.

Pause. Arthur begins to cry.

I can't live without you. I can't get through the day.

Maggie What else?

Arthur You said you loved me.

Maggie I did. I did love you. I loved you the way you used
to be.

Arthur But it's you that's made me the way I am now.

Maggie I know. That's what's called irony.

Pause.

We better go back.

Arthur Maggie.

She shouts into the night.

Maggie Nothing's going to stop me. No one. Ever. Let me
do what I want.

Pause. Arthur lying on the ground.

So much for small talk. Will you walk me back?

Arthur Right.

Maggie Poor Arthur. You'd like to be hip. But your
intelligence will keep shining through.

She laughs, and they begin to go.

Watch where you drop that fag.

Arthur Ha ha.

Maggie Don't want to start a . . .

She peals with laughter. At once the lights come up. The stage is empty. But thick with smoke. They've gone.

SCENE EIGHT

At once Laura wheels a flat porter's barrow on through the smoke. Inch appears from the other side.

Inch I jus' drove the van across the cricket pitch.

Laura Well done.

Inch I reckon it'll be takin' spin this year.

He and Laura begin to dismantle the equipment. Maggie and Arthur appear.

There some people lookin' for you.

Maggie Really? Where?

Inch About seven 'undred and fifty of 'em. An' all round, I'd say.

Saraffian appears squirting a soda syphon.

Saraffian My dear.

Maggie Saraffian.

Saraffian Well done. Very educational. We have all learnt something tonight.

Maggie What's that?

Saraffian Always put an arson clause in the contract. I'm going to have to pay for this.

He hands Inch the syphon.

Might as well nick it.

Inch Right.

Saraffian My God, but that was fun.

He bursts out laughing and embraces Maggie.

Bless you my dear. At a stroke the custard is crème brulée. You've totally restored my faith in the young.

Arthur Is anyone hurt?

Saraffian Can I tell you a story? I really must tell you a story now.

Wilson passes. He has scored a fireman's helmet.

Wilson Congratulations.

Maggie Thank you.

Wilson It's really beautiful.

He kisses her.

Maggie Better than taking your trousers down?

Wilson Oh yea. It's jus' a different thing.

Maggie Right.

Wilson If yer don't mind, I've 'eard there's a psychology tutor on fire, I'd really like to see it you know.

Maggie Sure.

Wilson heads out.

Wilson It's so stupid it's just wonderful.

Inch Hey, 'old on, Wilson, I think I'll come and drag some naked women from the flames.

205

Inch leaps off the stage and follows Wilson.

Saraffian I'll tell you of my evening at the Café de Paris. March 9th, 1941.

Nash crosses with a bucket of water.

Arthur You won't put it out with that.

Nash This ain't for the fire. It's for Peyote.

He laughs and goes into the dark.

Saraffian I was with this girl. She's related to a marquis on her mother's side and me a boy from Tottenham whose dad ran a spieler in his own back room. So I'm something of a toy, a bauble on her arm. And she said, please can we go to the Café de Paris, I think because she wants to shock her pals by being seen with me, but also because she does genuinely want to dance to the music of Snakehips Johnson and his Caribbean band.

Laura picks up as much equipment as she can manage and goes out. Saraffian, Maggie and Arthur left alone with the piano.

So I say fine, off to Piccadilly Circus, Coventry Street, under the Rialto cinema, the poshest . . . the jewelled heart of London where young officers danced before scattering across four continents to fight in Hitler's war. You won't believe this but you went downstairs into a perfect reproduction of the ballroom on the *Titanic*. I should have been warned. And there they are. A thousand young blades and a thousand young girls with Marcel waves in their hair. So out of chronic social unease, I became obstreperous, asking loudly for brown ale, and which way to the pisshouse, showing off, which gave me a lot of pleasure, I remember they enjoyed me, thinking me amusing. And I was pretty pleased with myself. The glittering heart of the empire, the waiter leaning over me

to pick up the champagne. And then nothing. As if acid
has been thrown in my face. The waiter is dead at my feet.
And the champagne rises of its own accord in the bottle
and overflows. Two fifty-kilo bombs have fallen through
the cinema above and Snakehips Johnson is dead and
thirty-two others. I look at the waiter. He has just one
sliver of glass in his back from a shattered mirror. That's
all.

Maggie gets up and moves away to sit on the stage.

So we're all lying there. A man lights a match and I can see
that my girl friend's clothes have been completely blown
off by the blast. She is twenty-one and her champagne is
now covered in a grey dust. A man is staring at his mother
whose head is almost totally severed. Another man is
trying to wash the wounded, he is pouring champagne
over the raw stump of a girl's thigh to soothe her. Then
somebody yells put the match out, we'll die if there's gas
about, and indeed there was a smell, a yellow smell.

I looked up. I could see the sky. It's as if we are in a huge
pit and above at the edges of the pit from milk bars all
over Leicester Square people are gathering to look down
the hole at the mess below. And we can't get out. There are
no stairs. Just people gaping. And us bleeding.

Then suddenly I realized that somebody, somehow,
God knows how, had got down and come among us. I
just saw two men flitting through the shadows. I close my
eyes. One comes near. I can smell his breath. He touches
my hand. He then removes the ring from my finger. He
goes.

He is looting the dead.

And my first thought is: I'm with you, pal.

I cannot help it, that was my first thought. Even here,
even now, even in fire, even in blood, I am with you in
your scarf and cap, slipping the jewels from the hands of
the corpses.

I'm with you.

So then a ladder came down and the work began. And we climbed out. There we are, an obscene parade, the rich in tatters, slipping back to our homes, the evening rather . . . spoilt . . . and how low, how low can men get stealing from the dead and dying?

And I just brush myself down and feel lightheaded, for the first time in my life totally sure of what I feel. I climb the ladder to the street, push my way through the crowd. My arm is grazed and bleeding. I hail a taxi. The man is a cockney. He stares hard at the exploded wealth. He stares at me in my dinner jacket. He says, 'I don't want blood all over my fucking taxi.' And he drives away.

There is a war going on. All the time. A war of attrition.

He smiles.

Good luck.

Maggie Bollocks. I just wanted to go to jail.

Silence. Then Laura appears.

Laura They really do seem to want you, Maggie. Can they have you now?

Maggie What a load of shit. You're full of shit, Saraffian. What a crucial insight, what a great moment in the Café de Paris. And what did you do the next *thirty years*?

Pause.

Well. I'm sure it gives you comfort, your nice little class war. It ties things up very nicely, of course, from the outside you look like any other clapped-out businessman, but inside, oh, inside you got it all worked out.

Pause.

This man has believed the same thing for thirty years. And

it does not show. Is that going to happen to us? Fucking hell, somebody's got to keep on the move.

Then she smiles, very buoyant.

Laura, come here, you look after Arthur.

Laura Yes.

Maggie You can have your hat back, all the hats he wants to give you, you can have. Anything I said about you, I withdraw. The tightness of your arse I apologize. You're Mahatma Gandhi, you're the Pope. Arthur, you're Cole Porter. Or at least you will be. Or at least nobody else ever will be.

She smiles again.

Laura Shall I let you know how it goes in Stoke?

Maggie If you make it.

Laura What?

Maggie I'm only guessing. But I'd take a bet this band never plays again. When did you cancel Stoke?

Saraffian About a week ago.

Maggie There.

Saraffian You know me too well.

He goes out.

Maggie So I go to jail. Nobody is to think about me, nobody is to say, 'How is she these days?' Nobody to mention me. Nobody to say, 'How much does she drink?' Nobody is to remember. Nobody is to feel guilty. Nobody is to feel they might have done better. Remember. I'm nobody's excuse.

If you love me, keep on the move.

*She heads out. She makes as if to take the bottle of
Scotch from on top of the piano but stops dead, her
back to us, and raises her hands instead. A pause. Then
she goes out. Silence. Arthur and Laura alone.*

Laura What are you on?

Arthur On?

Laura Transport.

Arthur Oh. Motor-sickle.

Laura Is there room on the back?

Arthur Sure.

Laura Will you give us a tune? One of those awful old
ones you like . . .

*He stares at her. Then Inch, Wilson, Nash and Smegs
return laughing.*

Wilson That was the best night I 'ad in years.

Nash Really brightened up the evenin'.

Wilson Yeah.

Nash I thought we was gonna 'ave a real flop on 'our
'ands.

Inch Funny 'ow plastic burns in' it?

Wilson Yeah, all sorta blue wiv little fringes.

Inch And formica doesn't.

Nash That's right. I noticed that.

Inch I kept 'oldin' it in the flames but nothin'.

He starts loading the equipment on to the barrow.

Smegs So what do we do?

Laura The police said we can all bugger off.

Inch Then we go 'ome, that's what we do.

Wilson Great.

Inch The van's over there.

Wilson Anyone fancy a game?

Smegs Sure.

Wilson Seven-card stud? I got some cards in the back. Perhaps we could try some new rules I got . . .

Nash, Wilson, Smegs, Inch go off, pulling off the trolley loaded with equipment.

Laura Where did you put your helmet?

Arthur I used to think it was so easy, you know. If I leave her, she'll kill herself. I thought she's only got one problem. She doesn't know how to be happy. But that's not her problem at all. Her problem is: she's frightened of being happy. And if ever it looked as if she might make it, if the clouds cleared and I, or some other man, fell perfectly into place, if everyone loved her and the music came good, that's when she'd kill herself. Not so easy, huh?

Pause.

Laura Play us a dreadful old tune.

Arthur Laura. It just wouldn't work between us. Not now.

Inch returns.

Inch There's 'ardly any petrol left in the van. I can't find the spare can.

Arthur Maggie took it. To burn down the tent.

Inch That's a bit fuckin' inconsiderate, she mighta noticed we was short o' gas. Lend us a couple of quid somebody. Arfer?

Arthur Don't have it.

Inch Well, sorry to say this, Laura, but we're gonna 'ave to sell your body. And pretty bloody fast. Somewhere between 'ere an' Baldock you're gonna 'ave to do it in the road.

Inch goes off.

Laura I've only waited six years. You might have mentioned it before.

Arthur Yes. Yes. It was silly.

Pause. Saraffian returns, picks up the situation at once.

Saraffian I had a look at the cellars.

Arthur Ah.

Saraffian The stock is remarkable. The 1949 Romanée St Vivant is like gold-dust you know.

Arthur Did you, er . . .

Saraffian Unfortunately, not. They'd padlocked the racks.

Arthur Ah.

Inch (*off*) Laura, get your fat butt in 'ere.

Saraffian looks at Laura who now has tears running down her face.

Saraffian Of course, this college was once famous for its port.

Arthur I didn't know that.

Saraffian The finest cellar of vintage port in England. Then in 1940 when the dons heard Hitler was coming . . . Hitler was coming . . .

They both look at her. She is now having hysterics, hitting the ground.

Arthur Laura, can you stop crying . . .

Saraffian Hitler was coming . . .

Arthur I can't hear what Saraffian is saying.

Saraffian They drank it. So he wouldn't get his fat
German hands on it. Their contribution to the war effort.
Four thousand bottles in just eleven months.

Saraffian as if to move.

Arthur Leave her.

Peyote enters.

Peyote Fantastic.

Arthur Yeah.

Peyote Fuckin' on a fire engine, you wouldn't believe it.

He goes.

Arthur What's the time?

Saraffian Just gone four.

Laura When are you going to tell them?

Saraffian Who?

Laura The band.

Saraffian Oh, tomorrow. Enough for one day.

Wilson has appeared upstage.

Wilson Laura. You comin' wiv us?

Laura Yes. Yes. I'm coming with you.

*She stands a moment crying. Wilson looks at them all as
if anew.*

Wilson I don't know why you lot make it so 'ard for
yerselves.

Laura picks up Maggie's bag and goes out.

Wilson Right. Well. Back into the little tin hell. Always makes me feel like bloody Alec Guinness. You know, into the 'ot metal 'ut. And at the other end, well we may be a little sweaty about the lip an' doin' that funny walk but fuck me if we ain't whistlin' Colonel Bogey. Goodnight all.

He goes.

Saraffian Goodnight lads.

Arthur Goodnight.

Saraffian and Arthur alone.

I knew a guy, played in a band. They were loud, they were very loud. What I mean by loud is: they made Pink Floyd sound like a Mozart quintet. I said to him, why the hell don't you wear muffs? In eighteen months you're going to be stone deaf. He said: that's why we play so loud. The louder we play, the sooner we won't be able to hear. I can see us all. Rolling down the highway into middle age. Complacency. Prurience. Sadism. Despair.

Saraffian gets out a hipflask.

Saraffian Don't worry. Have some brandy.

Arthur What?

Saraffian Napoleon. Was waiting till those buggers had gone.

He offers it. Arthur refuses. Arthur sits down at the upright piano on the deserted stage. Randolph comes in.

Randolph I rung the wife.

Saraffian Thank you.

Randolph Bloke answered.

Saraffian So.

Pause.

We must go.

Arthur Who's the bloke?

Saraffian Where did I put the car?

Arthur Who's the bloke?

Saraffian Oh, Mrs Saraffian's friend. Called Wetherby. Secretary of the local golf club, I'm afraid. Mean with a nine iron. She likes his manners. I rev the Jag in the drive, rattle the milk bottles, you know, wait ten minutes, then . . . enter my home.

Pause.

God bless you and . . . Saraffian goes. Come on, Tony, long way to go. Too late to count number plates, you'll just have to sit and think.

Saraffian and Randolph go out. Arthur alone on stage with the piano.

Arthur Where is the money? And where are the girls?

Pause. Then he begins to play.

Arthur's Song

My relatives and friends all think I'm barmy
Because I went away and joined the Foreign Legion
My funny little ways
Have got the others in a mess
I think it's time that I came clean
Decided to explain
It isn't just the season
That has given me the opportunity to do
What I have always wanted to do

And though we're stranded in the rain
Leaving on a midnight boat
At ease upon our chairs before the mast
The world round is spinning round decidedly too much
We must hang on or lose our sense of drama

Never seen faces so empty
Never spent money so fast
You can't touch the important things
They keep them under glass
Your good friends always tell you lies
Doing what your bad friends would never do
And nothing rhymes with orange
But
I love you

Never seen faces so empty etc.

ARTHUR'S SONG

Towards the end of the song Snead enters carrying two suitcases. He comes down towards Arthur at the very end.

Snead Sir.

Pause.

Left these.

Pause.

Left these behind.

Pause.

Sir.

Arthur Thank you, Mr Snead. Why are you frightened? Why's everyone frightened?

Pause. Then a blackout. Then projections large in the blackout, one by one.

ANDREW SMITH NICKNAME PEYOTE
INHALED HIS OWN VOMIT
DIED IN A HOTEL ROOM IN SAN ANTONIO TEXAS
APRIL 17TH 1973
MAGGIE
ARTHUR
SARAFFIAN
THE BAND
ALIVE
WELL
LIVING IN ENGLAND

Then:

Maggie's Song

Last orders on the Titanic
Set up the fol de rol

Tell the band to play that number
Better get it in your soul
Put the life boats out to sea
We've only got a few
Let the women and children drown
Man we've gotta save the crew

Because the ship is sinking
And time is running out
We got water coming in
Places we don't know about
The tide is rising
It's covering her name
The ship is sinking
But the music remains the same

Last orders on the Titanic
Put your life belts on
We can't hear the captain shouting
Cos the band goes on and on
I only want to tell you
That you have my sympathy
But there has to be a sacrifice
And it isn't going to be me

Because etc.

Last orders on the Titanic
Get up and paint your face
Deck hands in dungarees
And millionaires in lace
I only woke you baby
To say I love you so
But the water is up around
My knees goodbye I have to go

Because the ship is sinking etc.

The music remains the same

LAST ORDERS

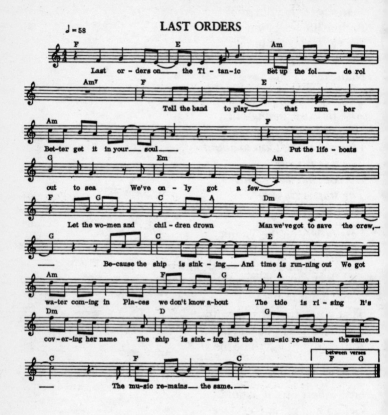

KNUCKLE

Characters

Curly Delafield
Jenny Wilbur
Grace Dunning
Patrick Delafield
Max Dupree
Barman
Storeman
Policeman
Porter
The Michael Lomax Trio

The main set is the Shadow of the Moon Club. The changes from scene to scene must always be very fast indeed. For this reason it is wiser not to drop a curtain between each scene.

Time – the present.

Knuckle was first presented by Michael Codron at the Comedy Theatre, London, on 4 March 1974. The cast was as follows:

Curly Delafield Edward Fox
Jenny Wilbur Kate Nelligan
Grace Dunning Shelagh Fraser
Patrick Delafield Douglas Wilmer
Max Dupree Malcolm Storry
Barman Leonard Kavanagh
Storeman David Jones
Policeman Stephen Gordon
Porter
The Michael Lomax Trio

Directed by Michael Blakemore
Settings by John Napier
Music by Marc Wilkinson

I had to admit that I lived for nights like these, moving across the city's great broken body making connections among its millions of cells. I had a crazy wish or fantasy that some day before I died, if I had all the right neural connections, the city would come all the way alive. Like the Bride of Frankenstein.

Ross Macdonald

Act One

SCENE ONE

The Shadow of the Moon Club. Night.
  There is a long, low bar; also a table, chairs and stools.
  When the curtain rises, **Jenny** *is sitting at a table,*
drinking and smoking. The **Barman,** *Tom, is behind the*
bar. **Lomax***'s voice is heard on the loudspeakers.*

Lomax (*off*) Ladies and Gentlemen, dance to the music of
Michael Lomax and the Freshman Three.

  A hick band starts playing 'String of Pearls', thin and
  distant. **Curly** *strides into the bar.*

Curly I'm having a lemonade.

Barman Fresh lemon, sir?

Curly Fresh lemon.

  The Barman sets to. Jenny goes up to Curly.

Jenny Is your name Curly?

Curly (*points to a table*) Just a moment.

Jenny Hullo.

Curly And a Scotch.

  Jenny goes and sits down. The Barman holds the glass
  against an upside-down whisky bottle.

Bottle.

Barman Sir?

Curly I want to look at the bottle.

227

The Barman hands over the bottle. Curly unscrews the measuring top and takes a wet wad out of it.

Blotting paper. That's a terrible trick.

Barman Sir.

Curly If you do that again I'll squeeze the lemon in your eye.

Barman Sir.

Curly And now I'll have the bottle.

He carries the bottle over to Jenny's table and puts it down. Jenny gives the Barman a nod. The Barman exits.

Got you a drink.

Jenny Thank you.

Pause.

You look like your sister.

Curly The Shadow of the Moon. Is this still the only club in Guildford?

He sits at the table.

Jenny This is it.

Curly Did Sarah come here?

Jenny You know Sarah?

Curly No, I don't. That's the whole point. I hadn't seen her for twelve years. I haven't seen anyone.

Jenny What made you come back?

Curly Was she friendly with men?

Jenny In a way. She went for a particular kind . . .

Curly I remember.

Jenny You know . . .

Curly Still the same kind?

Jenny These had a kind of Neanderthal gleam.

Curly That's them. And she was only eight at the time.

Jenny Did your father ask you to do this?

Curly Where was she working?

Jenny She'd been working as a nurse in a psychiatric hospital.

Curly Dangerous job.

Jenny Have you seen your father?

Curly Not yet. I'm staying with Patrick from tonight.

Jenny I see.

Curly How long's she been gone?

Jenny You take your conversation at a fair old lick.

Curly I'm transistorized. How long's she been gone?

  Jenny insists on a pause.

Jenny (*stubbing out her cigarette*) Eight weeks.

Curly Where exactly did she disappear?

Jenny Between Eastbourne and Pevensey Bay there's a stretch of beach about a mile long. Just dune and shingle. It's called the Crumbles.

Curly Had she been to Eastbourne before?

Jenny I don't know.

Curly What do the police have to say?

Jenny They think if she did drown herself in Eastbourne it would be six weeks yet before she was washed up in Herne Bay. A tribute to the strength of the English Channel.

Curly And Sarah's extraordinary buoyancy. Have a cigarette.

Jenny No, thank you.

Curly Was she suicidal?

Jenny I don't know what it means.

Curly Down in the dumps.

He puts down the cigarettes. He never smokes himself.

Jenny She was a paranoid. Of a particularly lethal type.

Curly Go on.

Jenny I know you don't like me, she used to say. Begging you to say, of course I like you. If you didn't say that, she was finished. And if you did say it, she didn't believe you. And once she couldn't believe that she couldn't believe anything. Everything you said had black wings and a bloodstained beak.

Curly And she was the nurse.

Jenny Yes.

Curly Have a cigarette.

Jenny No, thank you.

She deliberately lights her own cigarette.

Curly But not what you'd call suicidal.

Jenny She was depressed. So. Everyone's depressed. She used to say life was a plush abattoir. Fair enough.

Curly Fair enough.

Jenny She used to say – this is a very pretentious girl – she used to say she'd recognize a moment of happiness because – she remembered having one in 1965, and if another came along, she could compare.

Curly When was that?

Jenny Don't know. One evening, before dusk. She felt happy. For about twenty minutes . . .

Curly Well . . .

Jenny Well – what she said – more than her fair share.

Pause. The music ends, followed by clapping.

Curly Special friends, did she have?

Jenny A journalist called Dupree.

Curly Who else?

Jenny Just me.

Curly Like her pretty well?

Jenny Pretty well.

Curly Have another drink.

Jenny No.

Curly Not happy. Not liked. Pretentious.

Jenny We all told her she was pretentious. And she said certainly I am. That's because the world is unduly modest.

Curly Yes, well, there you are.

Jenny You left home much earlier she said.

Curly When I was fifteen.

Jenny She said you took four dozen rifles from the school cadet corps and sold them to the IRA.

Curly Old story. Not necessarily true.

Jenny Then sold the IRA to the British police.

Curly That sounds more like me. I was – loud. Had the second half of the pint. That sort of thing. Smoked twenty a day. But I've quietened down.

Lomax (*off, over the mike*) It's Hawaiian night in the Paradise Room.

> *Curly gets up and helps himself to lemonade from behind the bar.*

(*off*) Grass skirts, sweet music, and good food. The Paradise Room is situated on the first floor, just beyond William Tell's Alpine Grotto. Hurry up to Heaven.

> *A xylophonist starts playing 'Under A Blanket Of Blue'. Jenny does not look at Curly behind her.*

Jenny Are you afraid?

Curly Why?

Jenny If she was dead does that frighten you?

Curly I'm not afraid.

Jenny They found a purse on the beach. And a coat. Which is how they know she was there. And inside the purse they found two railway tickets. Returns to Victoria. Which means she was with someone. Which may mean she was killed.

Curly Is that consistent?

Jenny What?

Curly Is that consistent with how she lived?

Jenny Sarah? Sure. Like all women. Hanging out for it . . .

Curly All right.

Jenny Longs to be raped. Is that not what you think?

Curly All right.

Jenny Well . . .

Pause.

Curly Did she live with you?

Jenny The machine grinds on.

Curly Did she live with you?

Jenny She moved into my flat. She left Guildford to avoid her father. She ran away to Surbiton. Don't laugh. She couldn't gesture as big as you. Venezuela, wherever it was . . .

Curly Peru . . .

Jenny She ran away to Surbiton. That's the scale of her life.

Curly Had she been to Eastbourne before?

Jenny It's nice to hear the old ones again.

Curly Had she been to Eastbourne before?

Jenny Often.

Curly Why?

Jenny You could breathe in Eastbourne. That's what she said.

Curly You didn't tell me that before.

Jenny I was waiting for you to uncurl your lip.

Curly That's how I keep it. Catches crumbs. What do you do for a living?

Jenny I manage this club.

Curly Who owns it?

Jenny A man called Malloy. Runs it on the side.

Curly What else does he do?

Jenny What does everyone do in Guildford?

Curly Work in the City.

Jenny City. Right.

Curly Friend of Sarah's.

Jenny Friend of us all. This is our home.

Curly I used to come here . . .

Jenny Yes?

Curly It was skiffle. In my day. One time I . . .

Jenny Pissed in a bottle and made them sell it as Martini.

Curly You knew.

Jenny You're a legend.

Curly Sold like a bomb.

Jenny It's changed since then. It used to be the club of clubs. We all came here. Young Guildford, with our coke and Benzedrine. For a lot of us it was paradise. Loud and lovely. Then it lost its way. The lushes moved in and the middle-aged voyeurs. Now it's just a bomb site. Well, you can see . . .

Curly Why do you stay?

Jenny Not your business.

Curly I'm asking.

Jenny Do you know what Sarah said about you . . . ?

Curly Nice girl.

Jenny She said whenever you stood up there were two greasy patches on the seat of your chair.

Pause. The music ends, followed by clapping.

Curly I'm here for her sake. That's all.

Jenny Nobody asked you.

Curly And now I'm here I won't be put off. Nobody told me, do you know? I read it for myself, in an English paper. I reckon I'm far enough away from you all –

Jenny Don't count me . . .

Curly – to be the best person to find out what happened. I hold no brief for the Home Counties. Nor its inhabitants.

Jenny Best left to the police.

Curly They don't have my equipment. The steel-tipped boot, you know, the knuckleduster.

Jenny I can tell you've been out of the country.

Lomax (*off*) Ladies and gentlemen, for each and every one of us there must surely come the day when – we'll gather lilacs.

The band plays a reedy introduction to 'We'll Gather Lilacs'.

Curly Dance?

Jenny Dance with you?

Curly It's that or go home to my father.

Jenny You're squat and ugly.

Curly I am repulsive. That is true.

Pause.

Jenny Well, there you are.

Curly What I say is: don't piss in the well. One day you may want to drink from it.

Curly stands. Jenny begins to dance with him at arm's length. The music swells to very loud.

SCENE TWO

The drawing-room of the Delafields' Guildford house. Night.
*Everything is just so. As the curtain rises, **Mrs Dunning** is sitting on the sofa, sorting clothes from a box on the floor into a suitcase on the coffee table. She is Scottish.*
Curly comes through the door.

Curly Good evening. We haven't met yet. My name is Curly. Patrick's son Curly.

Mrs Dunning They let you into the country all right?

Curly No trouble. Where's Pa?

Mrs Dunning Upstairs.

Curly Have you lived here long?

Mrs Dunning About a year.

Curly fingers casually through a pile of clothes.

Curly There seems very little point in storing clothes –

Mrs Dunning Yes . . .

Curly – that are well past wearing.

He holds up an article of clothing.

Mrs Dunning That's a gymslip.

Curly She was twenty-one. White socks and a nice school blouse.

Mrs Dunning Excuse me.

She goes to the door.

Patrick. Somebody to see you.

Curly Your son.

Mrs Dunning I've given you your old room.

She sits again.

Curly Ah, next to the boiler.

Mrs Dunning Your father is greatly looking forward to seeing you.

Pause.

Patrick is a very Christian man.

Patrick *swings the door open.*

Patrick Curly. How wonderful. How good to see you.

Curly I'm over here.

Patrick Of course you are.

Pause.

Well, *Chara en thlipsae.* In the heart of sadness joy. Sit down.

Curly Thank you.

He sits.

Patrick Have you met Mrs Dunning?

Curly Yes, indeed.

Patrick Grace as we call her. I mean, that's her name. Grace.

Curly Sits pretty.

Patrick Good.

He sits. Pause.

Curly Pa . . .

Patrick Let me . . .

Curly The limits of the visit must be firmly set. You're the second on a list of people I'm to see.

Patrick Fine.

Curly I saw Jenny.

Patrick Nice girl.

Curly Yes.

Patrick A brightly painted object.

Curly So tell me what you know.

Patrick It was good of you to come.

Curly I was between wars. I was happy to come.

Patrick As you say.

Curly Well?

Patrick I only know what you've read in the paper. They say fifteen thousand Englishmen disappear every year – are never seen again. Amazing.

Curly But this is different.

Patrick Because she disappeared by the seashore. Not the kind of place where people disappear.

Curly She'd had a row with you . . .

Patrick That was a year ago.

Curly She'd left home.

Patrick A year ago. She was twenty-one. She was bound to leave.

Curly What were the reasons?

Patrick Curly, take the light bulb out of my eyes. Goodness me. Let's take it a little more slowly.

Curly She was suicidal.

Patrick Who says that?

Curly gets up.

Curly (*to Mrs Dunning*) He can't be trusted. He drops people like eggs.

He picks up a photo of Sarah as a young girl from a shelf.

Patrick I'm not expected to run her life for her.

Mrs Dunning (*holding it up*) Exercise book.

Patrick That would have been quite wrong.

Mrs Dunning (*reading*) 'Ah bonjour Monsieur le Corbeau que vous me semblez beau.'

Pause.

Curly Tell me the truth.

Patrick She wasn't impressed with my profession. The merchant bank. She didn't care much for yours, either.

Curly No.

Patrick But it's more glamorous than just making money.

Curly *Just* making money?

Patrick (*smiling*) I'm trying to see it from her point of view.

Pause.

Curly Is that why she left?

Patrick I suppose.

Curly It wasn't more personal? (*Pause.*) Had you spoken since she left?

Patrick Not really.

Curly The days I knew her she was brought up like an orchid.

Patrick Well . . .

Curly That's how she was cast.

Mrs Dunning Perhaps that was the trouble.

Curly What?

Patrick There isn't any trouble. She is highly strung. Like many of her generation without the broader-based values . . .

Curly Of a traditional education.

He replaces the photograph.

Patrick She was unsure of herself.

Curly Did she threaten to kill herself?

Pause.

Patrick She was self-critical, as you know. She thought she was a hateful kind of person. She used to say she had contracted one of Surrey's contagious diseases – moral gumrot, internal decay. Well, that's easy to say. She could say it. But nobody else. That's the point. So here we have paranoia. The fear of other people pointing out to you what you've been saying all the time about yourself, much louder, much longer.

Mrs Dunning (*still storing*) I wonder if Alice bands will ever come back into fashion again.

Curly And you?

Patrick What?

Curly What do you think?

Patrick I thought it was rather lame propaganda. (*Pause.*) Mrs Dunning, I think we could afford a cup of tea.

Mrs Dunning Of course.

She rises and closes the suitcase.

Patrick Not for me.

Curly Really?

Patrick I always have mine at half past four.

Curly It's a quarter to midnight.

Patrick Another would be decadence. Right, Mrs D?

Mrs Dunning Fine.

Curly Mrs Dunning. Use my father's old tea bag, if you like.

Mrs Dunning goes out with the suitcase.

Patrick Curly, you don't change.

Curly I recur.

Patrick Curly . . .

Curly Uh. Business, Father. Nothing at the human level, please. After all these years it would be hard to take. Just – tell me what you said to Sarah.

Pause.

Patrick I've always thought that life was – volatile. You should tread light. It's not a point of view Sarah could understand. I think everyone's entitled to their own illusions. Sarah thought not. Sarah thought everyone should know everything. She told the Bishop of Guildford that his son was known as Mabel and the toast of the Earl's Court Road.

Curly I see.

Patrick She said it was best he should know.

Curly What does she look like?

Patrick She's thin and angular. Wears grubby white jeans. Her hair always as if she's just been caught in a blaze. And the same expression of shock. All bones and big lips. Does that help?

Curly I . . .

Patrick How long since you saw her?

Curly Twelve years. Since I saw either of you.

Pause.

Patrick I hadn't seen her for six months. She went to live with Jenny. Then one day the police came to my door.

Curly Do you think she's dead?

Patrick I do rather. It's my experience of life that it never misses a trick. And murdered as well. I expect. (*Pause.*) She was like a buzz-saw in the inner ear. (*Pause.*) Some man she talked to on the beach.

Curly What about the police?

Patrick That's the current theory. There's apparently a man – well-known in Eastbourne – called Dawson.

Known as Dopey. Always out on the street. Reads the Bible to children. Shows them the meat hook he keeps in his mac. Used to be Borough Surveyor. Some years ago.

Curly Is there any evidence?

Patrick Lord, no, no evidence. Sounds rather easy but it's all they've got.

Curly There's a boyfriend . . .

Patrick Dupree . . .

Curly Yeah.

Patrick Not the right type . . .

Curly Not the right type for Sarah, eh?

Patrick Curly, you know better than that. Not the right type to kill, I meant.

Curly Which type is that?

Patrick Dupree is a remarkably fine young man.

Curly Solid sort of chap.

Patrick As you say.

Curly Must have been great for Sarah.

Patrick Well . . .

Curly (*breaking*) Pa . . .

Patrick The police visit me every night at eight. I will of course pass on to you everything they discover to help your – private search for justice . . .

Curly It's not justice I'm after.

Patrick I wish you well.

Curly Then tell me the truth. What about the club? The

man that owns it – Malloy. Do you know him?

Patrick Of course. Stockbroker. Not very successful. His hands tremble. It's – bad for business.

Curly Is that why he bought the club?

Patrick I should think so. He's almost my age, but he seems to enjoy the company of – young people.

Curly And what does that mean?

Patrick Curly . . .

Curly Why did Sarah leave home? Tell me why she left.

Patrick (*good-humouredly*) Life with Sarah was constant self-justification. I don't propose to start all over with you.

Curly When did the Scots haddock arrive?

Patrick Grace . . .

Curly The smell of starch and clean living when you come in that door . . .

Patrick Mrs Dunning . . .

Curly I bet she dabs Dettol behind her ears.

Patrick She wasn't here then.

Curly I'd have left home if I saw that coming. I can sympathize. This place is like silver paper between your teeth. I'm back five minutes and I'm . . .

Patrick As before.

Pause.

Curly (*quietly*) Don't cross your legs. It spoils the crease.

Pause.

Patrick Mrs Dunning is a pillar of strength. The best

244

housekeeper I've had. You can say anything at all to her. Anything you like. Grace, you have a very large mouth and very small heart. You could say that. She wouldn't mind. If it were true you could say that. Which it's not.

Curly Punchbag, eh?

Patrick Do you think, Curly, while you're here, a guest in my home, you could suppress the all-singing, all-dancing, all-fornicating side of your character which burst out so tellingly before you left – we do hope you've grown up.

Mrs Dunning enters with a laden tray.

Mrs Dunning I did know you were coming.

Patrick Matured.

Mrs Dunning I was told to get walnut whips. Your father said you loved . . .

Curly Yes, well . . .

Mrs Dunning Walnut whips.

Patrick I wasn't saying we should have them today.

Mrs Dunning You emphasized the point.

Patrick It was twelve years ago. After all . . .

Curly Mrs Dunning . . . (*Pause.*) You have a very large mouth . . .

Mrs Dunning (*with great pleasure*) And a very small heart. That's what your father always says.

She sits and pours tea.

Patrick I think I must be going to bed.

He rises.

Curly You haven't told me about Sarah.

Patrick There's plenty of time.

Curly You do want me to help?

Patrick Curly, I do indeed. Indeed I do.

Curly Then that's what I shall do. Help and then go.

Patrick Excellent. (*Pause.*) We'll wait and see if you measure up.

Curly Pa . . .

Patrick Ah – we'll talk more tomorrow. Grace, my Henry James.

Mrs Dunning By the bed.

Patrick (*looking at his watch*) The light will go out at a quarter past twelve.

> *Patrick exits.*

Mrs Dunning And now we'll have a cup of tea.

Curly (*dead quiet*) Sod the tea. (*Pause.*) Did you know Sarah?

Mrs Dunning I came after Sarah. I formed the impression of a tremendously vital girl.

Curly Vital?

Mrs Dunning She seemed to care so much about the world.

Curly Sarah and I went to a Martello tower on Aldeburgh beach when we were youngish – I think I was thirteen – there was a poodle playing inside which followed us to the top. Sarah – me – we didn't have a great deal in common, but at that moment, together, we simultaneously conceived the idea of throwing the poodle over the side of the tower. I can't tell you why but it was a hypnotic idea. Just to see it fall. So – we lifted this grey thing up to the edge, then we released at either end, at exactly the same moment – it's the firing squad idea – you don't know who's responsible. We felt terrible.

Mrs Dunning Worse for the dog.

Curly Bad for the dog. Also. But also terrible for us. The only barbaric thing I've ever done.

Mrs Dunning You've quite a reputation as a barbarian.

Curly Ignorance.

Mrs Dunning Ah.

Curly Ignorance and jealousy. Don't tell Pa.

Pause.

Mrs Dunning A wonderful man. He's undertaken an intensive study of Anglo-American literature.

Curly Mickey Spillane.

Mrs Dunning He's on the *Golden Bowl*. He knows an incredible amount.

Curly For a merchant banker.

Mrs Dunning He's a cultured man.

Curly Sure he's cultured. What good does that do?

Mrs Dunning His culture enlarges his . . .

Curly Mrs Dunning. Who ran Auschwitz? A pack of bloody intellectuals.

Mrs Dunning I must go up.

She rises.

Curly Is he your beau?

Mrs Dunning You must have lived in his shadow. When you were a child.

Curly We thought he was a fool.

Mrs Dunning Such a tremendously clever man.

Curly The trick of making money – is only a trick.

Mrs Dunning He said he thought – you'd have grown up.

She goes towards the door.

Curly Do the police always call?

Mrs Dunning At eight o'clock. That's it. A typical evening. Since Sarah.

Pause.

Curly What's he doing?

Mrs Dunning Reading his book. (*Pause.*) Did you never like him?

Curly Not very much.

Mrs Dunning I wonder why all the words my generation believed in – words like 'honour' and 'loyalty' – are now just a joke.

Curly I guess it's because of some of the characters they've knocked around with. Good night.

He picks up Sarah's photograph.

Mrs Dunning Good night.

As Mrs Dunning turns towards the door, music – 'For All We Know', with strings – fades up.

SCENE THREE

Acton Warehouse. Day.
   The stage is bare. A **Storeman** *wheels on a rack of rifles,
as large and as many as possible. Curly walks straight on.
He takes the revolver the Storeman offers him.*
   The music stops.
   *Curly takes two steps downstage. Then he aims with
great care and no fuss, and fires six times at six targets just
ahead into the audience. It must look perfect.*

Curly We'll take 2,000 Mannlicher-Carcanos, carbine and
ammunition, 1,500 Tokarevs, 1,400 Mosin-Nagants, what
few bolt-action Mausers you have, and the rest of the Lee-
Enfields. Knock-down job lot. My client is also in the
market for point thirty-o-six Springfield rifles with extra
long chrome-plated bayonets. Believe it or not. And he'd
also like an antique Mauser Nazi 'K' series Luger for
himself. As he's a bit of a raving lunatic on the side.

   *Curly stuffs a green wodge of money into the
   Storeman's pocket.*

And he'll be paying cash. Swiss francs.

Storeman Anything you say, Mr Delafield.

Curly And God help the poor bloody wogs.

   'For All We Know' swamps the action again.

SCENE FOUR

The Hospital Grounds. Day.
   *When the curtain rises the stage is in darkness except for
a spot on Curly.*

Curly Every man has his own gun. That's not a metaphor.

That's a fact. There are 750 million guns in the world in some kind of working order. Everyone can have one like every German was going to get a Volkswagen. I don't pick the fights. I just equip them. People are going to fight anyway. They're going to kill each other with or without my help. There isn't a civilization you can name that hasn't operated at the most staggering cost in human life. It's as if we *need* so many dead – like axle grease – to make civilization work at all. Do you know how many people have died in wars this century? One hundred million. And how many of those before 1945? Over 95 million. These last twenty-five years have been among the most restrained in man's history. Half a million in Biafra maybe, 2 million perhaps in Vietnam. Pinpricks.

The lights come up to reveal a stage bare except for a single bench. **Max** *is sitting on it, slumped forward. His face cannot be seen because he is staring at the ground.*

Things are actually getting better. The enormous continuing proliferation of arms since 1945 has actually led to a massive drop in the global numbers of dead. So there. I'm not ashamed of the trade, even if I'm a little tired of it. If every man on earth has a gun already, does he really need a second one? So now we can talk.

Max I asked Jenny what's his attitude to his profession, and she said – well, he says every man has his own gun, that's not a metaphor, that's a fact.

Curly It's my party piece. You sell guns, people come up to you. They can spot a moral issue. And I'm a tissue of moral issues. Like having a very loud suit. You get used to it.

Max OK.

Curly I have to get the subject out of the way.

Max OK. (*Pause.*) Well, she worked over there. In that lovely old house. And by all accounts was a very fine nurse.

Curly What would you say was wrong with her?

Max Why does there have to be something wrong? Sarah was unhappy, that's all. She needed character massage.

Curly She wasn't ill?

Max Ill?

Curly Mentally?

Max I've written stories about this hospital for the national newspapers. One about a man who wrapped his hands in copper wire and plugged himself into the mains. Another who believes there's a colony of rats lodged in his stomach wall. He drinks Domestos. Friend. So if a girl's unhappy because her father sits smiling all day with his arse in a bucket of cream, and because she thinks her brother's a twenty-four carat shark, I don't get very worked up. As far as I'm concerned she's just ambling round the foothills of the thing, and is unlikely to come to very much harm.

Curly (*sitting beside Max*) Is that true? About why she was unhappy?

Max Certainly . . .

Curly I'd heard she was living with you.

Max (*smiling*) Neanderthal type.

Curly Well?

Max She stopped over.

Curly Lucky girl.

Max She was free.

Curly Do you think she's run away?

Max No, I don't.

Curly Don't you think she's killed herself?

Max I don't understand your involvement.

Curly I'm her brother.

Max I thought she was just axle grease . . .

Curly This is different . . .

Max Make civilization work . . .

Curly You think she killed herself . . .

Max Mr Delafield . . .

Curly Mr Dupree . . . (*Pause.*) One shark to another: tell me the truth.

Max I'm not a shark. (*rising to behind the bench*) And I don't think she killed herself. (*Pause.*) But, of course, she had threatened it.

Curly Go on.

Max She wasn't quite mature. She had a misleading reputation. She was known as Legover Sarah. That was fine by me. But it wasn't true. In fact she was more possessive than she appeared. She blackmailed me – (*He smiles, embarrassed.*) – by saying she would kill herself. If I left her.

Curly Well . . .

Max So.

Curly Quite a man, Mr Dupree.

Max She was immature.

Curly Sure. Sure.

Max It was a terrific responsibility.

Curly Sure.

Max So when I first heard she'd disappeared I was terrified. But as soon as I heard about the purse   . . .

Curly Of course.

Max Two railway tickets on the beach . . .

Curly Right.

Max I knew she couldn't have killed herself.

Curly So that's all right. (*Pause.*) It's beautiful here.

Max It's a lovely place to go mad. There's a woman in there who thinks she's Napoleon.

Curly Sure. That I can understand. But who the hell did Napoleon think he was?

   Max smiles.

Mr Dupree, I'm told you're a Communist. What would you say?

Max Not a Communist exactly.

Curly That sort of thing.

Max Certainly.

Curly And you lived with Sarah . . .

Max Off and on . . .

Curly While entertaining other women . . .

Max That's true.

Curly Fair enough. I'm not accusing you. It seems a reasonable way of life.

Max Well?

Curly I just don't understand why a middle-aged, god-loving merchant banker should describe the lazy, promiscuous, self-righteous bolshevik who's meanwhile screwing his daughter as 'a remarkably fine young man'.

Max No.

Curly No.

Max Perhaps Patrick just liked me.

He moves away.

Curly Max, what's happened to Malloy?

Max What?

Curly The owner of the club, Malloy, what's happened to him?

Max I don't know.

Curly Why would it be he doesn't answer his door? And where was he on the night Sarah disappeared? Where is he now? Where indeed were you? Do you have an alibi?

Max Of course.

Curly All good questions. Plus: how does Jenny come into this?

Max Sarah's best friend, that's all.

Curly Not bad looking, Jenny.

Max If you say so . . .

Curly Oh, Max . . .

Max Nothing to do with me.

Curly Max. You and me. (*He gestures around him.*) The real world. And Jennifer. You're not saying you've missed Jennifer. The one with the legs. And the incandescent vagina. You of all people – Max – must have noticed. Being so intelligent. And ambitious. Yet choosing to go on living in this town, when you don't have to. Letting yourself become the Guildford stringer. Tying yourself down. Why would that be? Maximillian?

Max Maxwell.

Curly Max.

Max (*sitting*) Jenny and Sarah. Of course one would see them side by side. An unfair comparison. Jenny so bright and capable and lovely. Sarah ungainly with a slight moustache. And politically – erratic, I would say, an emotional kind of conviction. Whereas Jenny soars above us all. Just – beautiful. We all grew up together, went to the same club. Sniffed the same glue. Aspirins in the Pepsi, and French kissing. But Sarah was always – loss leader. And I'm afraid it seems to fit that she was killed. No doubt by some frightfully maladjusted person. (*Pause.*) And I promise you that's what I really think.

Curly I don't doubt your account.

Max Thank you.

Curly I just doubt the intense sense of relief with which you tell it. (*Pause.*) I'll see you tomorrow. Same time. Same place.

Max I . . .

Curly Tomorrow.

   Max goes out.

(*alone*) You chew all the meat until you hit the lump of gristle.

SCENE FIVE

The Delafields' drawing-room. Night.
  Patrick is sitting reading a sheet of music. Curly comes in.

Curly I've been to see Max Dupree.

Patrick Come in, come in. I'm reading some most enjoyable music.

Curly Great.

Patrick The horns have just come in. Would you like a drink?

Curly Do you want to know what Dupree said?

Patrick I have an idea.

Curly It's all right. He's very hopeful. He hopes she was murdered. Everyone hopes that. Including you. (*Pause.*) Not because you want her dead. I didn't say that. But given that she's dead you want her murdered because then it's nobody's fault except some poor psychopath and there's nothing anyone can do about those. Whereas if she killed herself she's going to squat on your shoulders for the rest of your life.

  Pause.

Patrick Have a drink.

  He rises.

Curly Never touch it. Time?

Patrick Ten to. The police will be here at eight. Are you staying?

Curly I'll stay – as long as I can.

Patrick You're living here . . .

Curly I know, but I couldn't last an evening. It's – what – not yet eight and already I'm half the man I am   . . .

Patrick It's just lack of practice. If we tried . . .

Curly Sure . . .

Patrick Sitting together . . .

Curly Sure . . .

Patrick Having a normal conversation . . .

Curly Sure . . .

Patrick Behaving normally . . .

Curly As if I hadn't been away twelve years.

Patrick Quite so. Ten minutes to eight.

Curly OK.

Pause. He takes off his coat and moves to sit.

I'd be pressed – Father – to put my finger on the quality that makes you impossible to spend an evening with . . .

Patrick That subject's taboo. Anything else . . .

Curly For God's sake . . .

He moves to leave.

Patrick Sit down.

Curly sits.

Have you read much Henry James? *Washington Square*.

Curly No.

Patrick Tremendous quality of civilization.

Curly That's what it is. (*Pause.*) I'm not getting very far. The man. The girl. And the father. She turns out to be a

hysterical kind of person whom nobody likes. Least of all
Max, who's meant to be the boyfriend. There's none of the
innocence that word suggests. In fact an outright
narcissist. And in love with Jenny I would say. Because he
thought they would look good together. Walking past
mirrors, that sort of thing. I don't think he enjoyed having
to make do with Sarah. I should think he winced every
time she opened her mouth. For myself I'd like to meet
Malloy. As he must have seen Sarah every night in the
club. But Malloy, everybody, has disappeared. Time?

Patrick Bit later.

Curly Yes, my friends, vanished. My day spent battering
at his door. But he has gone.

Patrick What's gun-running like?

Curly (*rising*) For Christ's sake.

Patrick Sit down. I'm asking.

Curly I don't run them. I sell them. It's a perfectly legal
profession. Like selling insurance.

Patrick Is there a great deal of travel?

Curly Lots. I was in Acton today.

Patrick Acton?

Curly There are 150,000 guns in Acton, west London. A
warehouse off the A40.

Patrick I always thought you were in Peru.

Curly I go where there's a war.

Patrick Acton?

Curly Or people want one.

Patrick I thought you were in danger.

KNUCKLE

Curly There's no danger. The people who supply the arms should not be confused with the soldiers. In the trade we tend to keep soldiers at some distance. They bring bad luck. There's one man – mercenary – claims a straight flush since 1939. Indo-China, Algeria, the Congo, the Yemen, Biafra, not forgetting Hitler's war – our side, of course – Cuba, South America, back to the Congo. Then Nigeria. There's a saying in the trade.

Patrick Yes?

Curly
You don't stand downwind
Of Franz Leopold von Lind.

Patrick I thought you said he was on our side in the Second World War.

Curly Eventually. (*Pause.*) Pa . . .

Patrick Yes?

Curly What do you like so much about Max?

Patrick Max called me. He said he'd seen you. All you've succeeded in doing is putting his back up. I'd miscalculated. Your particular talents seem quite useless in this matter.

Curly Listen . . .

Patrick You haven't grown up. You'll never grow up until you appreciate the value of tact.

Curly I'm off.

Patrick Sit down. (*Pause.*) That's typical. You've no self-control. (*Pause.*) You should be happy to sit and be humiliated.

Curly moves very slightly.

If you wish to destroy an ant heap, you do not use dynamite.

Curly You read them Henry James.

Patrick Just so. It's a question of noise. There is a saying in our trade. Or there ought to be. In the City. The saying is: 'The exploitation of the masses should be conducted as quietly as possible.'

Curly laughs slightly.

Quite right. I'll tell you of an incident before she left. It made me admire – my own daughter. I don't handle money as you know. I mean, actual notes.

Curly Cabbage.

Patrick (*trying it*) Yes, cabbage.

Curly Notes are cabbage. A bank is therefore a cabbage patch and a bouncing cheque is a bruised tomato.

Patrick Good. I had the cabbage. For various reasons – to do with Grace – I came home with two-fifty in ones.

Curly You had the hots in your pocket.

Patrick Quite. I brought them back home. I'm a romantic. I put them in the piano, played 'Scheherazade' and went to bed. The next morning they'd gone. And so had Sarah. She'd run away to Surbiton. (*Pause.*) I was furious. It was rude and messy and – loud. But last week I went to the flat for the first time. I went into the kitchen. She'd pasted them to the wall. I admired the elegance of the gesture. It was perfectly discreet. Bless her.

Pause.

Curly I saw a girl once in a bar in Laos, whose trick was an inverted sphincter. She smoked a cigarette through her arse. The most impressive feature was the hush. Just complete silence as this thing worked and blew and puffed. And nobody spoke. And the action itself was perfect. It summed up for me – the pleasures of the world.

Pause.

Patrick You get the idea.

Curly Do you know what Sam said?

Patrick Sam?

Curly Sam Cummings. International arms king.

Patrick Ah.

Curly Sam said to me: 'Open up. Let 'em have it.'

Patrick laughs.

Sam said to me: 'That's what civilization was, is and will always be. Open up. Let 'em have it.'

Patrick laughs again.

'That is why mine is the only business that will last for ever.'

Patrick Goodness me.

Curly He said that to me when I was fifteen.

Curly swings round the bottle of whisky to the table in front of him.

See that? I like the taste of whisky. Good whisky, Dad. But that's all I like. I don't like the effect.

He empties his pockets.

Fags. Two kinds. Cigars. Sweets. Condoms.

He puts them all down.

Do you know what I say?

Patrick No.

Curly No pleasure that isn't more pleasurable for being denied.

He gestures at the pile.

Don't use any of them.

Patrick Goodness me.

Pause.

Curly I need nothing.

Patrick Good. You're growing up.

Pause.

Curly How we doing?

Patrick (*looking at his watch*) Seven minutes.

Curly Bloody good. (*Pause.*) Did you ever talk to Sarah? After she left?

Patrick We met once. Neutral ground. Trafalgar Square. She took to wearing white. We had to argue things out. We talked about – no, I can't tell you . . .

Curly What?

Patrick We talked about what we believed.

Curly How disgusting.

Patrick I suppose you have to get your hands dirty sometimes.

Curly And what did she believe?

Patrick I can't remember.

Curly Well, no wonder, as you paid such close attention to her views . . .

Patrick Hush, hush. Over the top. Way over the top again.

We don't know she's dead. And if she is, there's no purpose to be served by booting your way through the local population like a mad Hussar. This is England. Surrey. Your approach is wrong. You're peg-legging along screaming your head off fifteen paces behind the local police. You've no idea.

Curly gets up.

Curly Jesus. I try to wipe my slate as clean as yours. Alcohol. Sex. I have left them behind. But I still can't quite manage your state of Zen. I still have a smudge of indignation. You still drive me fucking mad. I left this house because I was sick to death with Lord Earthly-bloody Perfection. If only you'd admit . . .

Patrick What?

Curly Just – something. Just own up. For instance, to your genius for mislaying your children.

Patrick Curly . . .

Curly I can't stand it.

Patrick Please.

Curly I thought when I came back you might be showing just a little petticoat below your hem. But no. (*He shows.*) Perfection. (*Pause.*) I'm clocking out. World Champion at nine minutes. I quit the game.

He makes to go out.

Patrick Curly.

Curly pauses.

Please take your condoms off my table.

Curly is about to exit and the music of 'We Gather Lilacs' is heard, as the curtain falls.

SCENE SIX

The Shadow of the Moon bar. Night.
  Jenny is sitting at the table, crying. The Barman is behind the bar. Curly enters and goes straight to him.

Barman The lemonade, is it, sir?

Curly No. Yes. I'll stick to lemonade.

Barman Pleasure to serve you, Mr Delafield.

  Curly just looks away.

You know this can be a pretty wild bar some nights.

Curly Lordy.

Barman A little too wild. Without a piece.

  Pause. Curly does not answer.

Oh, yes. Everyone needs a piece nowadays, eh?

Curly (*half at Jenny*) Who is this creep?

Barman Right, Mr Delafield.

Curly And a Scotch, I suppose.

Barman I'm talking about a hot rod, Mr Delafield. As you call it in the trade. (*Pause.*) Naturally we've got the security boys, private army, you know. But they don't have the lead . . .

Curly No . . .

Barman Perhaps you could – cross my palm with metal, Mr Delafield.

Curly Perhaps. (*He pauses, then smiles.*) Open up, let 'em have it.

Barman (*smiling*) Right, Mr Delafield.

Curly walks over to Jenny with the drinks.

Curly What a creep. I wouldn't sell him a water-pistol.

He sets down the bottle.

Well, Potato-face, your lucky day. This is Repulsive speaking. I am offering you a night on the tiles. What do you say? We could maybe both go look for Malloy.

Jenny You can find Malloy. Down the mortuary. (*Pause.*) The wrists are cut. With the razor blade. Not easy. You really have to go at them. He went at them. So it looked like gardening shears. The only way to do it.

Pause.

Curly Jen.

Jenny Who the hell am I? I bet you don't even know my second name.

Pause.

Curly Have another Scotch.

Jenny What's it to you? (*Pause.*) So that is why he does not answer the door. Because he is lying on the floor. With a suicide note. Bequeathing me the Shadow of the Moon. (*Pause.*) Malloy had ears like a dachshund. And a voice like two trees rubbing together. In short, a slob. He liked to put a brown paper bag over his head – this will amuse you – then take all his clothes off. He did this in the company of other Englishmen of the same age and class. They ran round in circles. With straps. They never saw each other's faces. Malloy said – the pleasure was not in the whipping. Or in the paper bags. The pleasure was in going to the Stock Exchange next day and trying to work out which of your colleagues you'd whipped the night before. (*Pause.*) He was funny. I liked him.

Curly Jen.

Jenny He sat in this bar, gin dripping from his chin, from his eyes, gin in the palms of his hands, talking about England. And the need to be whipped. His liver, at the end, was a little orange thing.

Curly Who found him?

Jenny I sent for the police.

Curly Does the note explain, say anything, to do with Sarah? The disappearance.

Jenny It depressed him. He says that.

Curly But . . .

Jenny But he knew nothing concrete. He'd told me that when he was alive. The note's mostly about my getting the club. He'd only bought it originally so that I could manage it. I was out of a job. So he set me up. A bauble.

Curly What did you do in return?

Jenny I did nothing. He was never my lover. It was Sarah he had. (*Pause.*) Getting Sarah to sleep with you. I don't know. I imagine rather a squalid operation. Some nights you could have gathered her up off the floor, and arranged the limbs how you wanted them. She was mad about him. He spilt a whole bottle of gin all over her. She never washed for weeks. Sentimental.

Curly What . . .

Jenny (*at once*) If you shut up I'll tell you. (*Pause.*) She thought he was like Patrick. Only human. She was obsessed with her father because he was so complete. Sarah used to say he had a personality like a pebble. There was no way in. Then she met Malloy. A man from her father's world. From her father's class. Of her father's age.

A man like her father. But able to be agonized. Capable of guilt. She was enthralled.

Curly How long did it last?

Jenny Few weeks.

Curly Then . . .

Jenny There was a row. A few months ago.

Curly What about?

Jenny Sarah said it was about the whipping. That she'd just found out.

Curly Did you believe her?

Jenny No – the whipping would have been an added attraction. Another weakness. She'd have loved him more.

Curly Then she lied.

Jenny Sarah never lied. She said people should know everything.

Pause.

Curly Have you ever met my father?

Jenny Yes.

Curly Have you seen inside the City of London? Inside the banks and the counting houses? It's perfect. Men with silver hair and suits with velvet pockets. Oiling down padded corridors. All their worries papered over with £10 notes and brilliantine. I first went there when I was seven. The crystal city. You could just hear the money being raked in like autumn leaves. My father moved as silkily as anyone. A clear leather desk in a book-lined room. A golden inkwell. That was all. That and the sound of money gathering like moss on the side of a wet building. When he got home at night, out with the cello and the

Thackeray. He made his money with silent indolence. Part of a club. In theory a speculator. But whoever heard of an English speculator who actually speculated and lost? Once you were in, you had it sewn up from paddock to post. Sarah would know what I'm talking about.

Jenny The two of you.

Curly So I chose guns. The noisiest profession I could find. I used to set up a client's demonstration of the AR10. You fire tracer bullets at tin cans filled with gasoline. Did you ever see a tracer bullet hit a bean can full of petrol? It's better than a John Wayne movie. The oohs and ahs. I used to saddle up and ride into the sunset leaving the range a smouldering ruin. We sold a hell of a lot of guns. Poor Sarah. I just know what she felt.

'Blanket Of Blue' is played off, Lomax-style.

Let me smell your Scotch. (*He smiles into the Scotch, then sniffs.*) Did anyone – love Sarah?

Jenny Bum business. Look what I got out of it. The Michael Lomax Trio scraping their balls off in an upstairs room. Dipso . . .

Pause.

Curly Tell me who killed her?

Jenny It would only have needed the barest suggestion. Sarah, just put your head under the water. Moving from grey to grey. She'd have done it. If you asked her. She would have covered herself in kerosene and set light to it. To win your affection. (*Pause.*) How Malloy could have touched her.

Curly Know what Bernie said?

Jenny Bernie?

Curly Bernie Cornfeld said to me: 'Humanity's a nasty racket to be in.' (*Pause.*) Miss Wilbur. You see, I even know your second name. I know everything I have been able to find out. A little obscure. I know all about your great-great-grandfather, the Armenian Jew who fucked his way through the nineteenth century like an Alka-Seltzer. I know it all since you came over here at fourteen. And I know dwelling-place, size of flat, name of dog, even dog's diet, even dog's distaste for Lassie meaty chunks. (*Pause.*) I'm propositioning you. (*Pause.*) You'd be the first for some time. For some years. The first in fact since the Sheikh of Mina Said's daughter. She went with an arms deal. A little Arab stardust might rub off.

Jenny What about Malloy?

Curly Laying Malloy aside. That's a very nice leg.

Jenny I've got another one just like it. What about Sarah?

Curly Laying Sarah aside. Listen, my dear . . .

Jenny What do you get out of it?

Curly Hopefully some change from a pound.

Jenny Listen – punk-face – I wouldn't buy what you've got if it was on refrigerated display.

Curly I don't suppose I'd be selling under those conditions. (*Pause.*) You come with me.

Jenny Me Jane.

Curly I'll show you the world.

Jenny Take me to Eastbourne then. Tonight.

Curly It's late.

Jenny Don't you want to go?

Curly Go some time.

Jenny About how you were the best man for the job.

Curly All right. I'll get Pat's car.

Jenny I'll get a wrap.

She laughs and moves to go.

Lassie meaty chunks.

Jenny exits.

Curly I was once stranded in Alaska for ten days with a single copy of G. E. Moore's *Principia Ethica*. And one copy of *My Gun Is Quick*. The work of Mickey Spillane. I was able in this period to make comparisons under scientific test conditions. The longest word in *Principia Ethica* is 'contrahydrapallotistic'. The longest word in Spillane is 'balloon'. Moore wins outright on length of sentence, number of words and ability to contradict yourself in the shortest space. Spillane won on one count only. It burns quicker.

Curly exits.

SCENE SEVEN

The Delafields' drawing-room. Night.
    Mrs Dunning is crocheting, Patrick reading. Peace. Patrick looks up, holds his look. Mrs Dunning looks across at him. They smile slightly. Patrick goes back to his book, sighs, puts it aside, gets up, sighs again.

Patrick Mrs Dunning.

Mrs Dunning smiles again, does not look up. He stands near her, does not touch her. She smiles at the crochet.

Mrs Dunning I love it when you call me that.

Patrick Hold on.

*Patrick loosens his tie, then goes out by the side door.
Mrs Dunning puts her crochet aside, kicks off her shoes,
then pulls off the jumper she is wearing and folds it on
the sofa. She takes off her skirt, folds that, then drops a
string of pearls into a little heap on the table. She stands
in a bra, pants, stockings and suspenders. She gapes a
moment. Pause.*

Mrs Dunning (*quietly*) Pat.

*She listens for an answer, then goes back to the sofa,
picks up her crochet, and continues to work. Pause.
Curly comes in from the main door, sees her, looks at
his feet. Mrs Dunning sees him and half-smiles. He
looks at her. Patrick comes in by the side entrance,
wearing only trousers and socks. He stops when he sees
Curly. Pause.*

Curly I called in on the police.

Patrick Ah.

Curly No news of Sarah. I want to borrow the car.

*Patrick takes the car keys out of his pocket and throws
them lightly across the room. Curly catches the keys and
goes out. Pause. Patrick stares a moment, then walks up
and down. Pause.*

Patrick Put your clothes on.

He moves to go out. Mrs Dunning turns away.

*Before the start of the next scene the sound of the sea is
heard.*

SCENE EIGHT

The Crumbles. Night.
   The curtain rises on a bare stage. At once, from downstage, soaking wet, Jenny comes running on, wearing a bathing costume.

Jenny Hallelujah.

   Curly runs on, also fresh from the sea, also in a bathing costume.

Curly Hallelujah.

   Curly cartwheels twice. Jenny does a handstand over. Curly turns her round in a wheel, then she runs towards his out-held hands. She steps up on to his shoulders. They stand in this position, looking out into the audience, as still as possible.

Jenny Right.

Curly So this is it.

Jenny The Crumbles.

Curly Christ.

Jenny It's strange. (*Pause.*) It's cold.

Curly Cold for September.

Jenny Cold for one o'clock in the morning.

Curly What do you see?

Jenny (*with relish*) I see suffering and pain and men not happy with their lot . . .

Curly Do you?

Jenny I do. I see heavy scowls and fists raised in anger, and I see tears of sorrow and of indignation. I see men

with axes in their backs, acid steaming off their skins,
needles in their eyeballs, tripping on barbed wire, falling
on broken bottles. That's what I see.

Curly Ah. Eastbourne. Quite unchanged.

Jenny I see the living dead.

Curly What do you see that's nice?

Jenny Nice?

Curly Yeah. You know. Nice.

Jenny I see men – born happy. It just doesn't show. Let me
down.

She climbs down from Curly's shoulders.

I'm going to get dressed.

Curly Stay.

Jenny Why?

Curly Sit.

Curly sits cross-legged. Jenny watches.

The colder you get the more you will enjoy being warm.

Jenny Oh yeah?

Curly The essence of pleasure is self-denial.

*Curly puts a tattered paper bag on his head. Jenny just
watches.*

I come to England maybe once a year. It's a shabby little
island, delighted with itself. A few months ago I decided to
return.

Jenny Where's the whip?

Curly I was ready for England. I was attracted by news of the property racket. Slapping people on top of people like layers of lasagne. Think about what I'm saying. Don't think about the cold.

Jenny Forget the cold. Listen to Curly.

Curly When I got back I found this country was a jampot for swindlers and cons and racketeers. Not just property.

Jenny goes out. Curly continues, unaware that she has gone.

Boarding-houses and bordellos and nightclubs and crooked charter flights, private clinics, horse-hair wigs and tin-can motor cars, venereal cafés with ice-cream made from whale blubber and sausages full of sawdust.

Jenny (*off*) Forget the cold. Listen to Curly.

Curly Money can be harvested like rotten fruit. People are aching to be fleeced. But those of us who do it must learn the quality of self-control.

Jenny reappears with duffel coat and sweater. She looks warm. She is carrying Curly's clothes.

Jenny Curly, is that why you came back?

Curly Wherever I've travelled, wherever I've been, there's been a tiny echo in my mind. The noise in my father's office. The slight squelch of Dad's hands in the meat.

Jenny Why did you come back?

She drops his towel near him. Curly takes his bag off.

Curly I came back because I'm ready. I've grown up.

Pause.

Jenny What about Sarah?

Curly Sarah. (*Pause.*) Yes, well. That as well.

Pause. He wraps himself in his towel.

When I went to get the car my father was with Mrs Dunning. I even detected a moment of shame. He's getting old. The first crack in the pebble. It made me sad. You should see her thighs. Like putting your hand between two slices of liver.

Jenny You horrible little man. (*Pause.*) Sarah was wide open. An ever-open wound. Her face was so – open, it just begged to be kicked. You had to put the boot in. It's . . .

Curly All right . . .

Jenny She was so naive. She used to tell Patrick your wealth is built on the suffering of the poor. And she expected an answer.

Curly All right.

Jenny (*screaming*) All right.

She throws his clothes to the ground.

Always ready with an innocent question. Why don't you share what you've got? Why can't people run their own lives? Why persist with a system you know to be wrong? How can you bear to be rich when so many people are poor?

Curly Did she say that?

Jenny Well, what did she expect? (*Pause.*) Christ Jesus. Doesn't she know there's a war on? She was asking for it.

Curly Do you know what Bernie said?

Pause.

Jenny No.

Curly Bernie Cornfeld said to me: 'Curly,' he said, 'there's nothing in this world so lovely it can't be shat on.'

Jenny Right.

Curly Right.

Jenny And this is where she died. (*She yells into the night air.*) Return John Bloom to your kingdom. Jack Cotton, arise from your grave. Harry Hyams, claim your children.

Pause.

Curly You know your way around.

He sits on the ground.

Jenny (*she sits*) I know them all. Their names. And I wonder about . . .

Curly (*smiling*) The state of their souls.

Jenny (*smiling*) All right.

Pause.

Curly I called in on the police when I was getting the car. The railway tickets were first-class. (*Pause.*) Can you imagine . . .

Jenny Sarah?

Curly First . . .

Jenny Never. (*Pause.*) God. (*Pause.*) Have you spoken to him?

Curly Couldn't. (*Pause.*) Look at the night.

Jenny Yeah.

Curly Just look at the water.

Jenny You don't want to be like them, Curly.

Curly smiles thinly.

Do you? (*Pause.*) It's such a beautiful night. Isn't it lovely?

Curly This is the loveliest it gets.

He gets up and smiles.

I'll take you home. You look wonderful.

Jenny Curly.

Curly Old bean.

Jenny Is that what you say?

Curly What?

Jenny Is that what you say to a girl you want? 'Old bean'?

Curly Sure.

Jenny I see.

Curly Well . . . (*Pause.*) Let's go.

Jenny Curly.

Curly What?

Jenny First-class.

Curly Yes, I know. (*Pause.*) It could have been Malloy.

Jenny No. Not his – manner. He would never. Especially with her. She wouldn't allow him.

Curly So.

Jenny So.

Curly I've thought of nothing else.

Jenny Why didn't you ask him?

Curly I will.

Jenny Are you afraid? (*Pause.*) That's what I asked you. When we first met.

Curly This place gives me the creeps. (*Pause.*) Let's go.

Jenny The essence of pleasure is self-denial.

She rises, picks up all his clothes and his car keys, and taunts him.

Curly Oh, Jenny, come on.

Jenny So.

Curly For Christ's sake.

She throws the keys up in the air as a taunt and catches them herself.

Jenny Wrap up warm.

She heads out fast.

Curly Christ.

Jenny goes out with the keys and clothes.

Jenny (*as she goes*) Forget the cold. Listen to Curly . . .

Curly (*bellowing after her*) Patrick's not the only man who travels first-class. (*Pause. Bellowing*) Christ. (*Pause.*) Christ. (*Pause. Muttering*) Christ. (*Pause.*) Control yourself. (*Pause.*) Control. (*Pause.*) I am a pebble. With self-control.

Pause. He drops the towel at his feet. The lights fade to a spot on Curly.

Eastbourne is a grey city. The lights shine less bright than in LA. I wanted to be on the Santa Monica freeway stopping over at Sloppy Joes for pastrami on rye and one cheese and tomato Anita Ek-burger. I wanted to be in Caracas paying $25 for a Venezuelan sauna. I wanted to be in the Persian mountains playing poker with Kurd guerrillas for lumps of hashish as big as a man's brain. I wanted to be in that bar in Laos watching that old inverted sphincter puffing and inhaling, puffing and

exhaling: a last inverted monument to human ingenuity
that not even the Americans could bomb into submission.

*The lights fade and music swells up, 'We'll Gather
Lilacs' – not the thin Lomax version, the full-bodied
BBC Concert Orchestra – as the curtain falls.*

Act Two

SCENE NINE

A Police Station. Day.
Apart from a single flat or cut-out to indicate the setting, the stage is bare except for the chair on which Jenny is sitting. A **Policeman** *stands by her.*

Policeman Spring of 1924 – April twelfth – a man called Patrick Mahon, lived in London, went to an ironmongers, bought a meat saw and a ten-inch knife. He then went to Waterloo station, collected his suitcase and then took a train to Eastbourne. Waiting in Eastbourne, a Miss Emily Kaye. A young stenographer he had met in London. The idea was to rent a small cottage on the beach to conduct what Mahon referred to as 'a love experiment'. Miss Kaye had prepared for the experiment by selling some bonds she owned and giving them to Mr Mahon. The cottage they rented was on the stretch of beach known as the Crumbles. They moved in. The experiment lasted three days. On the following Tuesday, Mahon strangled her and dismembered her body. He packed some pieces tightly into old boxes and filled biscuit tins with her innards. He attempted to boil down her fat in open saucepans. In the middle of the night, in savage weather, with thunder crashing outside he placed her severed head on the fire. The intense heat of the flames caused the eyes of the dead woman to open. Mahon, a thirty-three-year-old soda fountain salesman, ran from the house. For the first time, horrified. He returned to London. Later he was arrested and executed. (*Pause.*) Would anyone in the family have heard that story before?

Jenny Well – Patrick's the most highly educated.

A single cello plays.

SCENE TEN

The Hospital Grounds. Day.
  Max is discovered, in black, his hands in his pockets.
Curly appears, in quite a big overcoat.

Curly Glad you could make it. How was the funeral,
Max?

Max Subdued.

Curly Anyone there?

Max Just Malloy's mother.

Curly No one else?

Max And Jenny.

Curly And Jenny – ah.

Max Yes.

Curly How was that?

Max What?

Curly In black. Did that give you any kind of buzz?

Max Listen . . .

Curly Uh. Ignore it. Proceed. I'd like to hear your alibi for
the night Sarah disappeared.

Max It's dull.

Curly I'm sure it's dull. That's not the point.

Max That's a terrible cold you've got.

Curly Now you mention it, yes. I got left out on the beach, you see. Reconstructing the crime. Alibi.

Max I spent the evening with a man called Hart. H-a-r-t. A vet. Well, not a vet exactly. Michael Hart is a spiritualist. He claims that through animals we may talk to the other side.

Curly Go on.

Max The dead. Animals have a psychic flair for communicating with the dead.

Curly I see. So your alibi can be confirmed by a reliable dog.

Max No. No. Confirmed by your father. It was at his house.

Curly Yes?

Max You should talk to him.

Curly just stares at him.

It was Sarah's idea. I was working on a series about modern religions. Also Sarah's idea. She loved shopping around. She suggested taking Hart and his famous Alsatian to Patrick's. The idea was she would come with me. I just wanted to get her in the same room as her father. But she funked out – so – I was left with Mr Delafield. He wanted to communicate with his dead wife – your mother. I thought the whole thing was in very bad taste. Patrick was quite serious throughout. Hart's Alsatian kept snarling at him – then fell asleep. Without Sarah the whole exercise was hollow.

Curly She knew you were both there?

Max Oh, yes. She pushed us into it.

Curly And she went off to Eastbourne meanwhile?

Max We later found out. Yes.

Curly Did it occur to you afterwards she could have planned suicide all along and set you two up as a final gag?

Max Yes.

Curly Rather an elaborate gag.

Max Yes.

Curly Muttering away at an Alsatian.

Max But typical.

Curly From what you say.

Max Typical of her.

Curly No longer a nutcase?

Max smiles. Pause.

Max Check with your father, eh?

Curly Yaar. (*Pause.*) As Brigadier-General Bolivar Vallarino of Panama said to me: 'Put it there, pal.'

They shake hands. Salute.

Max What's it to be? Tomorrow – same time, same place?

Curly I don't think so, I don't think I want to see you again, Max. Something of the magic has died.

Max Well, well.

Curly heads out.

Abandoning the investigation?

Curly (*turning back*) Thinking about it.

Max That's what your father said you'd do.

Curly Did he say that?

Max He said being back in England made you want a nice job.

Curly I'm looking for an opening certainly.

Max I don't know what arms salesmen usually move on to.

Curly Allied Professions. The Church, you know, the Law.

He waves.

Max See you some day.

Curly Not if I see you first.

He sings.
Keep young and beautiful
It's your duty to be beautiful
Keep young and beautiful
If you want to be loved.

The lights fade to blackout.

SCENE ELEVEN

The Shadow of the Moon bar. Night.
In the darkness, Max follows on immediately with Curly's song from the previous scene.

Max
Keep young and beautiful
It's your duty to be beautiful
Keep young and beautiful
If you want to be loved.

The lights come up on the bar scene. Jenny is discovered behind the bar. She turns as she hears the singing. Max dances on.

Jenny I thought you were Curly.

Max What I say is: the world is a rice pudding. It's just waiting to be skinned.

Jenny You've met him too?

Max Oh yes. My dear.

Jenny The bar's closed.

Max Nice place. Where's the people?

Jenny Gone home.

Max Scotch.

Jenny Max. You look funny without her.

Max I feel funny. No longer the parrot on the shoulder. I get through whole sentences without interruption.

Jenny I warned you . . .

Max What?

Jenny That she'd kill herself.

Max Oh that.

Jenny That.

Pause.

Max Scotch.

Jenny I think she said, Max, I'm going to kill myself. And you said, 'Just show me.' And she did. (*Pause.*) How many times did I tell you?

Max Often. You leapt at the opportunity.

Jenny I was pointing out . . .

Max You did best all round.

Jenny What do you mean?

Max This place. You win the Shadow of the Moon.

Pause.

Jenny I see.

Max Well, so you're happy.

Jenny Max.

Max Now the lover is buried.

Jenny He was not my lover.

Max He just left you the club.

Jenny It was nothing to do with it.

Max Tell that to Mrs Malloy.

Jenny Malloy married . . .

Max Malloy's mother. At the funeral. Mrs Malloy.

Pause.

Jenny What are you talking about?

Max I have a photo of you in a gymslip.

He steps behind the bar to Jenny.

With a straw hat and black socks.

Jenny What about Mrs Malloy?

Max This is a knife. Kiss me. (*Pause.*) Hands behind head.

She does so.

Now follow me out from behind the bar.

They come out. We see the knife.

Sit down. Keep your hands there.

She sits down. He sits opposite.

I sit myself down. Don't move.

The knife is held by Max for the scene.

There aren't many girls left in Guildford.

Jenny No.

Max Speak up.

Jenny I said no, not many.

Max What with Juliet. And Fizz and Laura gone now. And the other Laura. And Jane Hammond got passed down the line. And the one with the lisp. They tell me Alice has been had by most of the Bank of England . . .

Jenny So I hear.

Max Sally and Pip . . .

Jenny Yes . . .

Max Both to chartered accountants, inevitably. Gloria, married. Janice. I'm scraping the very bottom of the barrel. Tamara. That doesn't leave many. Any. Of the ones who used to come here. And the ones who didn't come here were rubbish. Sarah would do anything you wanted. (*Pause.*) Rather a disgusting characteristic. (*Pause.*) Penny on her seventh actor and Jacqueline a nun. That leaves you. Oh, Jenny. What happens to people?

Jenny I don't know.

Max When we came here as teenagers – you and me and Sarah – you never knew what would happen. It seemed the most ambiguous place in the world. Like falling into satin in the dark. And look at it now. (*Pause.*) Tell me what you think of Curly. (*Pause.*) You know he's given up looking for Sarah already.

Jenny I didn't know that.

Max He's everything the world wasn't going to be. Blustering. And sneering. And insincere. Is that really what you want?

Jenny Then put the knife away.

Max Do you really want Curly?

Jenny He's never touched me, Max. (*Pause.*) Tell me about Mrs Malloy.

Max Do you really know nothing? (*Pause.*) She's in hospital. She may not have been mad when she went in. But she's certainly mad now. Jennifer. (*Pause.*) I find your innocence unforgivable. (*Pause.*) Take off your clothes.

   Nothing.

Lie down on the floor.

   Nothing.

Close your eyes, open your mouth, praise the Lord and thank God you're British. (*Pause.*) Goodnight.

   Max goes out immediately, putting the knife away. The lights change.

Jenny Young women in Guildford must expect to be threatened. Men here lead ugly lives and girls are the only touchstones left. Cars cruise beside you as you walk down the pavement, I have twice been attacked at the country club, the man in the house opposite has a telephoto lens, my breasts are often touched on commuter trains, my body is covered with random thumbprints, the doctor says he needs to undress me completely to vaccinate my arm, men often spill drinks in my lap, or brush cigarettes against my bottom, very old men bump into me and clutch at my legs as they fall. I have been offered drinks, money, social advancement and once an editorial position on the *Financial Times*. I expect this to go on. I expect to be bumped, bruised, followed, assaulted, stared at and propositioned for the rest of my life, while at the same time offering sanctuary, purity, reassurance, prestige – the only point of loveliness in men's ever-darkening lives.

SCENE TWELVE

Guildford Railway Station. Night.
    Jenny is sitting on a bench reading a newspaper. A **Porter** *and Curly enter from opposite sides. Curly has a briefcase and umbrella.*

Jenny Well. You're getting very hard to find.

Curly Get my luggage, will you? And a taxi.

Porter Sir.

    The Porter goes out.

Jenny (*allowing nothing*) They tell me your heart's gone out of it. The investigation.

Curly Can't do it all the time.

Jenny Even thinking of a job. Insurance. Something like Lloyd's.

Curly Well, I've been up to town. Just to talk it over.

Jenny Costs a lot of money.

Curly Seventy-five thousand entrance fee. That's all a chap needs. Buy himself a slice of security.

Jenny (*lethally*) I brought you the keys to your car.

    Jenny throws the keys over. Curly catches them, embarrassed.

Little man.

Curly (*smiling*) Jenny.

Jenny And some information. (*Pause.*) I've been to see a Mrs Malloy. She's seventy-three. Initials E. R. Malloy. As, she said, like the Queen. Am I keeping you?

Curly No, no.

Jenny Malloy's mother lived in one house for the whole of her life. A Victorian house in the centre of Guildford. Married for a month in 1918 before her husband was killed at Chemin des Dames. At the age of sixty-eight she transferred the house into her son's name. Tax dodge: you avoid death duties. Standard practice round here. She put it in her son's name. But she went on living there herself. So. Central Guildford. Torn apart as you know. And some developers bought the rest of the block. It tempted Malloy. He held the deeds. There was only one obstacle. His mother had lived there the whole of her life. He held out for a couple of months. Then suddenly cracked. He had her committed.

Curly Was she mad?

Jenny Oh, Curly, come on.

Curly Was she mad?

Jenny She was mad when enough people needed her to be. Let's face it. She was pushed. Malloy signed the committal order.

Curly Is there any actual evidence she was pushed?

Jenny Oh, Curly . . .

Curly How much did he make?

Jenny Two hundred thousand.

Pause.

Curly She was pushed.

Jenny (*rising*) And another property thrown in. A run-down old barn on the other side of town. A nightclub called the Shadow of the Moon. Mrs Malloy in the mental hospital sent her nurse on an errand. The nurse was Sarah. Where the old woman's house had been she found seventeen floors of prestige offices crowned with an antique supermarket. She went back to the hospital. Everyone should know everything. That's what she said. She told the old woman her house had gone. If she wasn't mad before, she certainly is now. (*Pause.*) Sarah was electrified when she found out. No wonder she rowed with Malloy. Can you imagine? Her friend Malloy – one of life's losers turns out to be a shark. She would have flipped. She would have told everyone. But the amazing thing is: she didn't. For the first time in her life she kept something secret. From me, from everyone. Except Max. Max was a journalist. He would have said what a wonderful story. 'Stockbroker Swindles His Own Mother In Property Deal'. But the story never appeared. I think he went to Malloy and blackmailed him. (*Pause.*) Do you want to go back to London?

Curly How do you know all this?

Jenny Partly from Max.

Curly Did he tell you?

Jenny He . . .

Curly What?

Jenny Signalled he knew.

Curly How?

Jenny With a knife. He came to the club last night. He

thought I knew.

Curly What made him think that?

Jenny Because Malloy was in love with me, that's why he left the Shadow of the Moon to me. Max thought it was because Malloy was my lover.

Curly Whereas in fact . . .

Jenny It was because he was never my lover.

Curly Yes. That makes perfect sense round here. So if Max did blackmail Malloy, you're saying he only had one problem . . .

Jenny The old problem we have met before.

Curly How to close Sarah's mouth.

Jenny Sarah will want to know why Max hasn't published the story.

Curly God . . .

Jenny How to shut her up . . .

Curly What a beautiful girl this Sarah is. Niagara. Vesuvius. Grinding on against injustice and the misery of the world.

Jenny Max's only problem . . .

Curly Yaaar.

   Pause.

Jenny Is that what happened?

Curly Why take her to the Crumbles?

Jenny Because in 1924 there was a particularly disgusting murder there.

Curly Well, exactly.

Jenny What?

Curly Why draw attention to yourself? The Crumbles. The worst possible place. It's the Wembley Stadium of murder already.

Jenny (*quietly*) Right.

Pause. Curly turns and looks at her.

Curly What do you mean he had a knife?

Jenny I've just said it.

Curly Tell me.

Jenny shakes her head.

What happened?

Jenny Why should I?

Curly Jenny.

Jenny He never came near.

Curly Jenny. (*Pause.*) I'm not telling you the truth.

Jenny I wouldn't expect it.

Curly I don't like to be honest. It's not in my nature.

Jenny (*smiling*) Go on.

Curly I'd heard a bit about Malloy, not about his mother, that surprises me, but about his house. You see, on a crooked deal a blackmailer will have a choice of targets. Malloy. Or the property company. Or the man who finances the property company. That old Victorian house? Patrick's money bought it.

Pause.

Jenny Max blackmails Patrick . . .

Curly Congratulations.

Jenny Max gets rid of Sarah, then forces Patrick into confirming his ludicrous alibi about the dog.

Curly You're very quick. (*Pause.*) They seem to have lost my luggage.

Jenny Which one will you go for first?

Curly You're very keen.

Jenny You getting frightened, Curly? Is that what it is? Losing your nerve? Frightened to hurt your father? Frightened to face up to him?

Curly Face up to Spats.

Jenny What luggage?

Curly All my things. I'm moving down here. Get a job. Get a house. I like the atmosphere. (*Pause.*) Don't stare at me, kid. (*Pause.*) Listen, the story's ridiculous. It's full of holes. If Max went to blackmail my father, he would have just said he didn't know.

Jenny But for the property company conning an old woman is bad publicity.

Curly It happens all the time. It's called business practice, people go to the wall.

Jenny Nobody would believe them.

Curly They'd say they didn't know. It's just a matter of keeping your nerve and a plausible story.

Jenny Who's to say it's plausible?

Curly Exactly. Newspapers can be bought, judges can be leant on, politicians can be stuffed with truffles and cognac. Life's a racket, that we know.

Jenny Christ, I'll make a person of you yet.

Curly Forget it. (*Pause.*) Listen – sugar plum – the horror of the world. The horror of the world is there are no excuses left. There was a time when men who ruined other men, could claim they were ignorant or simple or believed in God, or life was very hard, or we didn't know what we were doing, but now everybody knows the tricks, the same shabby hands have been played over and over, and men who persist in old ways of running their countries or their lives, those men now do it in the full knowledge of what they're doing. So that at last greed and selfishness and cruelty stand exposed in white neon: men are bad because they want to be. No excuses left.

Jenny You mean you're not going to see him?

Curly (*smiling*) No, I'm not.

Jenny Well, why not just say that? (*Pause.*) Like to have known you better, Curly.

The Porter wheels on Curly's luggage, a huge Singapore trunk. Jenny goes out.

Porter Here she is, sir. (*Pause.*) Moving down here, are you, sir?

Curly No. Change of plan. Left luggage. Twenty-four hours.

Curly heads off. 'We'll Gather Lilacs' is heard, Lomax-style.

SCENE THIRTEEN

The Shadow of the Moon bar. Night.
    The Barman is alone behind his bar. Curly walks in, vicious, drunk and smoking.

Curly Give me a Scotch.

Barman Right away, sir.

Curly And don't be so bloody pleasant.

Barman Sir.

Curly Now go upstairs, knock politely on her door and tell her there's something slimy to see her.

He takes the bottle and glass.

Barman Sir.

The Barman goes out.

Curly (*shouting*) For God's sake, Lomax, give us all a break. Just shut up.

'We'll Gather Lilacs' stumbles and stops.

(*sitting at the table*) Not as if anyone was dancing up there. Just looks like the bloody *Titanic*.

The Barman returns.

Barman She says . . .

Curly Yes, Barman?

Barman She says, 'Piss off.' Sir.

Curly White-knickered do-good cock-shrivelling cow.

Barman She wants you to go, sir.

Curly Want to make something of it, Barman?

He threatens the Barman with the bottle.

Barman Sir.

Curly I'm glad I didn't sell you a gun.

Jenny (*off*) Mike. Get scraping.

Curly turns at the strips.

Curly Down I go.

Curly exits.

Lomax (*off*) Come on, everybody. Let's bossa nova.

The Lomax Band plays a bossa nova.

SCENE FOURTEEN

The Hospital Grounds. Night.
Max is tapping his knife, unopened, against his hand.
After a moment Curly appears, in a big overcoat.

Curly Hullo, Max.

Max Hullo.

Curly I'm sorry to drag you out here in the middle of the night.

Max That's all right.

Curly At barely ten minutes' notice.

Max That's all right.

Curly No, it's not. You should be angry. (*Pause.*) You're an innocent party. Act angry. (*Pause.*) Story is you murdered Sarah. We don't believe that, do we, Max? We don't think you're the murdering type.

Max flashes his flick-knife out.

(*quickly taking out his gun*) Every man has his own gun. That's not a metaphor. That's a fact. Only some have more guns than others. Knife.

Max hands his knife to Curly.

I have a bottle in my pocket. Remove it.

Max tenderly takes the bottle from Curly's pocket.

And put it down there.

Max puts it on the ground.

And stay down. (*hard and fast*) I think you took money, Max. That was your crime. It's not the local custom, I have observed. In England they don't take money. They make money. Spot the difference. It's a country of opportunity. Everyone can run a racket of their own. Say I discover some property developers have used unusual pressures to achieve their aims. I don't go and ask for a share of their money. I go out and find a defenceless old cow of my own to swindle. That is the creative thing to do.

Max I'd never taken money before.

Curly I don't care. Your back is snapped. From now till the millennium. They have your number. (*Pause.*) Have a drink.

Max No, thank you.

Curly Have a drink.

Max takes a swig.

I don't think you have it in you to kill. But, Christ, you have it in you to wheedle. Have another drink.

Max takes a swig.

Sarah told you about the deal. You were to investigate. But you didn't go to Malloy. You went to Patrick. For cash. I have one question. Why did Patrick consent?

Max shrugs.

Please don't lie to me, Max. Have another drink.

Max drinks again.

Pretend you're Malloy.

Max drinks again.

Why did Patrick give you the money?

Max He . . .

Curly Have another drink.

Max drinks again.

Why did Patrick bother? He should have kept his nerve.
He had a perfectly plausible story . . .

Max He . . .

Curly Drink.

Max drinks again.

Have a cigarette.

*Curly throws down a cigarette and a box of matches.
Max lights up.*

He could have said he never knew. Is that not what people
say? In such circumstances.

Max He . . .

Curly Drink.

Max drinks again.

I understand he arranged the bridging loan for the
building. He would barely have been implicated.

Max There . . .

Curly Drink.

Max drinks again.

DAVID HARE

It's a half-baked sort of scandal that I can't quite understand. That's why I'm asking for your help. Have another cigarette.

Max lights a second cigarette, then lights two for Curly. Curly sticks one in Max's nose and one in Max's right ear.

Drink.

Max drinks, coughs and splutters and drops the cigarettes.

You're just about ready to tell me the truth.

Max They put a dog in . . .

Curly Dog?

Max Hart . . .

Curly The spiritualist . . .

Max Yes. Uses his dogs for other purposes . . .

Curly The ones that talk to the dead?

Max Can also be hired out on eviction jobs.

Curly But Malloy sold up.

Max Not at first. He wouldn't be bought. So they decided to flush him out of the house. Mrs Malloy was at the cinema. Malloy was alone. Hart stole the fuses. Then put an Alsatian in.

Curly What happened?

Max Malloy blew it apart with a shotgun.

Curly God almighty.

Max He did it in the dark. It was the fight of his life. He knew it was Hart's, he phoned him. I'm going to be sick.

Curly Don't – be sick. That means Patrick wasn't there that night. And it wasn't his dog. And it's not even publicly his profit. You had nothing on him. Why did he pay?

Max I had something on him. I had Sarah on him. He was terrified she'd find out that he was behind it. He was thinking of Sarah. He paid up. He loved her.

Curly Mistake.

Max On the last day – Sarah found out. It had been – it had been . . .

Curly Like holding Niagara . . .

Max Yes . . .

Curly Everyone should know everything.

Max Yes.

Curly How did she take it?

Max She was possessed. She'd killed a dog before.

Curly Yes.

Max When she was a child.

Curly Yes.

Max She kept saying: what happens to dogs.

Curly What happens to dogs.

Max What happens to people.

Pause.

Curly Finish the bottle.

Max I . . .

Curly Finish.

Max drinks again. Curly makes him finish; then bangs down his fist on the end; then gets up.

Now get up.

Max I can't.

Curly Take your empties. And go.

Max crawls off. Curly stamps out the cigarette ends. The lights change.

So it came back to Spats. It would always come back to Spats. The world is not run by innocents or small men who happen to believe the wrong thing. It is run by uncomfortably large, obscenely quiet men called Spats. The time was coming when I'd have to face Patrick. Patrick was no longer perfect. I had found a way in. In the thick, densely carpeted air of a merchant bank, the sound of a slight scuffle and the warm red smell of dog. Glimpsed for a second the implausible face of a man who loved his own daughter. I was in.

Music starts.

SCENE FIFTEEN

The Delafields' drawing-room. Night.
Curly is sitting in his overcoat with his feet up, waiting. The door opens and Patrick comes in, bleary-eyed, in dressing-gown and pyjamas.

Patrick Curly.

Curly Happy birthday, Spats.

Patrick Did you just wake me up?

Curly Come in. Sit down.

Patrick What's happened?

Curly You're OK. Sit down.

Patrick sits.

Patrick I'd like a glass of hot water.

Curly Not yet.

Patrick gets his little box out.

Put your eyes in. Attaboy.

Patrick leans back and dabs contact lenses on to his eyes.

Can you see me now?

Patrick Yes.

Curly I have my fingers on your throat. Feel anything? There's been a development. Stray dog. About a year ago. You were avoiding a public inquiry, I should think. Irreparable damage to the character of Guildford. So someone decided to flush out Malloy.

Patrick Well?

Curly Well?

Patrick I know what you're talking about. And I didn't condone their methods. Stupid. I was appalled.

Curly You didn't know at the time?

Patrick I run a merchant bank. I sanctioned the purchase – not the method of purchase.

Curly But he brought you the corpse.

Patrick The dead dog? Yes. He left it on my doorstep. A tuppenny gesture.

Curly How did he know that you were behind it?

303

Patrick He worked in the City. Remember. He could fight his way through. He knew the routes.

Curly But why did he sell? After he'd blown the dog apart. It was his victory. Why did he not seize it?

Pause.

Patrick Why do people give in? Because they recognize the way things are. He had made his point. He'd planted his tiny flag on the hillside and now – well, if you saw the site – there was just this old Victorian house, alone among the rubble of a demolition site. You looked at it. It was aching to come down. It had to.

Curly I don't understand.

Patrick Think. Even after that night, to hold on to the house would have meant turning your life into a battlefield, a constant act of self-assertion. Nobody wants to live like that. Straining endlessly to make your point. And why? He already had the moral victory. I glimpsed his face the following morning on the eight thirty-three. He looked up at me. A pleasurable glow of self-righteousness – the fight of his life and he'd won . . .

Curly Weren't you ashamed?

Patrick He had the righteousness. I had the house. (*Pause.*) Peace with honour. That is the phrase. It means surrender. But of a very special kind. With the sweet heart of your integrity intact. (*Pause.*) He had that. I had – well, so far it's nudging into its third million . . .

Curly This moral victory – the fight of his life . . .

Patrick Yes?

Curly Wasn't much use in his dying year.

Patrick That wasn't my fault. Peace with honour – peace

with shame. It's a very thin line. A matter of believing –
your own propaganda. (*Pause*.) And all for a girl.

Curly Everyone loves Jenny.

   Pause.

Patrick Stick to your story I used to say. When I met
Malloy later in the street. In the last days of alcoholic
collapse. I told him. Stick to your story. You killed the dog.
You revealed my corruption. Great victory. Old man.
(*Pause*.) Curly. Life is pain. Pure and simple. Pain. Around.
Below. All pain. But we have a choice. Either to protest
noisily – to scream against the pain, to rattle and wail – or
else – to submerge that pain, to channel it . . . (*Pause*.)
Preferably in someone else's direction. (*Pause*.) If I
admitted everything that had happened in my life, laid it
out in a field like the contents of an air disaster, would it
really help?

Curly Go back to Sarah.

Patrick No.

Curly Everyone should know everything. That's what I
believe.

Patrick Very well.

Curly You went to Max.

Patrick Not at all. He came to us. Saying he knew about
Mrs Malloy. We had nothing to fear . . .

Curly You'd have kept your nerve.

Patrick I should hope so . . .

Curly And a plausible story.

Patrick He said he knew about the dog. Again it was
nothing. We could have denied all knowledge.

Curly In fact you do.

Patrick Oh, yes. (*Pause.*) Of course. We sent him away. It was rubbish. But as an afterthought he said he'd tell Sarah. (*Pause.*) Curly. You may not believe it. The City of London once enjoyed a reputation for unimpeachable integrity. My word is my bond. So fabulously wealthy as to be almost beyond wealth. But in the last twenty years we've been dragged through the mud like everyone else. The wide boys and the profiteers have sullied our reputation. We work now like stallholders against a barrage of abuse. (*Pause.*) Who is to set standards? Curly. Who is to lead? You have to be able to believe – my daughter should not be given the chance to doubt – we were honest men . . . (*Pause.*) We are honest men. She had always abused me. But she had never been able to fault me. (*Pause.*) I had to buy Dupree. Do you understand? For her sake.

Curly smiles.

Curly How did you buy him?

Patrick A package. Rather lurid. I got him – a job in London and a series of leads on my younger, less scrupulous colleagues, gave him a little money . . .

Curly Is that all?

Patrick No. We negotiated.

Curly What?

Patrick A large anonymous donation to an anarchist party of his own choosing. (*Pause.*) On those terms he could take it. Do you see?

Curly Go on.

Patrick That was it.

Curly Apart from Sarah.

Patrick Apart from Sarah that was it. (*Pause.*) Sarah. Unquenchable. A deep well of unhappiness down which I could have thrown anarchist subscriptions, dead dogs, pints of my own warm blood, I could have turned on my head, destroyed my own life, and she would not have been satisfied. (*Pause.*) Like you. (*Pause.*) The two of you. Like woodpeckers. Nothing will stop you. In her case it was pity for the world. In yours . . .

Curly Go on.

Patrick In yours . . .

Curly Go on.

Patrick Disgust. (*Pause.*) You have a beady little heart, Curly. It pumps away. I've watched. One thing fires you. The need to ensure everyone is as degraded as you are.

Pause.

Curly Go on.

Patrick Max was like the rest of us. He got worn down. By the endless wanting to know. Now he wanted to know why the story had never appeared. (*Pause.*) He told her. Your father is financing the building. I have been paid off. Malloy was paid off. A dog is dead. Everyone should know everything. She went mad. (*Pause.*) The dog in particular. She was obsessed with the dog. She went straight to Victoria. I followed as soon as I could. (*Pause.*) I got into Eastbourne at midnight. The last train down. It was too late to try all the hotels. I went down to the promenade. By the silver railings there was a girl in a light-coloured raincoat. She had black frizzy hair. It was dark and drizzling and I couldn't see. She was squatting down. As I got nearer I could see she was pissing. On the promenade. She finished. She got up. And her coat was open. She was wearing nothing underneath. It was raining and it was very cold. She just wandered away. (*Pause.*) That's Eastbourne beach. (*Pause.*) I started to follow her. I had no choice.

Curly What did she say?

Patrick She said nothing.

Curly Go on.

Patrick We walked. A procession of two, through acres of bungalows to the open land. A flat rocky patch stretching away to the sea. The distance between us religiously observed. (*Pause.*) She sat down on the concrete jetty. (*Pause.*) Those who wish to reform the world should first know a little bit about it. I told her some stories of life in the City – the casual cruelty of each day; take-over bids, redundancies, men ruined overnight, jobs lost, trusts betrayed, reputations smashed, life in that great trough called the City of London, sploshing about in the cash. And I asked, what I have always asked: how will that ever change?

Curly Tell me of any society that has not operated in this way.

Patrick Five years after a revolution . . .

Curly The shit rises . . .

Patrick The same pattern . . .

Curly The weak go to the wall . . .

Patrick Somebody's bound to get hurt . . .

Curly You can't make omelettes . . .

Patrick The pursuit of money is a force for progress . . .

Curly It's always been the same . . .

Patrick The making of money . . .

Curly The breaking of men.

Patrick The two together. Always. The sound of progress.

Curly The making of money. The breaking of men.

Pause.

Patrick If I didn't do it . . .

Curly Somebody else would. (*Pause.*) And what did she say?

Patrick She said nothing. (*Pause.*) Finally, after twenty-one years she said nothing. Wrapped the mac tighter about her body. (*Pause.*) We watched the dawn. If I'd moved towards the jetty she would have thrown herself in. At five-thirty she was calm. She still said nothing. I took the decision. I walked into the town. I rang Hart from the Cavendish and told him to come and collect her. Then I got a train up to town.

Curly What?

Patrick I had a meeting. (*Pause.*) Money. (*Pause.*) Hart arrived to look after her at a quarter past seven. He was to drive her back. He followed my instructions to the beach. She was gone. Her raincoat was on the jetty. It was the only article of clothing she'd been wearing. It's safe to say she killed herself. (*Pause.*) The suicide was calculated from the start. Not uncommon. She had challenged Max to make me come to Eastbourne. Two malicious gestures. She had chosen to die at a place famous for a ghastly murder. And second, she had left two first-class tickets behind. The clearest possible way of saying – someone else is involved. (*Pause.*) It was me. (*Pause.*) She had to bang down her flag. Like everyone else.

Curly How do I know this is true? (*He rises.*) For all I know, you travelled down with her. You could have killed her.

Patrick Is that what you think?

Pause.

Curly No. I believe you absolutely. The story has just the right amount of quiet. She slipped obligingly into the sea. An English murder. Who needs ropes or guns or daggers? We can trust our victims to pass quietly in the night. Slip away into the bottle. Or the loony bin. Just – fall away with barely the crack of a knuckle as they go. (*Pause.*) I'm sure she died on the beach. I'm sure that you – were sixty miles away.

Patrick I didn't go to the police. I rigged up the alibi with Hart and Dupree.

Curly You left her to die.

Patrick No, that's what the police would have said.

Curly That's what you did.

Patrick It was a knife-edge decision. In the morning light. To stay or go. I had to decide which was better. Then something she said made up my mind for me.

Curly She spoke.

Patrick Just once.

Curly What did she say?

Patrick A single thing. 'What I despise most,' she said, 'is your pretence to be civilized.' (*Pause.*) I was reassured. The same old propaganda. The noise of someone who's going to live. The same old drivel. She was bleating again. So I left.

Curly In fact . . .

Patrick In fact she meant it. (*Pause.*) And that is the nail on which my life is hung. She meant it. (*Pause.*) But I see no reason to drag it out in public.

Curly Sure . . .

Patrick If I wish to continue . . .

Curly Making money . . .

Patrick The facts must be suppressed. The girl is dead. It makes no difference now.

    Pause.

Curly I possess a lethal combination of facts. Suppose I go to the press? The old woman, the dog, abandoning your daughter on the beach . . .

Patrick (*calling*) Mrs Dunning. (*to Curly*) You let it out. You ruin me. He left his daughter to kill herself. A despicable thing to do. Bad publicity. I leave my job. What happens? Someone else pops up in my place. Life covers up pretty fast. Only the people bleed. (*calling*) Mrs Dunning. (*to Curly*) Both of you did well. You wrung from me the same confession. You wanted me to say I was degraded. Well . . . (*Pause.*) I am. (*Pause.*) OK? So now can I please go back to work?

    Mrs Dunning comes in, also in a dressing-gown.

Mrs Dunning You must be quiet, Pat.

Patrick I'm sorry.

Mrs Dunning You must stay calm. You'd better go to bed.

Patrick I'm sorry.

Mrs Dunning That's all right. You'll be fine.

Curly I just want to say . . .

Mrs Dunning Sssh. Be quiet. Come to bed.

Curly Let me say . . .

Mrs Dunning Sssh. Quiet please. Let's everyone be quiet. (*Pause.*) All right, Pat?

She smiles and kisses Pat on the cheek.

Patrick My darling.

Mrs Dunning Good night.

Patrick Good night.

Patrick goes out.

Mrs Dunning (*at the door*) And we'll try to forget you were ever disturbed.

Mrs Dunning goes out. Curly is left alone. The lights change.

Curly Under the random surface of events lie steel-grey explanations. The more unlikely and implausible the facts, the more rigid the obscene geometry below. I was holding my father's life in my hands. I had to make up my mind. If I ditched my father, told the newspapers the story of those days, all I would be doing would be to bang down my tiny flag on the same mountain-side as Sarah. Somewhere every so often in this world there will appear this tiny little weed called morality. It will push up quietly through the tarmac, and there my father will be waiting with a cement grinder and a shovel to concrete it over. It is inadequate. It cannot help us now. There are no excuses left. Two sides. Two sides only. Lloyd's of London was beckoning me. I could feel its soft fiscal embrace. I wanted its quiet and its surety. I would sit in Lloyd's and wait for the end. I lay back. But I wanted Jenny beside me. I wanted to rest my head between her legs. I was ready to chase the same shadow, to tread the same path as Dupree and Malloy: all of us after

the same one thing: the hard, bright, glistening girl who
ran the Shadow of the Moon.

Music, 'We'll Gather Lilacs', very loud.

SCENE SIXTEEN

The Shadow of the Moon bar. Night.
Jenny is in the bar. As the music stops, Curly enters.

Curly Come for a quick one.

Jenny Come in.

Curly Bet I'm the worse soak you ever had.

Jenny smiles and gets him a bottle.

You're up pretty early.

Jenny Yes. Do you want some breakfast?

Curly I . . .

Jenny looks up.

I talked to Patrick.

Jenny What did he say?

Curly He knew nothing. It turned out.

Jenny You mean . . . ?

Curly He really is completely innocent.

Jenny What about Malloy?

Curly That was – quite another business.

Jenny I see.

Curly Nothing to do with it. Or with Patrick. He didn't
know.

Jenny Why did she kill herself?

Curly Well . . . (*Pause.*) You said it. She was paranoid. I think she got depressed.

Jenny Nothing to do with Malloy . . .

Curly No.

Jenny Or Patrick.

Curly No.

Jenny I see.

Curly She just wasn't quite cut out for things.

Jenny No. . . .

Curly Looking back. Inevitable. You understand.

Jenny Oh, yes.

Pause.

Curly Some people. You can see it coming.

Jenny I got a letter this morning. Shall I read it to you?

Curly Please.

Jenny takes out a sheet, leans against the bar, reads:

Jenny 'My darlings, whoops that's fig juice if you're wondering.
Let us rejoice in the ugliness of the world. Strangely, I am not upset. I am reassured. I think I left a finger pointing on the beach.
Jenny, keep Pat on the flat of his back. On his knees. Keep him confessing. Keep the wound fresh.
I walked five miles before I found any clothes.
Insist we are degraded.
Resist all those who tell you otherwise.
At all costs fight innocence.

Forbid ignorance.
Startle your children.
Appal your mothers.
Know everything.
Love everything.
Especially –
Decay.
Insist on decay.
I have twice been debauched in the open road. I am
travelling at this moment through France. Don't tell Pat.
Goodbye, sweet friends, goodbye.'

Pause.

I think it's from her. I don't know anyone else . . . (*Pause.*)
He called me up.

Curly Who?

Jenny Patrick.

Curly What did he say?

Jenny He said . . . (*Pause.*) Don't look so worried.

Curly (*smiling*) No, no . . .

Jenny This was yesterday.

Curly Ah.

Jenny He said he'd like to buy this place.

Curly Here?

Jenny Yeah.

Curly What did you say?

Jenny He's offering a very good price.

Curly I'm sure.

Jenny It's a crummy sort of building as you can see.

Curly Yeah . . .

Jenny You know . . .

Curly Yeah . . .

Jenny Some whisky stains and a few tears . . .

Curly Jenny . . .

Jenny I said no.

Pause.

Curly Jenny . . .

Jenny So . . .

Curly Oh, Jenny . . .

Pause.

Jenny Thanks for your help.

Curly What?

Jenny Sarah.

Curly Well . . .

Jenny Thank you. (*Pause.*) I had a long talk with Michael Hart. About Malloy. And the dog. And Patrick's behaviour on the beach. (*Pause.*) I know everything. (*Pause.*) So do you.

Pause.

Curly Keep your chin up.

Jenny And you.

Curly (*backing away*) I liked your legs. I've always liked your legs.

Jenny Goodbye.

Curly Goodbye.

Jenny goes out. The lights change.

Why should I feel ashamed of myself? Why should I feel inferior? Why should I feel anything? Jenny would go to the newspaper. They didn't believe her. And, anyway, Sarah was alive. It was autumn again. In the mean square mile of the City of London they were making money. (*smiling*) Back to my guns.

The lights fade.

LICKING HITLER

For Reg

Characters

Anna Seaton
Archie Maclean
Will Langley
John Fennel
Eileen Graham
Karl
Herr Jungke
Allardyce
Lotterby
Lord Minton

Chauffeur, Maids, Sergeant, Soldiers, Naval Commander,
Engineers, Officers, Nurse, Voice of Narrator

Licking Hitler was first shown on BBC TV on 10 January 1978. The cast was as follows:

Anna Seaton Kate Nelligan
Archie Maclean Bill Paterson
Will Langley Hugh Fraser
John Fennel Clive Revill
Eileen Graham Brenda Fricker
Karl Michael Mellinger
Herr Jungke George Herbert
Allardyce Patrick Monckton
Lotterby Jonathan Coy

Photography by Ken Morgan
Produced by David Rose
Directed by David Hare

1. EXT. HOUSE. DAY
An English country house. Perfect and undisturbed. Large and set among woods. The sun behind it in the sky. Loudly a bird tweets.

2. EXT. DRIVE. DAY
A convoy of military vehicles comes noisily up the long drive.

3. INT. CORRIDOR. DAY
A corridor inside the house. At the end of the corridor we can see through to the large hall where **Langley,** *a uniformed army officer, is standing. The sound of the convoy arriving. An elderly* **Chauffeur** *carries luggage out of the house. An even older* **Maid,** *in black-and-white uniform, follows with more.* **Lotterby,** *a young officer, comes into the house, salutes and begins reporting to Langley. All the time the camera is tracking back, drawn by the voice of* **Archie Maclean.**

Archie (VO) The question of Hess.

Pause.

Nobody really believes that Hess flew to Britain on the Führer's instructions. Hess flew to Britain for one simple reason: because he's a criminal lunatic.

The camera pans slowly round to a bare passage leading down to the servants' quarters. A few hunting and military pictures hang at random on the cream walls. At the bottom of the passage the sun shines brilliantly through the glass panes of the closed door of the gun room, from which Archie's voice is coming.

Now what is frightening about Hess is not what he has done. It is the fact he once found his way so easily into Hitler's confidence. As loyal Germans we have to face the

fact that Adolf Hitler chooses to surround himself with
fools, arse-lickers, time-servers, traitors, megalomaniacs
. . . and men who wish to rape their own mothers.

4. INT. GUN ROOM. DAY
*Archie Maclean is standing at one side of the room where
the shotguns are kept. It is mostly very dirty, full of fishing
rods, tennis rackets, golf clubs, mosquito nets, sola topees,
nails, hammers, saws, croquet mallets, polo sticks, riding
boots, skis, deerstalkers, wellingtons and husky jackets.
There is a table piled with cartridges where* **Eileen Graham**
*has cleared a space to take dictation. She is about twenty-
two, with very long legs and fashionably long and wavy
hair. She is efficient, self-contained, lower-middle-class.
Archie is in his late twenties but already looks much more
mature; squat, powerful, stocky, a Clydesider with a very
precise manner.*

Archie God . . . God . . . when I think of the . . . (*Pause.
Eileen catches up on her dictation, then looks away and
out of the window, while Archie searches for the right
word.*) . . . worms. When I think of the worms, when I
think of the cheapjacks, when I think of the human
excrement that is even now clogging up the innermost
councils of the Reich, when I think how badly divided our
leaders are, how grossly they have miscalculated, how the
pygmies scratch and . . .

    Pause. Action again suspended.

. . . jostle . . . jostle around the Führer's teats, how the
greybeard eunuchs and slug-like parvenues congest and
clot the bloodstreams of the nation, then I cry . . . Lord I
cry for Germany.

    *He turns and looks at Eileen still thinking. She looks up.
Then he waves a hand.*

Something like that.

5. EXT. COUNTRY LANE. DAY
Country lane in spring. A young girl of nineteen, struggling along the road, which is deserted, carrying two heavy suitcases which she has to put down every fifty yards. Her hair falls in front of her face. She is thin and very tired. **Anna.**

6. INT. HALL. DAY
A large hall with a fine staircase. The front doors of the house have been flung open and opposite them the military vehicles are now parked and are being unloaded by **Soldiers** *under the direction of the* **Sergeant**. *They are taking off office equipment, which they now bring into the house. Also waiting outside is an old Rolls-Royce. At the very centre of the hall* **Lord Minton** *is sitting on his suitcase. He has a stick, a big black coat and is very old and ill. Around him, and taking no notice, soldiers carry filing cabinets and wireless equipment through the hall and off down the corridor.*

Langley comes down the staircase. We see him to be in his thirties, thin, bony, with sleeked-down black hair and a very dry edge to his manner. **Allardyce,** *a young engineer, approaches him, carrying a green telephone.*

Allardyce The green line, sir – anywhere in particular?

Langley Best place is my study. I'll show you where that is.

Archie is standing in his shirt sleeves at the end of the corridor watching the arrivals. Langley gestures to him.

Archie, can you . . .

Langley nods, then disappears with Allardyce and the telephone equipment. Archie looks across at the

Chauffeur who is coming back from the car.

Archie Is he ready?

The Chauffeur looks down at Lord Minton and asks him a question in deaf and dumb language. Lord Minton replies vociferously, then turns to Archie. Gets up. He smiles and gestures wonderingly round the magnificent house. Then shrugs. Archie hands him his cane and gloves.

7. EXT. STEPS OF THE HOUSE. DAY
Archie shakes Minton's hand and shouts at him.

Archie Very kind. Of you. To lend us. Your place.

Minton turns and gets into the car, the door of which is held open for him by his Chauffeur.

Tell him we appreciate his sacrifice. Having to spend the rest of the war in that squalid wee single end in Eaton Square.

The Chauffeur smiles thinly as he closes the door, and goes round to drive away. Anna arrives just in time to hear Archie as he waves from the steps.

That's right Minton, you bugger off.

Anna looks up at him.

Anna Is this Wendlesham?

Archie You were due yesterday.

Anna The train . . . it stopped for the night outside Aylesbury. Nobody knew why.

But Archie has already turned to Lotterby, who is carrying a huge photograph of Goebbels into the house. Archie seizes it.

And it's taken all day just to get . . .

Lotterby Goebbels for you, sir.

Archie smiles and goes into the house.

Archie We'll hang him in the study. Is that not what people do?

8. INT. HALL. DAY
Archie passes quickly through with Lotterby carrying the portrait of Goebbels.

Archie Look at the face. Extraordinary face. The lips.

They go off down the corridor. Anna follows in through the door and looks round the hall which has suddenly emptied. She puts her bags down, looks round. Sudden quiet.

9. EXT. DRIVE. DAY
The military convoy disappears down the drive.

10. GUN ROOM. DAY
As before except now at the centre of the clutter is the large and magnificent portrait of Goebbels. Archie is standing at the window. It is darkening outside. Eileen is sitting at the desk reading back typed dictation.

Eileen The question of Hess, stop. Nobody believes that Hess came to Britain on the Führer's instructions, stop. Hess flew to Britain for one simple reason, colon. Because he's a criminal lunatic, stop.

Anna is standing at the door. She has taken her coat off and has tidied up. She carries a huge volume under her arm. Eileen stops reading. Archie turns.

Archie I take it you've signed the Act. (*Anna nods.*) Sit down.

Anna sits on a wooden chair among the tennis rackets.

Ihr Deutsch soll ausgezeichnet sein.

Anna Ja. Das war ja einfach für mich.

Archie Where did you learn?

Anna My family . . . my cousin was married to a German. I spent my summers in Oberwesel. They had a *Schloss* on the Rhine.

Archie Who vetted you?

Anna Naval Intelligence. My uncle is Second Sea Lord at the Admiralty.

Archie I see.

Anna I also have a cousin who's high-up in . . .

Archie Och yes, I can imagine.

There is a pause. Archie looks at Anna.

Well, there's nothing for you yet. But we do need somebody to make the tea.

11. INT. KITCHEN. EVENING
A large bare room with a gas range. The only provisions in view are a packet of tea, a packet of sugar and a bottle of milk. Anna comes in, looks around, then takes a saucepan over to the tap. We can hear Eileen in the distance repeating the Hess speech. Anna pauses uncertainly at the tap, then turns back, takes a decision. She confidently empties the whole packet of tea into the saucepan and pours on to it a good hard gush of cold water. She then puts the pan on to the gas and lights it.

12. INT. CORRIDOR. EVENING
Empty. Gun room door open.

Archie (VO) I'll do the blackout, it's a'right.

Eileen appears from the gun room, looks puzzled down the corridor, then goes one door down to the kitchen. Goes in.

13. INT. KITCHEN. EVENING
The tea is now boiling, Anna is staring at it. She looks up at Eileen as soon as she comes in. Eileen at once takes it off the stove, amazed, and looks at the empty packet.

Eileen That's a week's ration.

Anna I've never had to.

She is beginning to cry.

Eileen No.

Anna Just can't.

14. INT. BEDROOM. NIGHT
A darkened room, plain, once a servant's bedroom. An iron bed. Anna lying awake in the dark. Then quietly she slips the covers off and runs across to her suitcase at the far side of the room. Takes out her battered, yellowing teddy bear. Returns to bed with him. Stops in front of the bed.

Anna Which side do you want?

15. INT. DRAWING ROOM. DAY
A magnificent yellow room. High windows. Bright daylight. Armchairs and sofas. Superb full-length portraits on the walls. At one end Langley has set up a table behind which he and **Fennel** *sit. Fennel is almost forty, fat, boyish, an enthusiast, an intellectual enjoying his war. Scattered round the room are a mixture of* **Plainclothes People,** **Engineers** *and* **Officers** *from the three Services. Next to*

Anna on a sofa is **Karl**, *heavy, dark-jowled, bewildered.*
He seems to understand nothing of what is going on.

Fennel This is a research unit within the Political Warfare
Executive. How the rest of that department functions is
none of your concern. I am your only contact with the
world outside and I don't expect to visit you very often.
I'm afraid you will know very little about the success or
failure of your work. You are throwing stones into a pond
which is a very long way away. And there will be almost
no ripples. So your job must be to keep your heads down
and just . . . keep at it, even though you'll have almost no
idea of the effect you're having.

Karl leans across the sofa and whispers to Anna.

Karl Ich verstehe nicht.

Anna (*whispers in German*) Moment.

Fennel Perhaps even when the war is over you will not
know what good you did.

Fennel smiles.

16. INT. DRAWING ROOM. DAY
Anna leans alone against a window frame. Everyone is
now standing in cocktail positions. Two **Maids** *pass*
between groups of people pouring out beer from big,
stoppered two-pint bottles. In one group stand Fennel,
Langley, Allardyce.

Fennel I suppose you'd been hoping to represent your
country.

Langley That's right. I was aiming for the 1940 Olympics.

He smiles.

Fennel But you still have your blue?

Langley Half-blue.

Fennel Fencing is a half-blue?

Langley That's right. But I'm still hoping for national honour. I mean, after the war.

They smile. Archie is sitting alone on the sofa staring across the room at Anna. Anna raises the pint mug to her lips but takes as little as possible. She is very self-conscious and lonely. The Fennel conversation has moved on.

Fennel The boys on *The Times* actually got hold of an onion.

Langley Good Lord.

Fennel Can you imagine? Someone actually gave them one. A whole onion. Great big thing. So they auctioned it among the staff. Went to the night editor for £4 3s. 4d.

Allardyce Well.

Langley Worth it.

Now Fennel seems to catch Anna's eye. She looks away.

Fennel Certainly. Of course.

A gong sounds. The room goes silent, caught for a moment as they stand.

17. INT. DINING ROOM. DAY
The Unit sits round a large dinner table, overhung with chandeliers. The Older Maid dollops mashed potato on to each plate as the Young Maid passes with an ashet on which sits a piece of pork luncheon meat in the shape of a tin. She puts it down at the head of the table, and as the top seat is unoccupied, Archie rises and gravely begins to carve the luncheon meat. It makes a succulent, unpleasant

noise. Anna looks out of the window to the drive where Langley is talking animatedly to Fennel and a **Naval Commander**. *You can just hear them speaking.*

Fennel Goodbye. Good luck. I'll try and get down in a couple of months.

Fennel and the Commander climb into the car, gathering up piles of paper from off the back seat. They look to Anna romantic and attractive. Fennel's **Driver** *drives them away.*

An uneasy silence as the Unit eat. Karl leans to Anna and whispers in German. Apologetically, Anna speaks.

Anna He would like to know . . . what exactly we're all doing here.

Archie looks up from his food.

Archie Tell him it's a wireless station. Like the BBC.

18. INT. GUN ROOM. DAY
Archie at the window. Eileen with her dictation pad. Anna and Karl sitting useless at the other side of the room.

Eileen The question of Hess.

Archie The question of Hess.

He taps his knuckles on the windowpane in a gesture of frustration.

Anna Perhaps if you told us more about it we would be able to help.

Eileen smiles. Anna watches as Archie turns and stares at her.

Archie The game is. We are a radio station . . .

Anna Yes.

Archie Broadcasting to Germany. My job is to script the broadcasts. Your job is to interpret them.

Anna I see.

Karl Was sagt er?

Anna (*in German*) Propaganda.

Archie Yes.

Pause.

We are to pretend to be two German army officers stationed a thousand miles apart sending coded messages to each other nightly over short-wave radio. When the messages have been sent, the idea is that one of our officers – 'Otto' – will relax, he will talk more frankly, he will add his own personal comments on the conduct of the war. And those comments will not be complimentary to the Nazi leaders.

Anna I see.

Archie Does that make sense to you?

Anna Of course. But it does seem a little elaborate.

A moment. Archie looks beadily at Anna.

Archie You fight a war, you expect propaganda, you expect your enemy to tell you lies. Right?

He moves across the room towards them.

So people spend a good deal of their time on their guard. Now the beauty of this idea is that when we make our first broadcast tonight, maybe ten or fifteen people, radio hams mostly, will twiddle their dials and stumble on it. But because they have found us by accident, and because they appear to be eavesdropping on a purely private conversation, and that conversation is indubitably between loyal army officers on their own side . . . they will be inclined to trust everything we say. And from that trust our influence will grow.

Anna looks at Archie, then nods at Karl.

Anna Is he one of the officers?

Archie nods.

Who is he really?

Archie He's a Jew. From Frankfurt.

Anna Shall I tell him?

Archie nods. Anna turns to Karl. As Archie speaks Anna translates.

Archie He will be playing the part of Otto, a loyal Prussian officer, broadcasting to an old friend in another part of Germany . . .

Anna (*translating consecutively*) Sie sollen die Rolle von Otto spielen, einem treuen preussischen Offizier, der mit einem altern Kameraden in einem anderen Teil Deutschlands ein Rundfunkgespräch führt.

Karl Sie meinen, ich soll Theater spielen?

Anna Ja.

Archie The character of the Prussian must be authentic . . .

Anna Er muss authentisch sein.

Archie is staring at Anna, who has lost her nervousness for the first time.

Archie His language will therefore be rough . . .

Anna Er spricht sehr roh.

Archie Corrosive . . .

Anna Abrupt.

Archie Obscene.

Anna does not look up. A pause.

Anna Obszön.

Karl looks up.

19. INT. BILLIARD ROOM. NIGHT
The room has been converted into a wireless station, but signs of its original function remain. Racks of cues stand on the walls, and there is a prominent scoreboard. A green leather top has been laid over the baize.

Microphones have been placed at either end of the table, beside green light bulbs which flash to cue the broadcaster. At one end is Karl, at the other **Herr Jungke**. *He is a small, rather effete old man with pursed lips. In the middle, like a tennis umpire, sits Allardyce controlling the equipment.*

Along the side of the room sit the rest of the Unit watching: Archie, Anna, Eileen, Langley.

Allardyce Stand by, please.

A red light comes on and Allardyce nods at Karl who is looking more than usually nervous and distraught.

You have the air.

Langley makes a sign at Karl to sit forward. The green light comes on silently in front of him.

Karl Hier Otto-Abend Eins . . . Hier Otto-Abend Eins.

Karl's light goes out. He sits back. At the other end of the table Jungke's light comes on. He now cups one hand over his ear instinctively in response to Karl.

337

Jungke Ja . . . Otto . . . ich empfange . . . hast du 'ne Meldung?

A moment, then his light goes out. He sits back with an expression of relief. At the other end Karl becomes more apprehensive than ever. His light is on. Allardyce beckons at him.

Karl Jawohl. Die Meldung lautet. Mitzi muss ihren Vater treffen. Mitzi muss ihren Vater treffen.

Karl's light goes out. Jungke's light comes on. We see down the whole length of the billiard table, two ludicrous figures pretending to be miles apart.

Jungke Verstanden. Na, Otto, was hältst du denn von der Flucht von Hess?

The light bulbs change. Karl flinches.

Karl Ach ja, die Sache mit Hess. Tja, also . . .

He seems to have lost his place. Archie puts his head in his hands. Anna looks away.

Niemand glaubt, Hess sei auf Befehl des Führers nach England geflogen. Nein nein, er ist aus einem ganz anderen Grund nach England geflogen.

Archie gets up from his seat.

Der Grund ist – er ist ein grosser Verbrecher, ein Wahnsinniger.

20. INT. TRANSMISSION ROOM. NIGHT
A disc-cutting machine is the next room. Over it sits an Engineer wiping the floss from the disc as it cuts. Beside him stands Lotterby.

Karl (VO) Der Erschreckende an Hess ist nicht was er gemacht hat, sondern die Tatsache dass er so leicht ein

Vertrauter Hitlers werden konnte. Als treue Deutsche
müssen wir uns damit abfinden, dass Adolf Hitler bereit
ist, Idioten um sich zu dulden . . .

21. EXT. HOUSE. NIGHT
*The house from outside sitting confidently in the English
countryside. The moon beyond. Distorted across the
airwaves comes the continuous sound of Karl, now ranting
falteringly but with increasing vehemence. Some rabbits
pass across the lawn.*

Karl (VO) . . . Archlecker, Verbrecher, Verräter, solche die
an Grössenwahn leiden, oder die ihre eigenen Mütter
vergewaltigen wollen.

22. INT. BILLIARD ROOM. NIGHT
Jungke waves at Karl. Karl waves back.

Jungke Auf wiedersehen.

His light goes out. Allardyce turns to Karl.

Karl Auf wiedersehen.

*His light goes out. He sits back. Archie walks straight
out of the room. Silence. Karl spreads his palms on the
table.*

Am sorry.

*Langley acknowledges this with a nod. Karl speaks with
terrible seriousness and difficulty.*

Will be good.

Langley Yes.

Karl All Jews . . . good at showbiz.

Langley Yes. (*He gets up and smiles.*) All right everyone.

23. INT. HALL. NIGHT.
The Unit comes quietly into the hall and disperses upstairs, Anna and Eileen walking up together. Langley crosses with Jungke to the front door where Lotterby is waiting with Jungke's coat.

Lotterby Take Herr Jungke back, sir.

Langley Thank you.

Jungke confides in Langley as he puts his coat on.

Jungke The boy is nervous.

Langley Yes.

Jungke But also the script is not good. The writing . . . (*rubs his fingers together*) . . . not savage enough.

A pause. Langley remains expressionless.

Langley We'll try again tomorrow. Thank you for coming. Goodnight.

He reaches for the unseen light switch by the door and we are plunged into darkness.

24. EXT. SKY. NIGHT
Clouds move quickly across the moon.

25. INT. BEDROOM. NIGHT
As before, but this time Anna is asleep. Then suddenly the door crashes open, and Archie bursts into the room carrying a bottle of Scotch.

Archie I'll smash a bloody bottle in yer if yer bloody come near me.

He slips and falls at once to the floor. The bottle smashes. Silence.

26. INT. CORRIDOR. NIGHT
In the moonlight Anna's door opens and she appears
dragging Archie's body out into the upstairs corridor.
Then, when she's got him out, she turns him to point the
way the corridor goes. He does not wake. Then she goes
back in. A moment later she comes out with a blanket
which she lays over him. She goes back into her room,
closes the door.

27. INT. BEDROOM. DAY
Morning light at the window. Anna gets out of bed.
Avoids the broken glass on the floor. Takes away the chair
she has jammed under the door handle. She involuntarily
puts one arm over her chest as she opens the door. The
corridor is deserted. Even the blanket has gone.

28. INT. DINING ROOM. DAY
Archie sits alone at the far end of the table with a bottle of
milk and a plain glass. Anna goes over to the sideboard.
On the hot-plate there is a kettle, a pan and a tin. She
opens it. Powdered eggs. She attempts normality.

Anna Can I make you some egg?

Archie I've had yer tea. I'd want inoculation before I tried
yer egg.

Anna Look, I'm quite prepared not to mention the
fact . . .

Archie (*shouts*) What?

Anna looks at him and walks out of the room.

29. INT. HALL. DAY
Anna comes out into the deserted hall. At the bottom of
the staircase a teleprinter machine is clattering out
information. Then a **Voice** *comes from a distant wireless.*

Voice This is the first news bulletin of the day and Joseph McLeod reading it. The retreat of the defeated Italian army goes on. General Wavell's message to his troops . . .

Anna stands alone in the middle of the hall.

Anna Somebody talk to me.

30. MONTAGE SEQUENCE ONE
At once we hear Chopin's Waltz No. 3 in A Minor. A piano segment, no more than thirty seconds. Under it we see the following images: Archie standing watching the rain coming down outside the window; Allardyce looking regretfully away as Karl blunders through another broadcast; Anna and Eileen laughing together as Eileen elaborately shows Anna how to make a cup of tea; Langley and Allardyce playing croquet on the lawn as Eileen and Anna sit watching. Lotterby stands behind them and commentates. Long cool drinks are being sipped; Anna before she goes to bed putting the chair against her door. Fade. The Chopin ends.

31. INT. PASSAGE. DAY
Outside the gun room. Most of the sporting gear has been moved into the passage from which no one has had time to move it. It is oddly piled alongside overspill from inside the office. There is a pair of skis by the door. Nailed on to the door is a trophy, a Nazi noticeboard: JUDEN BETRETEN DIESEN ORT AUF EIGENE GEFAHR. The sound of Eileen's typewriter as Anna walks quickly down the passage and into the gun room.

32. INT. GUN ROOM. DAY
Eileen at work on a huge pile of notes. Anna comes in.

Anna Langley wants us. There's a morning conference.

Eileen I've still got all this stuff to do.

342

Anna They're going into Russia.

Eileen Who?

Anna The Germans.

Eileen Into Russia. What for?

Anna To make us work even harder, I suppose.

Eileen smiles.

33. INT. LANGLEY'S OFFICE. DAY
*A room in the front of the house. Once a gentleman's
study and library, now serving as Langley's office, it has a
large open fireplace and cleared desks. It is clean, manly
and well ordered. Flowers in vases. Langley sits behind his
desk opposite Archie. At one side Eileen sits taking
dictation; on the other side sits Anna. Langley is at his
most severe.*

Langley This discussion to be noted, minuted, dated 10th
June 1941.

Eileen's shorthand follows.

We have it from the War Cabinet that Hitler is invading
Russia within the next two weeks. I needn't stress how
important this news is to our work. It's a military step of
extraordinary foolishness, Hitler himself counsels against
it in *Mein Kampf*, and it gives us exactly the opportunity
we've been looking for to cast doubt on Germany's war
leadership. Our loyal German officer therefore is now in a
position to condemn the step as national suicide. He can
then go on to question the whole direction of the war.

Pause.

Archie May I ask a question, Will?

Langley Of course.

Archie Surely if there's a possibility of national suicide, that's something we'd be wanting to encourage, no?

Archie smiles.

Langley I'm sorry, I don't see your point.

Archie You see, I can't help looking at it another way. Your idea is nice, Will, I mean it's simple anyway, but surely one of the things we've learnt . . . attack the leadership direct and it always sounds like propaganda. And anything that sounds like propaganda is not good propaganda.

Langley Go on.

Archie I'd say if they're going to do something foolish, we should encourage them. I mean, let's have Otto right behind the idea.

Langley But you can't justify it, Archie. Otto's a military man . . .

Archie Look, Otto says . . .

Langley He'd know that going into Russia is insane. I mean, a war on two fronts.

Archie Look, Otto says . . . Otto says the real enemy of Germany has always been Bolshevism. And now the army is getting a chance to begin its real fight. But. It is hard to fight Bolshevism abroad, when there are known Bolsheviks inside the Nazi Party. So. The loyal German is happy to die in Russia, but he is not happy if there is any evidence of subversion at home. And anybody . . .
anybody at all who for whatever reason dares to oppose the Russian venture, or fails to support it with every sinew of their body is by definition . . . a Bolshevik. (*He smiles.*) Do y'see, everybody? Red-baiting! (*He laughs and claps his hands together.*) Anyone who speaks out is branded as a Bolshevik. Criticism silenced. Millions die.

Pause. Langley stares at him.

Well? Is that no' what ye want?

34. INT. GUN ROOM. NIGHT
*Blacked-out windows. A single green light. Eileen has a
single sheet of paper in her hand, which she reads out.
Archie is sitting on the desk. Langley, Anna are watching.
Karl is tucked away, his lips moving slightly as Eileen
reads. There is a new concentration in the work. Eileen
reads well.*

Eileen Many will die. Many will be happy to die on the
road to Moscow as long as they feel they have the efforts
of the whole nation concentrated behind them. For those
who stay at home have a duty too. They have a duty to
keep morale high, to silence dissent.

Archie nods at Langley to signal approval of the idea.

There will not be enough food this winter, there will not be
enough clothes. Everyone must therefore try to discover
those Party members who are taking more than their
rations. Everyone will have to be vigilant, everyone will
have to be a spy. It is a great adventure. We must all be
ruthless in its pursuit. Goodnight my friend. My dear, dear
friend.

She looks up. They look at her, awed.

35. INT. BILLIARD ROOM. NIGHT
*The red light goes on. Karl bends forward. He is
transformed. We follow his delivery – ironic, witty,
inflected. Sweat pours from him. His voice is much deeper
than before.*

Karl Viele werden sterben. Viele werden froh sein auf dem
Wege nach Moskau zu sterben, solange sie wissen, dass
das ganze Volk ihnen beisteht.

*We look at the Unit sitting at the side, as if deeply
moved by what he is saying.*

Aber die, die zu Hause bleiben, haben auch eine Aufgabe.
Ihre Aufgabe ist es, die Moral des Volkes zu heben und
Gegner zum Schweigen zu bringen. Es wird in diesem
Winter nicht genug zu essen geben, nicht genug Kleidung.

Archie smiles. We go back to Karl.

Jeder muss also versuchen herauszufinden, welche
Parteimitglieder mehr als ihre Rationen bekommen. Jeder
muss wachsam sein. Jeder muss Spion sein. Es ist ein
grosses Abenteuer. Wir müssen rücksichtslos sein. Gute
Nacht lieber Freund, mein lieber, lieber Freund.

*The red light goes off and Karl takes off his glasses.
Langley smiles.*

Langley Superb!

36. INT. HALL. NIGHT
*At once Chopin again. Odd, lilting, deft. Langley and
Archie seen from behind going down corridor together.*

Archie We've hit a vein.

Langley We have. More again tomorrow?

Archie Certainly.

Langley This Russian business . . . could be the making of
us.

*As they turn into the drawing room, Archie
uncharacteristically performs a tiny dance step.*

37. INT. DRAWING ROOM. NIGHT
*Jungke sits playing Chopin. His face is angelic, his feet
barely touch the pedals. The Steinway has been pulled out
from the wall, and the Unit has flopped down round the*

room. Eileen is reading Wellington Wendy, *Langley is reading* The Times. *The Engineers are playing chess. Anna sits staring on a sofa as behind her Archie moves very slowly, decanter in hand. He stops immediately behind her, pours out a glass very steadily and moves on. She does not turn. Jungke leans in to perform an intricate arpeggio. Then Lotterby appears at the door with Jungke's coat.*

Lotterby The car for Herr Jungke, sir.

Jungke stops playing. Langley gets up from his seat, speaks slowly to him.

Langley We have something for you.

Lotterby crosses to the piano and helps Jungke up as Langley goes to the sideboard where a bottle sits on a tray with a little dish beside it. Lotterby brings Jungke back and sits him in Langley's empty chair. Langley ceremoniously carries the tray and sets it down beside Jungke.

Langley Sambuca.

Jungke Do you have . . . a coffee bean?

Langley takes the dish and puts one coffee bean in the liquid, then takes out a box of matches and sets light to it. Jungke looks at the flame.

Jungke It is payment enough. Thank you.

Langley looks up at Lotterby.

Langley Ian, would you take Herr Jungke back to the internment camp?

Lotterby Sir.

38. INT. HALL. NIGHT
*Jungke is being escorted out by Langley, Lotterby waits
for them.*

Jungke It's not too bad. I have to be in solitary because of
this work but there are compensations. I have books, you
know. And I had a letter once.

    *Anna and Eileen cross the hall and go upstairs on their
    way to bed.*

Eileen Archie's drunk again.

Anna Why does he drink so much?

Eileen I don't know. Fleet Street, I suppose. They all do.

Anna Was he a journalist?

39. INT. STAIRS. NIGHT
Anna and Eileen on the servants' stairs.

Eileen By the time the war came he was on one of the big
national dailies. Fought his way up.

Anna From?

Eileen Poverty. Terrible. He comes from Glasgow, from
the Red Clyde. You must know that.

Anna I don't know anything.

40. INT. BEDROOM. NIGHT
*Anna comes into her bedroom. Closes the door. She then
picks up the chair to put it under the handle. But then
pauses with the chair in her hand. Turns. Puts the chair
back where it came from. Goes instead into the bathroom.*

41. INT. BEDROOM. NIGHT
As before. Anna's face, asleep. We are very close.

Archie (VO) Woman.

A moment, then Anna opens her eyes. She does not move. The sound of ripping material.

(VO) I'm at yer feet.

Anna scrambles up the bed and stands on top of it. By this time she can make out the figure of Archie at the bottom of the bed. He is very serious and very drunk.

The Scotsman's approach to the art a' love-makin'. (*Pause.*) The Scot makes love wi' a broken bottle. An' a great deal a' screamin'. (*Pause.*) There'll be a moment while I take off ma clothes.

He disappears beneath the end of the bed. There is a pause. Anna peers forward, into the dark.

42. INT. BEDROOM. NIGHT
Anna lying in bed with the sheet pulled up around her. She is soaked in sweat, her hair in strands. There is a light on in the bathroom and the door is ajar. You can see a trousered leg and hear the sound of water in a bowl. Anna barely turns towards the figure.

Anna I literally didn't know there was such a thing as an electricity bill. I was sheltered, I suppose. Where we live we just always left the lights on. I assumed the electricity just came . . . it just came and you paid your taxes and you got your light. Then the other day I was talking to Eileen and she said electricity prices had risen, and I said, you mean, you have to pay? For what you use? You have to pay? Gas, electricity, water. It had never occurred to me. (*Silence. She shivers.*) Archie. I am trying to learn.

The light goes out in the bathroom. Archie walks silently through the bedroom, opens the door and goes out. Anna alone.

43. INT. KITCHEN. DAY
*Daylight flooding in at the kitchen window. Anna is sitting
on the table with her back to us as Eileen carefully steams
open envelopes over a boiling kettle. She then sorts the
letters out into two piles.*

Eileen (*sorting through letters*) German . . . German for
you . . . English for me . . . German . . . English.

   Anna casually picks one up.

Anna Who wrote them?

Eileen Just ordinary people in Germany writing to their
relatives in the States.

Anna I didn't know they were allowed to.

Eileen Why not? America's neutral.

Anna Then how did we get hold of them?

Eileen Not that neutral, apparently. English . . .

Anna What are we meant to do with them?

Eileen You'll have to ask Genius.

Anna Is he down?

Eileen In the office.

Anna Ah.

   Anna goes. Eileen continues to read her letters.

Eileen Whoops. Somebody's dead.

44. INT. GUN ROOM. DAY
*Archie at his desk writing flowingly with a fountain pen.
Bright morning light behind him. Around him fresh
supplies of office stationery, including two piles of files
almost ceiling-high. On one wall is pinned a new map of*

*Germany. He does not look up as Anna comes in. She
stands at the door with a fistful of letters.*

Anna I want to know what to do with these.

Archie looks at her, referring to the piles of stationery.

Archie I shall be opening files on named individuals.
While their army is in Russia we shall be looking for
examples of favouritism at home. How Nazi Party officials
get more food, get more clothes, than ordinary people.
How they get sugar. How they get fruit. How they get
wine. How they give parties in private rooms where cakes
full of raisins and marzipan are eaten. Outrageous things.
You have to comb through these letters, and open files on
any named official, you have to pick out from the gossip
any hard fact, any details of their way of life, any
indiscretion, any sign that they're enjoying themselves
more than their brothers-in-arms. This way we drive a
wedge between the Party and the people. We broadcast
real names, plausible offences, backed up with thorough
research.

He looks at Anna, then returns to writing.

Anna And when we've finished with the letters . . . ?

Archie Yes.

Anna Do we send them on?

Archie stares at her.

Archie Yes. We send them on.

*Archie returns to writing. Anna moves across the room
sharply and puts the letters down on his desk.*

Anna Mr Maclean.

Archie Yes.

This time he does not look up at Anna.

Anna I have to go to the medicine cupboard.

Archie Yes.

Anna I have some bruises.

Archie Yes.

Nothing. Anna turns to go.

45. INT. LANGLEY'S OFFICE. DAY
Fennel in a big chair with a pot of coffee. He looks more crumpled and effusive then ever. He talks in a fast stream which Langley can barely intercept.

Fennel We now have four stations like yours, Will, each pretending to be an individual broadcasting from within Germany. Of course, none of this would be necessary if we could persuade the BBC to take a less literal attitude to what they like to call the truth, but I'm afraid that they do go on insisting that when the Navy says it's sunk a sub, it does actually have to have sunk a sub. So I can't see us getting much joy out of them. So what I'd like to do is co-ordinate all intelligence outlets, and start a Rumour Committee which will take charge of all misleading information, so we don't find ourselves with lots of little rumours popping up all over the place, but put all our efforts into good big sharp vicious rumours that really do the job. . . .

A knock at the door.

Langley Come in.

Anna enters.

Anna I'm sorry, I just want the medicine chest.

Langley Yes, of course. Come in.

Langley goes to get it down from a high cabinet. Fennel goes on, ignoring Anna.

Fennel It'll be a high-level committee; Sandy, Gargs, Freddy, if we have to, God help us, weekly meetings, decide who to go for . . .

Langley Yes.

Fennel Mostly the smaller fish, but go hard . . .

Langley Yes.

Fennel It's the little chap, the local leader we can really destroy, smears, innuendo, well co-ordinated . . .

Langley Yes.

Fennel Anyway we'll send you Rumour Directives. They'll come on G2s, of course. When you get the G2, for Christ's sake don't forget to cross-file.

Langley hands a white box with a red cross to Anna.

Langley Here you are.

Anna Thank you.

Fennel I hope you're settling down all right, my dear. Don't find it all too high-powered.

Anna smiles, not knowing what to say. She clutches the box.

Your uncle was very angry with me. Said I'd sent you to work for a savage.

Anna looks at Langley.

Langley I think he means Maclean.

Anna I see.

Fennel That's right.

Anna opens the medicine box and searches through it.
They look at her as if expecting her to say more.

The Celtic race, you know: a cloven-hoofed people. They
do seem to be fighting quite a different war.

Anna He seems . . . he just seems a very extraordinary
man to me.

She turns and looks at them defiantly. Then refers to a
bottle.

Is this Dettol?

Langley That's what it says.

46. INT. BEDROOM. DAY
Anna sitting on the edge of her bed. She lifts her skirt up
and undoes a suspender. Pulls down her stocking. On her
upper thigh, scratch and bruise marks. She applies the
Dettol with cotton wool. Tears come into her eyes. She
works down her thigh. Tears flow now, silently. Without
sobbing, she just lets the tears run down her cheek.

47. MONTAGE SEQUENCE TWO
Chopin again. The same segment. Under it we see: Eileen
hard at work at night, typing furiously; Karl broadcasting,
a look of extreme vindictiveness colouring his face; The
Unit sitting round a dinner table heavy with Christmas
decoration. Anna comes into the dining room with a
soufflé she has obviously just cooked. Everyone applauds.
Anna getting out of bed in the morning. She removes an
empty whisky bottle from the bedside table and takes it to
the wardrobe. There she sets it in a rank next to six other
empty bottles which are stacked on a high shelf next to her
teddy. Fade. Chopin ends.

48. INT. PASSAGE. DAY

Now almost impassable. A line of filing cabinets is banked along one wall. Opposite, several thousand loose files and complete editions of German and English newspapers. Langley comes down with a file and finds Anna sitting on the floor in the corridor doing her work. She is wrapped in many sweaters against the cold. He refers into the gun room.

Langley What's happening?

Anna One of his moods. What's that?

Langley German prisoners of war. Interrogated by Intelligence. Very gratifying. Look.

He opens the file and hands it to Anna. From inside the room you can hear Eileen's typewriter and Archie's odd bad-tempered grunt.

They report a run on clothing in Berlin. It's impossible to buy an overcoat because of rumours that Nazi Party officials are soon to get special clothing privileges.

Anna Amazing.

Langley They're issuing denials but to no effect. All our own work. It's proof someone's listening. I'll show it to him.

Anna He wouldn't want to know. It would spoil the game.

They smile.

Archie (*VO, rudely*) Anna.

49. INT. GUN ROOM. DAY

The room is now a fat stew of paperwork. Towers of documents take up most of the room. Archie is strained and tired. Eileen, who like Anna is well wrapped, is barely keeping her patience with him. Anna comes in.

Archie I have chosen Cologne. I have chosen the Burgomaster in Cologne. Now what do we have?

Anna looks round the room confused.

Anna Eileen, is Cologne in the lavatory?

Eileen No, no it's over there somewhere.

Anna heads where Eileen pointed, flicks through.

Archie Eileen. Prisoner interrogation. Anything we have from the cages to do with Cologne.

Eileen gets up and goes out.

50. INT. PASSAGE. DAY
Langley is standing listening outside the door, unseen by Archie. As Eileen comes out to get a file, she turns back towards the room and mimes machine-gunning Archie to death. Langley smiles and squeezes her arm. Eileen just nods and sets to work. Langley heads off down the corridor, casually tossing the file he has brought on to a random pile.

51. INT. GUN ROOM. DAY
Anna lays out what she's collected on Archie's desk, taking it all from one fat file.

Anna Street directory. Train timetable. Party structure.

Archie Ah.

He takes that out and studies it.

Anna Bus timetables. Guide to the museum. Plan of the sewers, any use?

She smiles; he takes no notice.

Archie His name is Duffendorf. Lutz Duffendorf, Burgomaster of Cologne, please.

This last to Anna, who goes to a wall cabinet for a file-card system. Eileen meanwhile is back from the corridor.

Eileen Cologne's pretty good. Eighteen separate interrogations. Three or four look good.

Anna (*to herself*) D – Duffendorf.

Archie I need a woman, Eileen. Find me a woman of doubtful reputation.

Eileen I'll see.

As she goes to search, Anna returns, with a white card.

Anna Lutz Duffendorf. Age 43. Bookseller's son. Married. No children.

Archie No children.

Anna His wife is blind.

Archie Wife blind. How wonderful.

Anna There's a picture.

She detaches a newspaper photo from the card and shows it to Archie, holding a pencil over the man's face. An official dinner at which a group of Germans are conspicuously well fed. Duffendorf is fat and slack. Archie stares at him. Meanwhile, Eileen has found a suitable detail.

Eileen Someone in the parachute regiment mentions a greengrocer, and his wife, in Blumenstrasse. She sounds what you're looking for.

Archie Good.

He reaches down behind his desk and gets out three large volumes.

Krafft-Ebing. Havelock Ellis. And Kleinwort's *Dictionary of Sexual Perversion*. Start at the index, right?

He hands the dictionary to Anna. Eileen is about to protest.

Eileen Is this . . . ?

But Archie just looks at her and she turns away. Anna opens the book, then begins reading dispassionately.

Anna Fantasies?

Archie Yes.

Anna Male fantasies. Judge. Air pilot. Hanged man. Horse. Snake charmer. Roman Catholic Priest . . .

Archie All right. Off fantasies.

Anna Fetishes?

Archie Yes.

Anna Food. Rope. Rubber. Leather . . .

Archie Look up leather.

Anna looks at Archie, but he cuts her off before she speaks.

It will do. Eileen.

Eileen waits, pad in hand, patiently. Anna looks up the reference.

You won't believe this, old friend, what . . .

Eileen Duffendorf.

Archie . . . what Duffendorf's been up to. Everyone in Cologne is talking about what the telegram boy saw when he looked through the letterbox trying to deliver. What he saw was the Burgomaster trying to deliver to Frau . . .

Anna (*not looking up*) That pun won't translate.

Eileen Ilse Schmidt.

Archie Trying to deliver to Frau Ilse Schmidt. Well we know how many people have been down that particular path before. But what is unusual is what she was wearing . . .

Archie holds out his hand. Anna heaves across the open book.

A leather bathing costume.

Eileen is about to protest, when Archie jabs viciously at the book with his finger.

It says here.

Anna smiles.

A leather bathing costume. And him standing with a hosepipe in his hand. (*A pause. He closes his eyes.*) Well, well, you ask why does she consent? It doesn't sound like pleasure in the ordinary sense of the word. It is not. It is corruption. In return for her performance the Burgomaster is using his influence to secure her a supply of fresh fruit and vegetables which she will sell at inflated prices. While our countrymen are dying on the Russian front, she will exploit their families at home. And meanwhile even as they romp, above the obscene display there sits an old woman locked in her room. The Burgomaster's wife. (*His coup de grâce.*) Alone. Listening. And blind.

52. INT. EILEEN'S ROOM. NIGHT
An identical room to Anna's but Eileen has made it more homely with photographs and a dressing table stacked with make-up. Eileen is sitting at it in her slip, getting

ready for dinner. Anna stands behind her, already dressed.
They are laughing.

Eileen He is going mad.

Anna D'you think so?

Eileen I'm sure. He is barking mad.

They both laugh. Eileen looks at herself in the mirror
intently. Then at Anna pacing behind her.

Are you having a thing with him?

Anna I suppose so. I suppose that's what a thing is. (*A*
pause. Eileen smiles.)

Eileen What does he really think about . . . ?

Anna I don't know. I don't know what he thinks about
anything. We've never had a conversation. We just have a
thing.

She looks down at Eileen. Then bursts out laughing.

Isn't life wonderful?

53. INT. HALL. NIGHT
The Unit going in to dinner. Anna and Eileen come down
the stairs together. Langley is standing outside his office as
they come down. He moves across to intercept them.

Langley Eileen. There's somebody to see you.

Eileen Oh, really?

Langley Would you like to use my room?

Eileen goes in. Langley closes the door behind her but
we just glimpse a uniformed Officer as the door shuts.
Anna is left standing looking across at Langley.

Her brother has been killed. Singapore.

Anna stands completely stunned by the news. Langley
watches. Then she speaks quietly.

Anna Oh God . . .

54. INT. EILEEN'S ROOM. NIGHT
Anna and Eileen in each other's arms rocking backwards
and forwards. Eileen is hysterical with grief, wild, out of
control, like a drowning woman. The make-up has scarred
her face. She is screaming.

Eileen All the time . . .

Anna Yes, I know . . .

Eileen All the time . . .

Anna I know.

Eileen All the time we've been here . . .

Anna Yes.

Eileen All the time, all the time we've been here.

Anna Yes, I know.

Eileen I can't stand it. I can't stand it.

Anna No.

Eileen I can't stand what we've done.

55. INT. HALL. NIGHT
In the darkness a single shaft of light falls on Eileen's cases
stacked by the door. The Officer we have glimpsed comes
across and picks up her coat which is draped across them.
Then Eileen comes into frame, still crying gently. He puts
the coat round her shoulders, picks up her handbag. Then
leans across her and whispers quietly. The tiny scuffles of
grief. Anna watches in an upstairs doorway.

DAVID HARE

56. INT. GUN ROOM. NIGHT

Anna enters the darkened room with a cup of tea. Archie is standing staring at the blacked-out window, his back to the door.

Anna Do you want this?

Archie Just put it down.

Anna crosses to the desk and puts tea on it.

Archie What time is it?

Anna Two.

Archie Has she gone?

Anna Mmm-mm. (*Pause.*) You should have said goodbye to her.

Archie What?

Anna That was the decent thing to do.

Archie turns and moves towards the desk.

Archie There's a broadcast here. I've just completed. I want it transmitted as fast as possible. You'll also have to take on Eileen's secretarial tasks. Get right down to it in the morning, will you?

Anna No, I won't.

Pause. Archie looks at Anna.

Archie I set ma'self the task. Get through the war. Just get through it, that's all. Put it no higher than that. Accept it. Endure it. But don't think, because if you begin to think, it'll all come apart in your hands. So. Let's all have the time of our lives not bothering to think about a bloody thing. Just . . . get on with it. This house is the war. And I'd rather be anywhere, I'd rather be in France, I'd rather be in the desert, I'd rather be in a Wellington over Berlin,

anywhere but here with you and your people in this
bloody awful English house . . . but I shall spend it here.

(Pause.)

Anna Strange thing; as if to suffer and say nothing were
clever. As if to do this degrading work were clever. As if
that were clever.

Long pause.

Will you hold me? Will you touch me?

Archie No.

He looks down.

57. INT. BEDROOM. NIGHT
*Anna sits dressed on her bed reading Archie's script. We
look at the pages. They are a mass of scrawled instructions
and underlinings. There are Stars of David scratched in
bright red ink, there are exclamation marks and enormous
phrases like 'Now look here', and 'Stress this'. Some
phrases refer to disease and corruption. We look at Anna
again. She regularly puts the sheets aside. Her face is dead.*

58. INT. LANGLEY'S OFFICE. DAY
*Langley working at his desk, looks up. Anna standing at
the door. Bright morning light.*

Anna There's a broadcast here. I'm not sure it's quite
right.

Langley Come in.

Anna comes in and sits down opposite him at the desk.

Tell me about it.

Anna Well . . . apparently one of Goebbels's newspapers
has singled out for special praise the work of some doctors

363

on the Russian front who run blood transfusion units and who've been successful in saving many, many lives.

Langley Yes.

Anna Now our idea in reply is to say that the units are getting their supplies of blood not from good clean fellow Germans, but from Polish and Russian prisoners who have not even had a Wassermann test. In other words, our job is to convince an army which we believe has just sustained the most appalling losses in the history of human warfare that those of them who have managed to escape death are on the point of being consumed with venereal disease.

There is a pause. Langley spreads his hands.

Langley It sounds a very good idea.

Anna You don't think he's mad? You don't think, clinically, Archie Maclean is mad?

Pause.

Langley We don't really know what's happening on the Russian front. But people are telling us that one million Germans have died in Russia in the last eight months. And of those maybe half have been killed in battle. The rest have just curled up in their greatcoats and died. Of frostbite. Exposure. Well nobody in that party went of their own accord. They went because they were inspired to go. By that great genius Joseph Goebbels. And they stayed, in part, because of the work he is doing. And because of that work, they are still there. And they are still dying. Now if you want to tell me that you can't draft that broadcast, then you had best return to your country estate, because we have as much duty to assist our side as he has his. And we must bring to it the same vigour, the same passion, the same intelligence that he has brought to his. And if this involves throwing a great trail of aniseed across

Europe, if it means covering the whole continent in obloquy and filth . . . then that is what we shall do.

A pause. Anna quite lost. Langley looks across at her.

There has been a complaint about you. From Maclean. He spoke to me this morning. Your German is good and so is your application. But he feels from the start you have tried to compromise him. I put it another way. You have tried unsuccessfully to get him to sleep with you. Please. There is the question of legality – your age. Also Maclean knows something of your background, your family, how little you know of the world, and felt to take advantage would be indefensible. And he has come to feel that the pressure is now intolerable and rather than have to upset you in person, he has asked me to request you to resign.

Anna But it's not true.

Langley I don't care if it's true. You have unbalanced one of our most gifted writers. That is unforgivable.

A pause. Langley takes out a clean piece of stationery from his desk drawer and pushes it across the desk with a fountain pen.

A letter of resignation.

Anna No.

Langley Otherwise I shall have to speak to your father, tell him what's occurred.

Anna But it's not true, it's not what happened. None of it's true.

Langley Then why did he say it?

Silence. We look at Anna.

Anna No.

59. BLANK SCREEN

Voice Five months later, in July 1942, Otto-Abend Eins made his final broadcast.

60. INT. BILLIARD ROOM. NIGHT
The Unit gathered round the table, minus Anna, Eileen and Archie. But Fennel is present this time, watching from the side. Karl is in full flood. Jungke is listening.

Karl Die deutsche Wehrmacht muss härter kämpfen, muss den Krieg mit einer Rücksichtslosigkeit führen, die sie bisher nicht gezeigt hat. Dieser Defaitismus frisst den Willen der deutschen Nation auf.

> *Langley cues Lotterby, who then bangs his rifle butt against the inside of the door very loudly, so loudly the door almost splinters. Then the door is thrown open from the other side and Archie is revealed standing with a machine-gun. He runs into the room and jumps on top of the billiard table.*

Um Gotteswillen!

Archie Also. Otto. Wir haben ihn gefunden.

> *He points the machine-gun at Karl.*

Karl Nein, nein! Bitte! Nicht!

> *Langley cues again. Archie fires the machine-gun deafeningly loud. Karl reels back clutching himself and moaning. His chair goes over and he falls to the floor.*

Archie Also . . .

> *Archie strides to the wireless equipment and in a huge gesture rips the cables out. Moves to stand over.*

Otto ist tot.

With a creak Karl sits up from his dead position. His
face breaks into a huge grin.

61. EXT. HOUSE. DAY
The house seen from the outside. Its main doors are
opened and out from it come the Soldiers and their
Sergeant carrying out office and wireless equipment.
Fennel, with his Naval Commander, follows them and gets
into his car. Langley shakes his hand.

Voice The work of the department continued until the end
of the war when all its official records were destroyed.
Many of the most brilliant men from the Propaganda and
Intelligence Services went on to careers in public life, in
Parliament, Fleet Street, the universities and the BBC.

62. EXT. COUNCIL ESTATE. DAY
Fennel moves in an election van, speaking on the back of a
jeep which is plastered with photos of himself and the
slogan 'Let's Go With Labour'.

Voice John Fennel resumed a career in politics which took
him in 1968 to a Cabinet rank which he lost with Labour's
subsequent defeat in 1970.

63. EXT. NURSING HOME. DAY
Langley in his bathchair being wheeled across a lawn by
an obviously expensive **Private Nurse**. *He looks ill and*
drawn.

Voice Will Langley went on to become a world-famous
thriller writer in the mid-fifties. His work helped to
establish a genre notable for its sustained passages of
sexuality and violence. He died in 1962.

64. EXT. GOLF COURSE. DAY
Amateur film. The sound of a projector. Eileen Graham

*on the golf course, looking much older, in a sensible skirt
and windcheater. She fools around for the camera.*

Voice Eileen Graham started a chain of employment
agencies specializing in temporary secretaries. She is
President of the Guild of British Businesswomen. She has
never married.

65. INT. VIEWING THEATRE. NIGHT
*Archie Maclean viewing rushes. He is sitting forward, the
beam of the projector behind his shoulder.*

Voice Archie Maclean was transferred that year to the
Crown Film Unit, where he made distinguished
documentaries. He became known in the fifties for his
award-winning feature films . . .

66. INT. SLUM HOUSE. DAY
*A sequence from Archie's black-and-white film, made in
the late fifties. A small boy watches as his father is washed
in a tin bath by his mother.*

Voice . . . which he both wrote and directed. The most
famous example is *A Kind of Life*, a loving and lyrical
evocation of his own childhood in Glasgow. But his most
recent work starring some of Hollywood's best loved
names . . .

67. EXT. SEA. DAY
*A sequence from one of Archie's latest films. A runaway
car speeds off the end of a pier and crashes into the water.*

Voice . . . has commanded little of the same critical
attention or respect.

68. BLANK SCREEN
Voice Anna Seaton.

69. STILLS SEQUENCE
Anna in a sequence of black-and-white stills is seen in an advertising agency leaning over an artist's shoulder to look at a drawing of a comic dog.

Voice Entered advertising in 1946 where she remained for ten years, increasingly distressed at the compromises forced on her by her profession. In 1956 she resigned and announced her intention to live an honest life.

70. STILLS SEQUENCE
A semi-detached in Fulham, seen from outside.

Voice She told her husband she was having an affair with another man, and could no longer bear the untruths of adultery. Her husband left her.

71. STILLS SEQUENCE
A brightly lit hospital seen from outside.

Voice After a period of lavish promiscuity she suffered an infected womb and an enforced hysterectomy.

72. STILLS SEQUENCE
Grosvenor Square demonstrations, 1968.

Voice She became a full-time researcher for the Labour Party, until she left during the Vietnam demonstrations and went to live with a young unmarried mother in Wales.

73. STILLS SEQUENCE
Anna, much older, playing on a Welsh hillside with a small girl and a dog.

Voice Having travelled to see Maclean's latest film at a seaside Odeon, she was driven to write to him for the first time since 1942, complaining of the falseness of his films, the way they sentimentalized what she knew to be his appalling childhood and lamenting, in sum, the films' lack of political direction. The last paragraph of her letter read:

74. INT. HOUSE. DAY
Shots of the empty rooms inside the house after the Unit has gone. Dining room. Drawing room. Bedroom. Gun room. All empty, standing deserted.

Anna (VO) It is only now that I fully understand the events that passed between us so many years ago. You must allow for my ignorance, I was born into a class and at a time that protected me from even a chance acquaintance with the world. But since that first day at Wendlesham I have been trying to learn, trying to keep faith with the shame and anger I saw in you. In retrospect what you sensed then has become blindingly clear to the rest of us: that whereas we knew exactly what we were fighting against, none of us had the whisper of an idea as to what we were fighting for. Over the years I have been watching the steady impoverishment of the people's ideals, their loss of faith, the lying, the daily inveterate lying, the thirty-year-old deep corrosive national habit of lying, and I have remembered you. I have remembered the one lie you told to make me go away. And I now at last have come to understand why you told it. I loved you then and I love you now. For thirty years you have been the beat of my heart. Please, please tell me it is the same for you.

75. EXT. HOUSE. DAY
The house seen from outside.

Voice He never replied.

The house sits in the sun. A few seconds, then:

76. END CREDITS
Chopin's Waltz No. 3 in A Minor

PLENTY

For Kate

Characters

Susan Traherne
Alice Park
Raymond Brock
Code Name Lazar
A Frenchman
Sir Leonard Darwin
Mick
Louise
M. Aung
Mme Aung
Dorcas Frey
John Begley
Sir Andrew Charleson
Another Frenchman

Plenty was first performed at the Lyttelton Theatre, London, on 7 April 1978. The cast was as follows:

Susan Traherne Kate Nelligan
Alice Park Julie Covington
Raymond Brock Stephen Moore
Code Name Lazar Paul Freeman
A Frenchman Robert Ralph
Sir Leonard Darwin Basil Henson
Mick David Schofield
Louise Gil Brailey
M. Aung Kristopher Kum
Mme Aung Me Me Lai
Dorcas Frey Lindsay Duncan
John Begley Tom Durham
Sir Andrew Charleson Frederick Treves
Another Frenchman Timothy Davies

Directed by David Hare
Settings by Hayden Griffin
Costumes by Deirdre Clancy
Music by Nick Bicât

SCENE ONE

Knightsbridge. Easter 1962.

*A wooden floor. At the back of the stage high windows
give the impression of a room which has been stripped
bare. Around the floor are packing cases full of fine
objects. At the front lies a single mattress, on which a
naked man is sleeping face downwards.*

Susan *sits on one of the packing cases. In her middle
thirties, she is thin and well presented. She wastes no
energy. She now rolls an Old Holborn and lights it.*

Alice *comes in from the street, a blanket over her head.
She carries a small tinfoil parcel. She is small-featured,
slightly younger and busier than Susan. She wears jeans.
She drops the blanket and shakes the rain off herself.*

Alice I don't know why anybody lives in this country.
No wonder everyone has colds all the time. Even what
they call passion, it still comes at you down a blocked
nose.

*Susan smokes quietly. Alice is distracted by some stray
object which she tosses into a packing case. The man
stirs and turns over. He is middle-aged, running to fat
and covered in dried blood. Susan cues Alice.*

Susan And the food.

Alice Yeah. The wet. The cold. The flu. The food. The
loveless English. How is he?

Susan Fine.

Alice kneels down beside him.

Alice The blood is spectacular.

Susan The blood is from his thumb.

Alice takes his penis between her thumb and forefinger.

377

Alice Turkey neck and turkey gristle, isn't that what they say?

A pause. Susan smokes.

Are you sure he's OK?

Susan He had a couple of Nembutal and twelve fingers of Scotch. It's nothing else, don't worry.

Alice And a fight.

Susan A short fight.

Alice takes the tinfoil parcel and opens it. Steam rises.

Alice Chinese takeaway. Want some?

Susan It's six o'clock in the morning.

Alice Sweet and sour prawn.

Susan No thanks.

Alice You should. You worked as hard as I did. When we started last night, I didn't think it could be done.

Alice gestures round the empty room. Then eats. Susan watches, then gets up and stands behind her with a key.

Susan It's a Yale. There's a mortise as well but I've lost the key. There's a cleaning lady next door, should you want one, her work's good but don't try talking about the blacks. You have a share in that garden in the centre of the square, you know all those trees and flowers they keep locked up. The milkman calls daily, again he's nice, but don't touch the yoghurt, it's green, we call it Venusian sperm.

Pause.

Good luck with your girls.

Susan turns to go. Alice gets up.

378

Alice Are you sure you can't stay? I think you'd like them.

Susan Unmarried mothers, I don't think I'd get on.

Alice I'm going to ring round at nine o'clock. If you just stayed on for a couple of hours . . .

Susan You don't really want that, nobody would.

Pause.

You must tell my husband . . .

Alice You've given me the house, and you went on your way.

Susan Tell him I left with nothing that was his. I just walked out on him. Everything to go.

Susan smiles again and goes out. There is a pause. The man stirs again at the front of the stage. Alice stands still holding the sweet and sour prawn.

Brock Darling.

Brock *is still asleep. His eyes don't open as he turns over. Alice watches very beadily. There is a long pause. Then he murmurs:*

What's for breakfast?

Alice Fish.

SCENE TWO *Time jump*

St Benoît. November 1943.
 Darkness. From the dark the sound of the wireless. From offstage a beam of light flashes irregularly, cutting up through the night. Then back to dark.

Announcer Ici Londres. Les voix de la liberté. Ensuite

379

quelques messages personnels. Mon Oncle Albert a perdu
son chien. Mon – Oncle – Albert – a– perdu – son – chien.

*A heavy thump in the darkness. Then the sound of
someone running towards the noise. A small amount of
light shows us the scene. Lazar is trying to disentangle
himself from his parachute. He has landed at the edge of
the wood. At the back Susan runs on from a great
distance, wrapped in a greatcoat against the cold. She
has a scarf round her face so that only her eyes can be
seen. She is extremely nervous and vulnerable, and her
uncertainty makes her rude and abrupt.*

Susan Eh, qu'est-ce que vous faites ici?

Lazar Ah rien. Laisse-moi un moment, je peux tout
expliquer.

*Susan takes a revolver from her pocket and moves
towards him. She stoops down, feels the edge of Lazar's
parachute.*

Susan Donnez-moi votre sac.

*Lazar throws across the satchel which has been tied to
his waist. Susan looks through it, then puts the gun back
in her pocket.*

And your French is not good.

*Susan moves quickly away to listen for sounds in the
night. Lazar watches then speaks quietly to her back.
Lazar is a code name; he is, of course, English.*

Lazar Where am I?

Susan Please be quiet. I can't hear when you speak.
(*Pause.*) There's a road. Through the wood. Gestapo
patrol.

Lazar I see.

Susan I thought I heard something.

Lazar Are you waiting for supplies?

Susan On the hour. There's meant to be a drop. I thought it was early, that's why I flashed.

Lazar I'm sorry. We had to take advantage of your light. We were losing fuel. I'm afraid I'm meant to be eighty miles on. Can you . . . could you tell me where I am?

Susan You've landed near a village called St Benoît. It's close to a town called Poitiers, all right?

Lazar Yes. I think. I have heard of it you know.

Pause. She half-turns but still does not look at him.

Susan Hadn't you better take that thing off?

Lazar We are in the same racket, I suppose?

Susan Well we're pretty well dished if we aren't. Did you spot any movement as you came down?

Lazar None at all. We just picked out your light.

Susan If you didn't see anything I'd like to hold on. We need the drop badly – explosives and guns.

Lazar Have you come out on your own?

A pause. He has taken off his jump-suit. Underneath he is dressed as a French peasant. Now he puts a beret on.

You'd better tell me, how does this look?

Susan I'd rather not look at you. It's an element of risk which we really don't need to take. In my experience it is best, it really is best if you always obey the rules.

Lazar But you'd like me to hold on and help you I think?

Pause.

Listen, I'm happy I might be of some use. My own undertaking is somewhat up the spout. Whatever happens I'm several days late. If I could hold on and be of any help . . . I'm sure I'd never have to look you in the face.

Susan All right, if you could just . . .

Lazar Look the opposite . . . yes. I will. I'm delighted.

He does so.

All right?

Susan If you could hold on, I'm sure I could find you a bike.

Lazar Would you like a cigarette?

Susan Thank you very much.

Pause.

Cafés are bad meeting places, much less safe than they seem. Don't go near Bourges, it's very bad for us. Don't carry anything in toothpaste tubes, it's become the first place they look. Don't laugh too much. An Englishman's laugh, it just doesn't sound the same. Are they still teaching you to broadcast from the lavatory?

Lazar Yes.

Susan Well don't. And don't hide your receiver in the cistern, the whole dodge is badly out of date. The Gestapo have been crashing into lavatories for a full two months. Never take the valley road beyond Poitiers, I'll show you a side-road.

Pause.

And that's it really. The rest you know, or will learn.

Lazar How long have you been here?

Susan Perhaps a year. Off and on. How's everyone at
home?

Lazar They're fine.

Susan The boss?

Lazar Fine. Gave me some cufflinks at the aerodrome.
Told me my chances.

Susan Fifty-fifty?

Lazar Yes.

Susan He's getting out of touch.

Pause.

Lazar How has it been?

Susan Well . . . the Germans are still here.

Lazar You mean we're failing?

Susan Not at all. It's part of our brief. Keep them here,
keep them occupied. Blow up their bridges, devastate the
roads, so they have to waste their manpower chasing after
us. Divert them from the front. Well that's what we've
done.

Lazar I see.

Susan But it's the worst thing about the job, the more
successful you are, the longer it goes on.

Lazar Until we win.

Susan Oh yes.

Pause.

A friend . . . a friend who was here used to say, never kill a
German, always shoot him in the leg. That way he goes to
hospital where he has to be looked after, where he'll use

383

up enemy resources. But a dead soldier is forgotten and replaced.

Pause.

Lazar Do you have dark hair?

Susan What?

Lazar One strand across your face. Very young. Sitting one day next to the mahogany door. At the recruitment place. And above your shoulder at the other side, *Whitaker's Almanack.*

Susan turns.

Susan You know who I am.

The sound of an aeroplane. Susan moves back and begins to flash her torch up into the night. Lazar crosses.

Lazar That's it over there.

Susan Wait.

Lazar Isn't that it?

Susan Don't move across. Just wait.

Lazar That's the drop.

The light stops. And the sound of the plane dies. Susan moves back silently and stands behind Lazar looking out into the field.

Susan It's all right, leave it. It's safer to wait a moment or two.

Lazar Oh my God.

Susan What?

Lazar Out across the field. Look . . .

Susan Get down.

They both lie down.

Lazar He's picking it up. Let's get away from here.

Susan No.

Lazar Come on, for God's sake . . .

Susan No.

Lazar If it's the Gestapo . . .

Susan Gestapo nothing, it's the bloody French.

From where they have been looking comes a dark figure running like mad with an enormous parcel wrapped in a parachute. Susan tries to intercept him. A furious row breaks out in heavy whispers.

Posez ça par terre, ce n'est pas à vous.

Frenchman Si, c'est à nous. Je ne vous connais pas.

Susan Non, l'avion était anglais. C'est à nous.

Frenchman Non, c'est désigné pour la résistance.

Lazar Oh God.

*He stands watching as Susan, handling the **Frenchman** very badly, begins to lose her temper. They stand shouting in the night.*

Susan Vous savez bien que c'est nous qui devons diriger le mouvement de tous les armements. Pour les Français c'est tout à fait impossible . . .

Frenchman Va te faire foutre.

Susan Si vous ne me le donnez pas . . .

Frenchman Les Anglais n'ont jamais compris la France. Il faut absolument que ce soit les Français qui déterminent notre avenir.

Susan Posez ça . . .

Frenchman C'est pour la France.

The Frenchman begins to go. Lazar has walked quietly across to behind Susan and now takes the gun from her pocket. The Frenchman sees it.

Arr yew raven mad?

Lazar Please put it down.

Pause.

Please.

The Frenchman lowers the package to the ground. Then stands up.

Please tell your friends we're sorry. We do want to help. Mais parfois ce sont les Français mêmes qui le rendent difficile.

Frenchman Nobody ask you. Nobody ask you to come. Vous n'êtes pas les bienvenus ici.

Susan about to reply but Lazar holds up his hand at once.

Lazar Compris.

Frenchman Espèce de con.

There is a pause. Then the Frenchman turns and walks out. Lazar keeps him covered, then turns to start picking the stuff up. Susan moves well away.

Lazar Bloody Gaullists.

Pause.

I mean, what do they have for brains?

Susan I don't know.

Lazar I mean really.

Susan They just expect the English to die. They sit and watch us spitting blood in the streets.

Lazar looks up at Susan, catching her tone. Then moves towards her as calmly as he can.

Lazar Here's your gun.

Lazar slips the gun into Susan's pocket, but as he does she takes his hand into hers.

We must be off.

Susan I'm sorry, I'm so frightened.

Lazar I must bury the silk.

Susan I'm not an agent, I'm just a courier. I carry messages between certain circuits . . .

Lazar Please . . .

Susan I came tonight, it's my first drop, there is literally nobody else, I can't tell you the mess in Poitiers . . .

Lazar Please.

Susan My friend, the man I mentioned, he's been taken to Buchenwald. He was the wireless operator, please let me tell you, his name was Tony . . .

Lazar I can't help.

Susan I have to talk . . .

Lazar No.

Susan What's the point, what's the point of following the rules if . . . ?

Lazar You mustn't . . .

Susan I don't want to die. I don't want to die like that.

Suddenly Susan embraces Lazar, putting her head on his shoulder and crying uncontrollably. He puts his hand through her hair. Then after a long time, she turns and walks some paces away, in silence. They stand for some time.

Lazar Did you know . . . did you know sound waves never die? So every noise we make goes into the sky. And there is a place somewhere in the corner of the universe where all the babble of the world is kept.

Pause. Then Lazar starts gathering the equipment together.

Come on, let's clear this lot up. We must be off. I don't know how I'm going to manage on French cigarettes. Is there somewhere I can buy bicycle clips? I was thinking about it all the way down. Oh yes and something else. A mackerel sky. What is the phrase for that?

Susan Un ciel pommelé.

Lazar Un ciel pommelé. Marvellous. I must find a place to slip it in. Now. Where will I find this bike?

Lazar has collected everything and gone out. Susan follows him.

Susan I don't know your name.

occupation of France
talking about the
hold of politics in
Britain?

SCENE THREE

Brussels. June 1947.
From the dark the sound of a small string orchestra gives way to the voice of an **Announcer**.

Announcer Ici Bruxelles – INR. Et maintenant notre soirée continue avec la musique de Victor Sylvester et son orchestre. Victor Sylvester est parmi les musiciens anglais les plus aimés à cause de ses maintes émissions à la radio anglaise pendant la guerre.

Evening. A gilt room. A fine desk. Good leather chairs. A portrait of the King. Behind the desk **Sir Leonard Darwin** *is working, silver-haired, immaculate, well into his late forties. A knock at the door and* **Raymond Brock** *comes in. An ingenuous figure, not yet thirty, with a small moustache and a natural energy he finds hard to contain in the proper manner. He refers constantly to his superior and this makes him uneasy.*

Brock Sir Leonard . . .

Darwin Come in.

Brock A few moments of your time. If I could possibly . . .

Darwin You have my ear.

Brock The case of a British national who's died. It's just been landed in my lap. A tourist named Radley's dropped dead in his hotel. It was a coronary, seems fairly clear. The Belgian police took the matter in hand, but naturally the widow has come along to us. It should be quite easy, she's taking it well.

Darwin nods. Brock goes to the door.

Mrs Radley. The ambassador.

Susan has come in. She is simply and soberly dressed. She looks extremely attractive.

Darwin If you'd like to sit down.

She sits opposite him at the desk. Brock stands respectfully at the other side of the room.

Please accept my condolences. The Third Secretary has

told me a little of your plight. Naturally we'll help in any way we can.

Brock I've already taken certain practical steps. I've been to the mortuary.

Susan That's very kind.

Brock Belgian undertakers.

Darwin One need not say more. Your husband had a heart attack, is that right?

Susan Yes. In the foyer of our hotel.

Darwin Painless . . .

Susan I would hope. He was packing the car. We were planning to move on this morning. We only have two weeks. We were hoping to make Innsbruck, at least if our travel allowance would last. It was our first holiday since the war.

Darwin Brock, a handkerchief.

Susan No.

Pause.

Brock I was persuaded to opt for an embalming, I'm afraid. It may involve you in some small extra cost.

Susan Excuse me, but you'll have to explain the point.

Brock Sorry?

Susan Of the embalming I mean.

Brock looks to his superior, but decides to persist.

Brock Well, particularly in the summer it avoids the possibility of the body exploding at a bad moment. I mean any moment would be bad, it goes without saying, but on the aeroplane, say.

Susan I see.

Brock You see, normally you find the body's simply washed . . . I don't know how much detail you want me to provide . . .

Darwin I would think it better if . . .

Susan No, I would like to know. Tony was a doctor. He would want me to know.

Brock pauses, then speaks with genuine interest.

Brock To be honest I was surprised at how little there is to do. There's a small bottle of spirit, colourless, and they simply give the body a wash. The only other thing is the stomach, if there's been a meal, a recent meal . . .

Susan Tony had . . .

Brock Yes, he had breakfast I think. You insert a pipe into the corpse's stomach to let the gases out. They insert it and there's a strange sort of sigh.

Darwin shifts.

Darwin If, er . . .

Brock It leaves almost no mark. Apparently, so they told me, the morgue attendants when they're bored sometimes set light to the gas for a joke. Makes one hell of a bang.

Darwin Shall we all have a drink?

Darwin gets up. Brock tries to backtrack.

Brock But of course I'm sure it didn't happen in this particular case.

Darwin No. There is gin. There is tonic. Yes?

Susan Thank you.

Darwin mixes drinks and hands them round.

Brock I'm afraid we shall need to discuss the practical arrangements. I know the whole subject is very distressing but there is the question . . . you do want the body flown back?

Susan Well, I can hardly stash it in the boot of the car.

A pause. Darwin lost.

Darwin What the Third Secretary is saying . . . not buried on foreign soil.

Susan No.

Brock Quite. You see for the moment we take care of it, freight charges, and His Majesty's Government picks up the bill. But perhaps later we will have to charge it to the estate, if there is an estate. I'm sorry, I don't mean to interfere . . .

Susan I'm sure there'll be enough to pay for it all. Tony made a very reasonable living.

Darwin gets up.

Darwin Well, I think we now understand your needs. I shall go downstairs and set the matter in train.

Brock Would you prefer it if I did that, sir?

Darwin No, no. You stay and talk to Mrs Radley. I'll have a word with the travel people, make a booking on tomorrow morning's flight, if that suits?

Susan Yes, of course.

Darwin You will be going back with the body, I assume?

Susan Yes.

Darwin Are there other dependants? Children?

Susan No.

Darwin goes out. A pause.

Brock If . . .

Susan He doesn't like you.

Brock Sorry.

Susan The ambassador.

Brock Oh. Well, no.

Pause.

I don't think he's over the moon about you.

Susan I shouldn't have said that.

Brock No, it's just . . . Darwin thinks disasters are examinations in etiquette. Which fork to use in an earthquake.

Susan Darwin, is that his name?

Brock Yes, the mission all thinks it's God's joke. God getting his own back by dashing off a modern Darwin who is in every aspect less advanced than the last. (*He smiles alone.*) I'm sorry. We sit about in the evenings and polish our jokes. Brussels is rather a debilitating town.

Susan Is this a bad posting for you?

Brock I'd been hoping for something more positive. Fresher air. The flag still flies over a quarter of the human race and I would like to have seen it really. Whereas here . . . we're left with the problems of the war . . . (*He smiles again.*) Have you met any prison governors?

Susan No.

Brock It's just they talk exactly like us. I was hoping for Brixton but I got the Scrubs. Just the same.

Susan Does nobody like it here?

Brock The misery is contagious, I suppose. You spend the day driving between bombsites, watching the hungry, the homeless, the bereaved. We think there are thirty million people loose in Europe who've had to flee across borders, have had to start again. And it is very odd to watch it all from here. (*He gestures round the room.*) Had you been married long?

Susan We met during the war.

Brock I did notice some marks on the body.

Susan Tony was a wireless operator with SOE. Our job was harassment behind the lines. Very successful in Holland, Denmark. Less so in France. Tony was in a circuit the Gestapo destroyed. Then scattered. Ravensbrück, Buchenwald, Saarbrucken, Dachau. Some were tortured, executed.

Brock What did you do?

Susan I was a courier. I was never caught.

She looks straight at Brock.

I wasn't his wife.

Brock No.

Susan Had you realized that?

Brock I'd thought it possible.

Pause.

Susan What about Darwin, did he realize?

Brock Lord, no, it would never occur to him.

Susan Motoring together it was easier to say we were man and wife. In fact I was barely even his mistress. He simply

394

rang me a few weeks ago and asked if I'd like a holiday abroad. I was amazed. People in our organization really didn't know each other all that well. You made it your business to know as little as possible, it was a point of principle. Even now you don't know who most of your colleagues were. Perhaps you were in it. Perhaps I met you. I don't know.

Pause.

Tony I knew a bit better, not much, but I was glad when he rang. Those of us who went through this kind of war, I think we do have something in common. It's a kind of impatience, we're rather intolerant, we don't suffer fools. And so we get rather restless back in England, the people who stayed behind seem childish and a little silly. I think that's why Tony needed to get away. If you haven't suffered . . . well. And so driving through Europe with Tony I knew that at least I'd be able to act as I pleased for a while. That's all.

Pause.

It's kind of you not to have told the ambassador.

Brock Perhaps I will. (*He smiles.*) May I ask a question?

Susan Yes.

Brock If you're not his wife, did he have one?

Susan Yes.

Brock I see.

Susan And three children. I had to lie about those, I couldn't claim them somehow. She lives in Crediton in Devon. She believes that Tony was travelling alone. He'd told her he needed two weeks by himself. That's what I was hoping you could do for me.

Brock Ah.

Susan Phone her. I've written the number down. I'm afraid I did it before I came.

Susan opens her handbag and hands across a card. Brock takes it.

Brock And lie?

Susan Yes. I'd prefer it if you lied. But it's up to you.

She looks at Brock. He makes a nervous half-laugh.

All right, doesn't matter . . .

Brock That's not what I said.

Susan Please, it doesn't matter.

Pause.

Brock When did you choose me?

Susan What?

Brock For the job. You didn't choose Darwin.

Susan I might have done.

Pause.

Brock You don't think you wear your suffering a little heavily? This smart club of people you belong to who had a very bad war . . .

Susan All right.

Brock I mean I know it must have put you on a different level from the rest of us . . .

Susan You won't shame me, you know. There's no point.

Pause.

It was an innocent relationship. That doesn't mean

unphysical. Unphysical isn't innocent. Unphysical in my view is repressed. It just means there was no guilt. I wasn't particularly fond of Tony, he was very slow-moving and egg-stained if you know what I mean, but we'd known some sorrow together and I came with him. And so it seemed a shocking injustice when he fell in the lobby, unjust for him of course, but also unjust for me, alone, a long way from home, and worst of all for his wife, bitterly unfair if she had to have the news from me. Unfair for life. And so I approached the embassy.

Pause.

Obviously I shouldn't even have mentioned the war. Tony used to say don't talk about it. He had a dread of being trapped in small rooms with big Jewesses, I know exactly what he meant. I should have just come here this evening and sat with my legs apart, pretended to be a scarlet woman, then at least you would have been able to place me. It makes no difference. Lie or don't lie. It's a matter of indifference.

Brock gets up and moves uncertainly around the room. Susan stays where she is.

Brock Would you . . . perhaps I could ask you to dinner? Just so we could talk . . .

Susan No. I refuse to tell you anything now. If I told you anything about myself you would just think I was pleading, that I was trying to get round you. So I tell you nothing. I just say look at me – don't creep round the furniture – look at me and make a judgement.

Brock Well.

Darwin reappears. He picks up his drink and sits at his desk as if to clear up. There is in fact nothing to clear up, so mostly he just moves his watch round. He talks the while.

397

Darwin That's done. First flight tomorrow without a hitch.

Brock stands as if unaware Darwin has come back.

Susan Thank you very much.

Darwin If there's anything else. There is a small chapel in the embassy if you'd like to use it before you go.

Susan Thank you.

Brock turns and walks abruptly out of the room. Susan smiles a moment. Darwin puts on his watch.

Have you been posted here long?

Darwin No, not at all. Just a few months. Before that, Djakarta. We were hoping for something sunny but Brussels came along. Not that we're complaining. They've certainly got something going here.

Susan Really?

Darwin Oh yes. New Europe. Yes yes.

Pause.

Reconstruction. Massive. Massive work of reconstruction. Jobs. Ideals. Marvellous. Marvellous time to be alive in Europe. No end of it. Roads to be built. People to be educated. Land to be tilled. Lots to get on with.

Pause.

Have another gin.

Susan No thanks.

Darwin The diplomat's eye is the clearest in the world. Seen from Djakarta this continent looks so old, so beautiful. We don't realize what we have in our hands.

Susan No.

Brock reappears at the door.

Brock Your wife is asking if you're ready for dinner, sir.

Darwin Right.

Brock And she wants your advice on her face.

Darwin gets up.

I'll lock up after you, sir.

Darwin You'll see Mrs Radley to her hotel?

Brock Of course.

Darwin Goodbye, Mrs Radley. I'm sorry it hasn't been a happier day.

Darwin goes out. Brock closes the door. He looks at Susan.

Brock I've put in a call to England. There's an hour's delay.

Pause.

I've decided to lie.

Brock and Susan stare at each other. Silence.

Will you be going back with the body?

Susan No.

Brock goes to the door and listens. Then turns back and removes the buttonhole. He looks for somewhere to put it. He finds his undrunk gin and tonic and puts it in there. Then he takes his jacket off and drops it somewhat deliberately on the floor. He takes a couple of paces towards Susan.

Brock Will you remind me to cancel your seat?

SCENE FOUR

Pimlico. September 1947.

From the dark the sound of a string quartet. It comes to an end. Then a voice.

Announcer This is the BBC Third Programme. Vorichef wrote *Les Ossifiés* in the year of the Paris Commune, but his struggle with Parkinson's disease during the writing of the score has hitherto made it a peculiarly difficult manuscript for musicologists to interpret. However the leader of the Bremen Ensemble has recently done a magnificent work of reclamation. Vorichef died in an extreme state of senile dementia in 1878. This performance of his last work will be followed by a short talk in our series 'Musicians and Disease'.

> *A bed-sitter with some wooden chairs, a bed and a canvas bed with a suitcase set beside it. A small room, well maintained but cheerless. Alice sits on the floor in a chalk-striped men's suit and white tie. She smokes a hookah. Susan is on the edge of the bed drinking cocoa. She is wearing a blue striped shirt. Her revolver lies beside her. Brock is laid out fast asleep across two chairs in his pinstripes. Next to him is a large pink parcel, an odd item of luxury in the dismal surroundings. By the way they talk you know it's late.*

Susan I want to move on. I do desperately want to feel I'm moving on.

Alice With him?

Susan Well that's the problem, isn't it?

Pause. Alice smiles.

Alice You are strange.

Susan Well, what would you do?

Alice I'd trade him in.

Susan Would you?

Alice I'd choose someone else off the street.

Susan And what chance would you have tonight, within a mile, say, within a mile of here?

Alice Let me think. Does that take in Victoria Coach Station?

Susan No.

Alice Then pretty slim.

Susan Is that right?

They smile. The hookah smokes.

That thing is disgusting.

Alice I know. It was better when the dung was fresh.

Susan I don't know why you bother . . .

Alice The writer must experience everything, every kind of degradation. Nothing is closed to him. It's really the degradation that attracted me to the job.

Susan I thought you were going to work tonight . . .

Alice I can't write all the time. You have to live it before you can write it. What other way is there? Besides nicking it.

Susan Is that done?

Alice Apparently. Once you start looking it seems most books are copied out of other books. Only it's called tribute. Tribute to Hemingway. Means it's nicked. Mine's going to be tribute to Scott Fitzgerald. Have you read him?

Susan No.

Alice *Last Tycoon.* Mine's going to be like that. Not quite the same of course. Something of a bitch to make Ealing Broadway hum like Hollywood Boulevard but otherwise it's in the bag.

Brock grunts.

He snores.

Susan You should get a job.

Alice I've had a job, I know what jobs are like. Had a job in your office.

Susan For three days.

Alice It was enough.

Susan How are you going to live?

Alice Off you mostly. (*She smiles.*) Susan . . .

Susan I want to move on. I do desperately want to feel I'm moving on.

Pause.

I work so hard I have no time to think. The office is worse. Those brown invoices go back and forth, import, export . . .

Alice I remember.

Susan They get heavier and heavier as the day goes on, I can barely stagger across the room for the weight of a single piece of paper, by the end of the day if you dropped one on the floor, you would smash your foot. The silence is worse. Dust gathering. Water lapping beyond the wall. It seems unreal. You can't believe that because of the work you do ships pass and sail across the world. (*She stares a moment.*) Mr Medlicott has moved into my office.

Alice Frightful Mr Medlicott?

402

Susan Yes.

Alice The boss?

Susan He has moved in. Or rather, more sinister still he has removed the frosted glass between our two offices.

Alice Really?

Susan I came in one morning and found the partition had gone. I interpret it as the first step in a mating dance. I believe Medlicott stayed behind one night, set his ledger aside, ripped off his tweed suit and his high collar, stripped naked, took up an axe, swung it at the partition, dropped to the floor, rolled over in the broken glass till he bled, till his whole body streamed blood, then he cleared up, slipped home, came back next morning and waited to see if anything would be said. But I have said nothing. And neither has he. He puts his head down and does not lift it till lunch. I have to look across at his few strands of hair, like seaweed across his skull. And I am frightened of what the next step will be.

Alice I can imagine.

Susan The sexual pressure is becoming intolerable.

They smile.

One day there was a condom in his turn-up. Used or unused I couldn't say. But planted without a doubt. Again, nothing said. I tried to laugh it off to myself, pretended he'd been off with some whore in Limehouse and not bothered to take his trousers off, so that after the event the condom had just absent-mindedly fallen from its place and lodged alongside all the bus tickets and the tobacco and the Smarties and the paper-clips and all the rest of it. But I know the truth. It was step two. And the dance has barely begun.

Pause.

Alice. I must get out.

Alice Then do. Just go. Have you never done that? I do it all the time.

Susan They do need me in that place.

Alice So much the better, gives it much more point. That's always the disappointment when I leave, I always go before people even notice I've come. But you . . . you could really make a splash.

Brock stirs.

He stirs.

Susan I'd like to change everything but I don't know how.

She leans under her bed, pulls out a shoebox, starts to oil and clean her gun.

Alice Are you really fond of him?

Susan You don't see him at his best. We had a week in Brussels which we both enjoyed. Now he comes over for the weekend whenever he can. But he tends to be rather sick on the boat.

Alice You should meet someone younger.

Susan That's not what I mean. And I don't really like young men. You're through and out the other side in no time at all.

Alice I can introduce you . . .

Susan I'm sure. I've only known you three weeks, but I've got the idea. Your flair for agonized young men. I think you get them in bulk from tuberculosis wards.

Alice I'm just catching up, that's all.

Susan Of course.

Alice I was a late starter.

Susan Oh yes, what are you, eighteen?

Alice I started late. Out of guilt. I had a protected childhood. Till I ran away. And very bad guilt. I was frightened to masturbate more than once a week, I thought my clitoris was like a torch battery, you know, use it too much and it runs out.

Brock wakes.

He wakes.

They watch as he comes round.

Brock What time is it?

Alice Raymond, can you give us your view? I was just comparing the efficiency of a well-known household object with . . .

Susan Alice, leave him alone.

Alice It's getting on for five.

Brock I feel terrible.

Susan (*kissing his head*) I'll get you something to eat. Omelette all right? It's only powder, I'm afraid . . .

Brock Well . . .

Susan Two spoons or three? And I'll sprinkle it with Milk of Magnesia. (*She goes out into the kitchen.*)

Brock It seems a bit pointless. It's only twelve hours till I'm back on the boat. (*He picks up the gun.*) Did I miss something?

Alice No. She's just fondling it.

Brock Ah.

He looks round. Alice is watching him all the time.

I can't remember what . . .

Alice Music. On the wireless. You had us listening to some music.

Brock Ah that's right.

Alice Some composer who shook.

Brock I thought you'd have gone. Don't you have a flat?

Alice I did. But it had bad associations. I was disappointed in love.

Brock I see.

Alice And Susan said I could sleep here.

Brock (*absently admiring her suit*) I must say I do think your clothes are very smart.

Alice Well I tell you he looks very good in mine. (*She nods at the parcel.*) Do you always bring her one of those?

Brock I certainly try to bring a gift if I can.

Alice You must have lots of money.

Brock Well, I suppose. I find it immoderately easy to acquire. I seem to have a sort of mathematical gift. The stock exchange. Money sticks to my fingers I find. I triple my income. What can I do?

Alice It must be very tiresome.

Brock Oh . . . I'm acclimatizing, you know. (*Smiles.*) I think everyone's going to be rich very soon. Once we've got over the effects of war. It's going to be coming out of everyone's ears.

Alice Is that what you think?

Brock I'm absolutely sure. (*Pause.*) I do enjoy these weekends you know. Susan leads such an interesting life. Books. Conversation. People like you. The Foreign Office can make you feel pretty isolated – also, to be honest, make you feel pretty small, as if you're living on sufferance, you can imagine . . .

Alice Yes.

Brock Till I met Susan. The very day I met her, she showed me you must always do what you want. If you want something you must get it. I think that's a wonderful way to live don't you?

Alice I do. (*Pause. She smiles.*) Shall I tell you how my book begins?

Brock Well . . .

Alice There's a woman in a rape trial. And the story is true. The book begins at the moment where she has to tell the court what the accused has said to her on the night of the rape. And she finds she can't bring herself to say the words out loud. And so the judge suggests she writes them down on a piece of paper and it be handed round the court. Which she does. And it says, 'I want to have you. I must have you now.' (*She smiles again.*) So they pass it round the jury who all read it and pass it on. At the end of the second row there's a woman jurist who's fallen asleep at the boredom of the trial. So the man next to her has to nudge her awake and hand her the slip of paper. She wakes up, looks at it, then at him, smiles and puts it in her handbag. (*She laughs.*) That woman is my heroine.

Brock Well, yes.

Susan returns, sets food on Brock's knee. Then returns to cleaning her gun. Alice tries to re-light her hookah.

Susan Cheese omelette. What were you talking about?

Alice The rape trial.

Susan Did you tell Raymond who the woman was?

Brock What do you mean?

Susan I'm only joking, dear.

Alice and Susan laugh.

Brock I'm not sure it's the sort of . . .

Alice Oh sod this stuff.

Susan I said it was dung.

Alice I was promised visions.

Brock Well . . .

Alice It's because I'm the only Bohemian in London. People exploit me. Because there are no standards, you see. In Paris or New York, there are plenty of Bohemians, so the kief is rich and sweet and plentiful but here . . . you'd be better off to lick the gum from your ration card.

Susan Perhaps Raymond will be posted to Morocco, bring some back in his bag . . .

Brock I don't think that's really on.

Susan Nobody would notice, from what you say. Nobody would notice if you smoked it yourself.

Alice Are they not very sharp?

Susan Not according to Raymond. The ones I've met are buffoons . . .

Brock Susan, please . . .

Susan Well it's you who call them buffoons.

Brock It's not quite what I say.

Susan It's you who tells the stories. That man
Darwin . . .

Brock Please . . .

Susan How he needs three young men from public schools
to strap him into his surgical support.

Brock I told you that in confidence.

Susan In gloves.

Alice Really?

Brock Darwin is not a buffoon.

Susan From your own lips . . .

Brock He just has slight problems of adjustment to the
modern age.

Susan You are laughing.

Brock I am not laughing.

Susan There is a slight smile at the corner of your
mouth . . .

Brock There is not. There is absolutely no smile.

Susan Alice, I will paraphrase, let me paraphrase
Raymond's view of his boss. I don't misrepresent you,
dear, it is, in paraphrase, in sum, that he would not trust
him to stick his prick into a bucket of lard.

Brock puts his omelette to one side, uneaten.

Well, is he a joke or is he not?

Brock Certainly he's a joke.

Susan Thank you.

Brock He's a joke between us. He is not a joke to the entire world.

A pause. Brock looks at Alice. Then he gets up.

I think I'd better be pushing off home.

Brock goes and gets his coat. Puts it on. Susan at last speaks, very quietly.

Susan And I wish you wouldn't use those words.

Brock What?

Susan Words like 'push off home'. You're always saying it. 'Bit of a tight corner', 'one hell of a spot'. They don't belong.

Brock What do you mean?

Susan They are not your words.

Pause.

Brock Well, I'm none too keen on your words either.

Susan Oh yes, which?

Brock The words you've been using this evening.

Susan Such as?

Brock You know perfectly well.

Susan Such as, come on tell me, what words have I used?

Brock Words like . . .

Pause.

Bucket of lard.

Pause.

Susan Alice, there is only the bath or the kitchen.

Alice I know.

*Alice goes out. Susan automatically picks up the
omelette and starts to eat it.*

Brock Are you going to let her live with you?

Susan I like her. She makes me laugh.

Pause.

Brock I'm sorry, I was awful, I apologize. But the work I
do is not entirely contemptible. Of course our people are
dull, they're stuffy, they're death. But what other world do
I have?

Pause.

Susan I think of France more than I tell you. I was
seventeen and I was thrown into the war. I often think of
it.

Brock I'm sure.

Susan The most unlikely people. People I met only for an
hour or two. Astonishing kindnesses. Bravery. The fact
you could meet someone for an hour or two and see the
very best of them and then move on. Can you understand?

Pause. Brock does not move.

For instance, there was a man in France. His code name
was Lazar. I'd been there a year I suppose and one night I
had to see him on his way. He just dropped out of the sky.
An agent. He was lost. I was trying to be blasé, trying to
be tough, all the usual stuff – irony, hardness, cleverness,
wit – and then suddenly I began to cry. On to the shoulder
of a man I'd never met before. But not a day goes by
without my wondering where he is.

*Susan finishes her omelette and puts the plate aside.
Brock moves towards her.*

411

Brock Susan.

Susan I think we should try a winter apart. I really do. I think it's all a bit easy this way. These weekends. Nothing is tested. I think a test would be good. Then we would know. And what better test than a winter apart?

Brock A winter together.

Pause. They smile.

Susan I would love to come to Brussels, you know that. I would love to come if it weren't for my job. But the shipping office is very important to me. I do find it fulfilling. And I just couldn't let Mr Medlicott down.

Pause.

You must say what you think.

Brock looks at Susan hard, then shrugs and smiles.

I know you've been dreading the winter crossings, high seas . . .

Brock Don't patronize me, Susan.

Susan Anyway, perhaps in the spring, it would be really nice to meet . . .

Brock Please don't insult my intelligence. I know you better than you think. I recognize the signs. When you talk longingly about the war . . . some deception usually follows.

Brock kisses Susan.

Goodbye.

Brock goes out. Susan left standing for a few moments. Then she picks up the plate and goes quickly to the kitchen. Alice comes out of the bathroom at once in a dressing-gown. She has a notebook in her hand which

she tosses the length of the room, so it lands on a chair.
She settles on her back in the camp bed. Susan reappears
at the door.

Susan Did you hear that?

Alice Certainly. I was writing it down.

Susan looks across at her, but Alice is putting pennies
on her eyes.

My death-mask.

Susan Don't.

Alice I dream better.

Pause.

Susan Do you know what you're doing tomorrow?

Alice Not really. There's a new jazz band at the One-O-
One. And Ken wants to take me to Eel Pie Island in his
horrid little car. I say I'll go if I get to meet Alistair. I really
do want to meet Alistair. Everyone says he's got hair on his
shoulder-blades and apparently he can crack walnuts in
his armpits.

Susan Oh well, he'll never be short of friends.

Alice Quite.

Susan turns out one light. Dim light only. She looks at
the parcel.

Susan What should I be doing with this?

Alice If we can't eat it, let's throw it away.

Susan turns out the other light. Darkness. The sound of
Susan getting into bed.

Your friend Brock says we're all going to be rich.

Susan Oh really?

Pause.

Alice Peace and plenty.

SCENE FIVE

Temple. May 1951.
  Music, a cello leading. The Embankment, beside a lamp, overlooking the river.
  Night. Susan stands, thickly wrapped. For the first time, she is expensively dressed. She is eating hot chestnuts.
Mick *appears at the back. He is from the East End. He looks twenty, smart and personable. He speaks before she knows he's there.*

Mick Five hundred cheese-graters.

Susan Oh no.

Mick I got five hundred cheese-graters parked round the side. Are you interested?

Susan I'm afraid you're too late. We took a consignment weeks ago.

  Susan laughs. Mick moves down beside her.

Mick Where we looking?

Susan Across the river. Over there.

Mick Where?

Susan South Bank. That's where the fireworks are going to be. And there's my barrage balloon.

Mick Oh yeah. What does it say?

Susan Don't say that, that's the worst thing you can say.

Mick It's dark.

Susan It says 'Bovril'.

Mick Oh, Bovril.

Susan Yes. It's meant to blaze out over London.

Mick Surprised it hasn't got your name on.

Susan What do you mean?

Mick Everywhere I go.

Pause. They look at each other. Susan smiles and removes a napkin from her coat pocket, and unfolds its bundle.

Susan I managed to steal some supper from the Festival Hall. There's a reception for its opening night. They're using your cutlery, I'm happy to say.

Mick I wish I could see it.

Susan Yes, yes, I wish you could too. (*She smiles.*) I've actually decided to leave the Festival now. Having worked so hard to get the wretched thing on. I'm thinking of going into advertising.

Mick Ah very good.

Susan I met some people on the Bovril side. It's . . . well I doubt if it'll stretch me, but it would be a way of having some fun. (*Pause.*) Would you like a canapé?

Mick How's Alice?

Susan She's very well.

Mick Haven't seen her lately.

Susan No.

Mick She went mainstream you see. I stayed revivalist.

Different religion. For me it all stops in 1919.

He takes a canapé.

So how can I help?

Susan I'm looking for a father. I want to have a child.

Pause.

Look, it really is much easier than it sounds. I mean, marriage is not involved. Or even looking after it. You don't even have to see the pregnancy through. I mean, conception will be the end of the job.

Mick smiles.

Mick Ah.

Susan You don't want to?

Mick No, no, I'm delighted, I'm lucky to be asked.

Susan Not at all.

Mick But it's just . . . your own people. I mean friends, you must have friends.

Susan It's . . .

Mick I mean . . .

Susan Sorry.

Mick No, go on, say.

Susan The men I know at work, at the Festival, or even friends I've known for years, they just aren't the kind of people I would want to marry.

Mick Ah.

Susan I'm afraid I'm rather strong-minded, as you know, and so with them I usually feel I'm holding myself in for fear of literally blowing them out of the room. They are

kind, they are able, but I don't see . . . why I should have
to compromise, why I should have to make some sad and
decorous marriage just to have a child. I don't see why any
woman should have to do that.

Mick But you don't have to marry . . .

Susan Ah well . . .

Mick Just go off with them.

Susan But that's really the problem. These same men,
these kind and likeable men, they do have another side to
their nature and that is they are very limited in their ideas,
they are frightened of the unknown, they want a quiet life
where sex is either sport or duty but absolutely nothing in
between, and they simply would not agree to sleep with
me if they knew it was a child I was after.

Mick But you wouldn't have to tell them.

Susan I did think that. But then I thought it would be
dishonest. And so I had the idea of asking a person whom
I barely knew.

Pause.

Mick What about the kid?

Susan What?

Mick Doesn't sound a very good deal. Never to see his
dad . . .

Susan It's not . . .

Mick I take it that is what you mean.

Susan I think it's what I mean.

Mick Well?

Susan The child will manage.

Mick How do you know?

Susan Being a bastard won't always be so bad.

Mick I wouldn't bet on it.

Susan England can't be like this for ever.

Mick looks at her.

Mick I would like to know . . .

Susan Yes?

Mick Why you chose me. I mean, how often have you met me?

Susan Yes, but that's the whole point . . .

Mick With Alice a few times . . .

Susan And you sold me some spoons.

Mick They were good spoons.

Susan I'm not denying it.

Mick smiles.

Mick And Alice says what? That I'm clean and obedient and don't have any cretins in the family?

Susan It's not as calculated as that.

Mick Not calculated? Several hundred of us, was there, all got notes . . .

Susan No.

Mick . . . saying come and watch the Festival fireworks, tell no one, bring no friends. All the secrecy, I thought you must at least be after nylons . . .

Susan I'll buy nylons. If that's what you want.

They stare at each other.

Mick So why me?

Susan I like you.

Mick And.

Susan 'I love you'?

  Pause.

I chose you because . . . I don't see you very much. I barely ever see you. We live at opposite ends of town. Different worlds.

Mick Different class.

Susan That comes into it.

  There is a pause. Mick looks at her. Then moves away. Turns back. Smiles.

Mick Oh dear.

Susan Then laugh.

  Pause.

I never met the man I wanted to marry.

  They smile.

Mick It can't be what you want. Not deep down.

Susan No.

Mick I didn't think so.

Susan Deep down I'd do the whole damn thing by myself. But there we are. You're second-best.

  They smile again.

Mick Five hundred cheese-graters.

Susan How much?

Mick Something over the odds. A bit over the odds. Not much.

Susan Done.

Pause.

Don't worry. The Festival will pay.

Susan moves across to Mick. They kiss. They look at each other. He smiles. Then they turn and look at the night. He is barely audible.

Mick Fireworks. If you . . .

Susan What?

Mick Stay for the fireworks.

Susan If you like.

Pause.

Mick Great sky.

Susan Yes.

Mick The light. Those dots.

Susan A mackerel sky.

Mick What?

Susan That's what they call it. A mackerel sky.

SCENE SIX

Pimlico. December 1952.
   From the dark the sound of Charlie Parker and his saxophone.
   Night. The bed-sitting room transformed. The beds have gone and the room is much more comfortable. Three

people. Susan is working at her desk which is covered with papers and drawings. Alice is standing over a table which has been cleared so that she may paint the naked body of **Louise** *who lies stretched across its top. She is in her late teens, from Liverpool. Alice is a good way on with the job. The record ends.*

Susan This is hell.

Alice No doubt.

Susan I am living in hell.

Susan sits back and stares at her desk. Alice goes to the record player.

Alice Shall we hear it again?

Susan You're only allowed it once. Hear it too much and you get out of hand.

Alice It's true. (*She turns it off and returns to painting.*) I'd give that up if I were you. We have to go pretty soon.

Susan Why do I lie?

Alice We have to get there by midnight.

Susan What do I do it for?

Alice It's your profession.

Susan That's what's wrong. In France . . .

Alice Ah France.

Susan I told such glittering lies. But where's the fun in lying for a living?

Alice What's today's?

Susan Some leaking footwear. Some rotten shoe I have to advertise. What is the point? Why do I exist?

Alice Sold out.

Susan Sold out. Is that the phrase?

Pause. Alice paints. Susan stares.

Alice Turn over, let me do the other side.

Louise moves on to her stomach.

Susan To produce what my masters call good copy, it is simply a question of pitching my intelligence low enough. Shutting my eyes and imagining what it's like to be very, very stupid. This is all the future holds for any of us. We will spend the next twenty years of our lives pretending to be thick. 'I'm sorry, Miss Traherne, we'd like to employ you, but unfortunately you are not stupid enough.'

Susan tears up the work she is doing and sits back glaring. Alice explains to Louise.

Alice You're all trunk up to here, OK?

Louise Yeah, right.

Alice The trunk is all one, so you just have to keep your legs together. Then you break into leaf, just above the bust.

Louise Do I get conkers?

Alice No. If you were a chestnut, you'd get conkers. But you're an oak.

Louise What does an oak have?

Alice An oak has acorns.

Louise Acorns?

Alice But you won't need them, I promise. We scorn gimmicks. We will win as we are.

Susan (*to herself*) The last night of the year . . .

Alice And I will sell a great many paintings.

Pause. Alice paints.

Louise is staying with Emma and Willy . . .

Susan Oh yes?

Louise I met them in the street, I'd just left home, come down the A6.

Susan Good for you.

Louise I couldn't believe my luck.

Alice Willy's going as a kipper, I do know that. And Emma's a prostitute though how we're meant to know it's fancy dress I really can't think.

Louise I've gathered that.

Alice Otherwise I expect the usual historical riff-raff. Henry VIII, that sort of thing. We ought to walk it with a naked oak.

Louise Will that friend of yours be there?

A moment. Susan looks across at Alice and Louise.

Alice No. He'll be tucked up with his syphilitic wife.

Louise Why doesn't he . . . ?

Susan Shut up, Louise.

Alice It's all right. Ask what you want.

Pause.

Louise How do you know she's syphilitic?

Alice How do you think? She passed it down the line.

Louise Oh God.

Alice Or somebody passed it and I've decided to blame

her. It seems right somehow. She's a very plausible incubator for a social disease. Back over.

Louise turns again.

Louise Why doesn't he leave?

Alice Who?

Louise Your friend.

Alice Ah well, if they ever did leave their wives, perhaps the whole sport would die. For all of us.

Susan Roll on 1953.

Alice smiles and resumes painting.

Alice Actually the clinic say it's non-specific urethritis, which I find rather insulting. I did at least expect the doctor to come out and apologize and say, I'm sorry not to be more specific about your urethritis, but no, they just leave you in the air.

As she is talking Mick has appeared at the door.

Mick I wonder, does anyone mind if I come in?

Alice Mick?

Mick moves into the room.

Mick Would you mind if I . . . ?

Susan How did you get this address?

Alice Do you two know each other?

Mick Happy New Year.

Pause.

Alice Mick, may I introduce you to Louise?

Louise Hello, Mick.

Mick Hello, Louise.

Alice Louise is going to the Arts Ball, I'm painting her . . .

Mick Ah.

Alice She's going as a tree.

Susan Mick, I really don't want to talk to you.

Alice What's wrong?

Mick Is she really going to walk down the street . . .

Susan I thought we'd agreed. You promised me, Mick. You made a promise. Never to meet again.

A pause. Mick looks down.

Mick I just thought . . . well it's New Year's Eve and well . . . one or two weeks have gone by . . .

Susan Have you been watching the house? Is that how you found me? Have you been following me home?

She stares across at him.

Look, Mick, I suggest that you leave while you still have the chance.

Louise has swung down from the table.

Louise Does anyone mind if I put my clothes on?

In the silence she picks up her clothes and goes into the kitchen. Alice speaks quietly.

Alice She's not finished. She'll look good when it's done.

Pause.

Susan I asked Mick to father a child, that's what we're talking about.

Mick Oh Christ.

Symbolic of the political climate, trying to create and new future.

Susan Well we have tried over eighteen months, that's right? And we have failed.

Mick Right.

Susan Which leaves us both feeling pretty stupid, pretty wretched I would guess, speaking for myself. And there is a point of decency at which the experiment should stop.

Mick Susan . . .

Susan We have nothing in common, never did, that was part of the idea . . .

Mick It just feels bad . . .

Susan The idea was fun, it was simple, it depended on two adults behaving like adults.

Mick It feels very bad to be used.

Susan I would have stopped it months ago, I would have stopped it in the second month . . .

Mick You come out feeling dirty.

Susan And how do I feel? What am I meant to feel? Crawling about in your tiny bedroom, paper-thin walls, your mother sitting downstairs . . .

Mick Don't bring my mum into this.

Susan Scrabbling about on bombsites, you think I enjoy all that?

Mick Yeah. Very much. I think you do.

Pause. Alice looks away. Susan moves quietly away as if to give it up. Mick calms down.

I just think . . .

Susan I know what you think. You think I enjoy slumming around. Then why have I not looked for

426

another father? Because the whole exploit has broken my heart.

Pause.

Mick You think it's my fault.

Susan Oh Lord, is that all you're worried about?

Mick You think it's something to do with me?

Susan That was part of it, never to have to drag through this kind of idiot argument . . .

Mick Well it is quite important.

Susan You don't understand. You don't understand the figures in my mind.

Pause.

Mick, there is gentlemen's footwear. It must be celebrated. I have to find words to convey the sensation of walking round London on two pieces of reconstituted cardboard stuck together with horseglue. And I have to find them tonight.

Susan goes to her desk, takes out fresh paper. Starts work. Louise comes from the kitchen, plainly dressed.

Louise I'll tell the others. You may be late.

Alice stoops down and picks up a couple of papier-mâché green branches.

Alice There are some branches. You have to tie them round your wrists.

Louise Thanks all the same. I'll just go as myself.

Louise goes out. There is a silence, as Susan works at her desk. Alice sits with her hand over her eyes. Mick sits miserably staring. This goes on for some time until

427

*finally Susan speaks very quietly, without looking up
from her desk.*

Susan Mick, will you go now please?

Mick You people are cruel.

Susan Please.

Mick You are cruel and dangerous.

Susan Mick.

Mick You fuck people up. This little tart and her string of
married men, all fucked up, all fucking ruined by this tart.
And you . . . and you . . .

*Mick turns to Susan. Susan gets up and walks quietly
from the room. A pause. Alice is looking at him.*

She is actually mad.

*Susan reappears with her revolver. She fires it just over
Mick's head. It is deafeningly loud. He falls to the
ground. She fires three more times.*

Mick Jesus Christ.

SCENE SEVEN

Knightsbridge. October 1956.
  From the dark, music, emphatic, triumphant.
  *The room we saw in Scene One. But now decorated
with heavy velvet curtains, china objects and soft
furniture. A diplomatic home. Both men in dinner-jackets:
Brock smokes a cigar and drinks brandy. Opposite him is
an almost permanently smiling Burmese,* **M. Aung,** *short,
dogmatic. The music stops.*

Aung Two great nations, sir. The Americans and the

428

English. Like the Romans and the Greeks. Americans are the Romans – power, armies, strength. The English are the Greeks – ideas, civilization, intellect. Between them they shall rule the world.

Darwin appears putting his head round the door. He is also in a dinner-jacket. He appears exhausted.

Darwin Good Lord, I hope you haven't hung on for me.

Brock Leonard, come in, how kind of you to come.

Darwin Not at all.

Brock ushers him in. Aung stands.

Brock Our little gathering. We'd scarcely dared hope . . .

Darwin There seemed nothing left to do.

Brock Leonard, you know M. Aung, of course?

Aung Mr Darwin.

Darwin Rangoon.

Brock Now First Secretary, Burmese Embassy.

Aung An honour. A privilege. A moment in my career. I shake your hand. (*He does so.*)

Darwin Good, good. Well . . .

Brock Let me get you a drink.

Darwin That would be very kind.

Brock I'll just tell my wife you're here.

Brock goes out. Aung smiles at Darwin.

Aung Affairs of state?

Darwin Yes, if you . . .

Aung Say no more. We have eaten. We did not wait. In

Burma we say if you cannot be on time, do not come at all.

Darwin Really?

Aung But of course the English it is different. At your command the lion makes its bed with the lamb.

Darwin Hardly.

Aung Don't worry. All will be well. Ah Darwin of Djakarta, to have met the man, to have been alone with him. I shall dine in on this for many years.

Darwin Dine out on this.

Aung Ah the English language, she is a demanding mistress, yes?

Darwin If you like.

Aung And no one controls her so well as you sir. You beat her and the bitch obeys. (*He laughs.*) The language of the world. Good, good. I have learnt the phrase from you. Out of your mouth. Good, good. I am behind you sir.

Susan appears in a superbly cut evening dress. She is dangerously cheerful. Brock follows her.

Susan Leonard, how good of you to make an appearance.

Darwin I'm only sorry I've been delayed.

Susan and Darwin kiss.

Susan Brock says you're all ragged with fatigue. I hear you've been having the most frightful week . . .

Darwin It has been, yes.

Susan Well, don't worry. Here at least you can relax. You've met Mr Aung?

Darwin Indeed.

Susan You can forget everything. The words 'Suez Canal' will not be spoken.

Darwin That will be an enormous relief.

Susan They are banned, you will not hear them.

Darwin Thank you, my dear.

Susan Nasser, nobody will mention his name.

Darwin Quite.

Susan Nobody will say 'blunder' or 'folly' or 'fiasco'. Nobody will say 'international laughing stock'. You are among friends, Leonard. I will rustle up some food.

She smiles at Aung.

Mr Aung, I think the gentlemen may wish to talk.

Aung Of course, in such company I am privileged to change sex.

Aung gets up to follow Susan out.

Susan Nobody will say 'death-rattle of the ruling class'. We have stuck our lips together with marron glacé. I hope you understand.

Susan and Aung go out. Pause.

Brock Sorry, I . . .

Darwin It's all right.

Brock I did ask her to calm down.

Darwin I'm getting used to it.

Brock She's been giving me hell. She knows how closely you've been involved . . .

Darwin Do you think we could leave the subject, Brock?

Pause.

I'm eager for the drink.

Brock Of course.

Darwin At least she got rid of that appalling wog. I mean, in honesty, Raymond, what are you trying to do to me?

Brock I'm sorry, sir.

Darwin This week of all weeks. He had his tongue stuck so far up my fundament all you could see of him were the soles of his feet.

Brock takes over a tray of drinks.

Mental illness, is it? Your wife?

Brock No, she just . . . feels very strongly. Well, you know . . .

Darwin But there has been mental illness?

Brock In the past.

Darwin Yes?

Brock Before we were married. Some years ago. She'd been living very foolishly, a loose set in Pimlico. And a series of jobs, pushing herself too hard. Not eating. We got engaged when she was still quite ill, and I have tried to help her back up.

Darwin That's very good.

Brock Well . . .

Darwin Second marriage, of course. Often stabilizes.

Brock What?

Darwin The chap in Brussels.

Pause.

The stiff.

Brock Ah yes.

Darwin You don't have to be ashamed . . .

Brock No, I'm not, it's . . .

Darwin In the diplomatic service it isn't as if a mad wife is any kind of professional advantage. On the contrary, it almost guarantees promotion.

Brock Well . . .

Darwin Some of the senior men, their wives are absolutely barking. I take the word 'gouache' to be the giveaway. When they start drifting out of rooms saying, 'I think I'll just go and do my gouaches dear,' then you know you've lost them for good and all.

Brock But Susan isn't mad.

Darwin No, no.

Pause.

Is there a Madame Aung?

Brock In the other room.

Darwin I knew there had to be. Somehow. And no doubt culturally inclined. Traditional dance, she'll tell us about, in the highlands of Burma. Or the plot of *Lohengrin*.

Brock Leonard . . .

Darwin I'm sorry. I think I've had it, Brock. One more Aung and I throw in the can.

Pause.

Do you mind if I have a cherry?

Brock What?

Darwin The maraschinos. I'm so hungry. It's all those bloody drugs we have to take.

Brock Let me . . .

Darwin Stay.

Pause.

We have been betrayed.

Darwin reaches into the cocktail cherries with his fingers, but then just rolls them slowly in his palm.

We claim to be intervening as a neutral party in a dispute between Israel and Egypt. Last Monday the Israelis launched their attack. On Tuesday we issued our ultimatum saying both sides must withdraw to either side of the canal. But, Raymond, the Israelis, the aggressors, they were nowhere near the canal. They'd have had to advance a hundred miles to make the retreat.

Brock Who told you that?

Darwin Last week the Foreign Secretary went abroad. I was not briefed. We believe he met with the French and the Israelis, urged the Israelis to attack. I believe our ultimatum was written in France last week, hence the mistake in the wording. The Israelis had reckoned to reach the canal, but met with unexpectedly heavy resistance. I think the entire war is a fraud cooked up by the British as an excuse for seizing the canal. And we, we who have to execute this policy, even we were not told.

Pause.

Brock Well . . . what difference does it make?

Darwin My dear boy.

Brock I mean it.

Darwin Raymond.

Brock It makes no difference.

Darwin I was lied to.

Brock Yes, but you were against it from the start.

Darwin I . . .

Brock Oh come on, we all were. The Foreign Office hated the operation from the very first mention, so what difference does it make now?

Darwin All the difference in the world.

Brock None at all.

Darwin The government lied to me.

Brock If the policy was wrong, if it was wrong to begin with . . .

Darwin They are not in good faith.

Brock I see, I see, so what you're saying is, the British may do anything, doesn't matter how murderous, doesn't matter how silly, just so long as we do it in good faith.

Darwin Yes. I would have defended it, I wouldn't have minded how damn stupid it was. I would have defended it had it been honestly done. But this time we are cowboys and when the English are the cowboys, then in truth I fear for the future of the globe.

> *A pause. Darwin walks to the curtained window and stares out. Brock left sitting doesn't turn as he speaks.*

Brock Eden is weak. For years he has been weak. For years people have taunted him, why aren't you strong? Like Churchill? He goes round, he begins to think I must find somebody to be strong on. He finds Nasser. Now he'll show them. He does it to impress. He does it badly. No one is impressed.

Darwin turns to look at Brock.

Mostly what we do is what we think people expect of us. Mostly it's wrong.

Pause.

Are you going to resign?

*The sound of laughter as Susan, **Mme Aung**, M. Aung and Alice stream into the room. Mme Aung is small, tidy and bright. Alice is spectacularly dressed.*

Susan Mme Aung has been enthralling us with the story of the new Bergman film at the Everyman.

Darwin Ah.

Brock Ah yes.

Susan Apparently it's about depression, isn't that so, Mme Aung?

Mme Aung I do feel the Norwegians are very good at that sort of thing.

Susan Is anything wrong?

Susan stands and looks at Brock and Darwin.

Please do sit down everyone. I'm sorry, I think we may have interrupted the men.

Brock It's all right.

Susan They were probably drafting a telegram . . .

Brock We weren't . . .

Susan That's what they do before they drop a bomb. They

send their targets notice in a telegram. Bombs tonight, evacuate the area. Now what does that indicate to you, M. Aung?

Brock Susan, please.

Susan I'll tell you what it indicates to me. Bad conscience. They don't even have the guts to make a war any more.

   Pause.

Darwin Perhaps Mme Aung will tell us the story of the film. This is something I'd be very keen to hear.

Mme Aung I feel the ladies have already . . .

Alice We don't mind.

Susan It's all right. Go ahead. We like the bit in the mental ward.

Mme Aung Ah yes.

Susan Raymond will like it. You got me at the Maudsley, didn't you dear?

Brock Yes, yes.

Susan That's where he proposed to me. A moment of weakness. Of mine, I mean.

Brock Please, darling . . .

Susan I married him because he reminded me of my father.

Mme Aung Really?

Susan At that point, of course, I didn't realize just what a shit my father was.

   Pause.

Alice I'm sorry. She has a sort of psychiatric cabaret.

437

Susan laughs.

Susan That's very good. And there's something about Suez which . . .

Brock Will you please be quiet?

Pause.

The story of the film.

Mme Aung is embarrassed. It takes her considerable effort to start.

Mme Aung There's a woman . . . who despises her husband . . .

Pause.

Susan Is it getting a little bit chilly in here? October nights. Those poor parachutists. I do know how they feel. Even now. Cities. Fields. Trees. Farms. Dark spaces. Lights. The parachute opens. We descend.

Pause.

Of course, we were comparatively welcome, not always ecstatic, not the Gaullists, of course, but by and large we did make it our business to land in countries where we were wanted. Certainly the men were. I mean, some of the relationships, I can't tell you. I remember a colleague telling me of the heat, of the smell of a particular young girl, the hot wet smell, he said. Nothing since. Nothing since then. I can't see the Egyptian girls somehow . . . no. Not in Egypt now. I mean, there were broken hearts when we left. I mean, there are girls today who mourn Englishmen who died in Dachau, died naked in Dachau, men with whom they had spent a single night. Well.

Pause. The tears are pouring down Susan's face, she can barely speak.

438

But then . . . even for myself I do like to make a point of sleeping with men I don't know. I do find once you get to know them you usually don't want to sleep with them any more . . .

Brock gets up and shouts at the top of his voice across the room.

Brock Please can you stop, can you stop fucking talking for five fucking minutes on end?

Susan I would stop, I would stop, I would stop fucking talking if I ever heard anyone else say anything worth fucking stopping talking for.

Pause. Then Darwin moves.

Darwin I'm sorry. I apologize. I really must go.

He crosses the room.

M. Aung. Farewell.

Aung We are behind you, sir. There is wisdom in your expedition.

Darwin Thank you.

Aung May I say, sir, these gyps need whipping and you are the man to do it?

Darwin Thank you very much. Mme Aung.

Mme Aung We never really met.

Darwin No. No. We never met, that is true. But perhaps before I go, I may nevertheless set you right on a point of fact. Ingmar Bergman is not a bloody Norwegian, he is a bloody Swede. (*He nods slightly.*) Good night, everyone.

Darwin goes out. Brock gets up and goes to the door, then turns.

439

Brock He's going to resign.

Pause.

Susan Isn't this an exciting week? Don't you think? Isn't this thrilling? Don't you think? Everything is up for grabs. At last. We will see some changes. Thank the Lord. Now, there was dinner. I made some more dinner for Leonard. A little ham. And chicken. And some pickles and tomato. And lettuce. And there are a couple of pheasants in the fridge. And I can get twelve bottles of claret from the cellar. Why not?

There is plenty.

Shall we eat again?

INTERVAL

SCENE EIGHT

Knightsbridge. July 1961.
*From the dark the voice of a **Priest**.*

Priest Man that is born of woman hath but a short time to live and is full of misery. He cometh up and is cut down like a flower. He fleeth and never continueth in one stay. In the midst of life we are in death. Of whom may we seek for succour but of thee, O Lord, who for our sins art justly displeased?

The room is dark. All the chairs, all the furniture, all the mirrors are covered in white dust-sheets. There is a strong flood of light from the hall which silhouettes the group of three as they enter, all dressed in black. First Brock, then **Dorcas**, *a tall heavily-built, 17-year-old blonde and then* Alice *who, like the others, does not remove her coat. Alice's manner has darkened and sharpened somewhat. Brock goes to take the sheets off two chairs.*

440

Brock I must say, I'd forgotten just how grim it can be.

Alice All that mumbling.

Brock I know. And those bloody hymns. They really do you no good at all. (*He wraps a sheet over his arm.*) Would you like to sit down in here? I'm afraid the whole house is horribly unused.

The women sit. Brock holds his hand out to Dorcas.

You and I haven't had a proper chance to meet.

Alice I hope you didn't mind . . .

Brock Not at all.

Alice . . . my bringing Dorcas along.

Brock She swelled the numbers.

Dorcas I had the afternoon off school.

Brock I'm not sure I'd have chosen a funeral . . .

Dorcas It was fine.

Brock Oh good.

Dorcas Alice told me that you were very good friends . . .

Brock Well, we are.

Dorcas . . . who she hadn't seen for a very long time and she was sure you wouldn't mind me . . . you know . . .

Brock Gatecrashing?

Dorcas Yes.

Brock At the grave.

Dorcas It sounds awful.

Brock You were welcome as far as I was concerned.

Dorcas The only thing was . . . I never heard his name.

Brock His name was Darwin.

Dorcas Ah.

Susan stands unremarked in the doorway. She has taken her coat off and is plainly dressed in black, with some books under her arm. Her manner is quieter than before, and yet more elegant.

Susan Please, nobody get up for me.

Susan moves down to the front where there are two cases filled with books on the floor.

Brock Ah Susan . . .

Susan I was just looking out some more books to take back.

Brock Are you all right?

Susan Yes, fine.

Alice Susan, this is Dorcas I told you about.

Susan How do you do?

Dorcas How do you do?

Susan tucks the books away.

Alice I teach Dorcas history.

Brock Good Lord, how long have you done that?

Alice Oh . . . I've been at it some time.

Dorcas Alice is a very good teacher, you know.

Brock I'm sure.

Alice Thank you, Dorcas.

Dorcas We had a poll and Alice came top.

They smile at each other. Unasked, Dorcas gives Alice a cigarette.

Alice Ta.

Brock Where do you teach?

Alice It's called the Kensington Academy.

Brock I see.

Alice It's in Shepherd's Bush.

Dorcas It's a crammer.

Alice For the daughters of the rich and the congenitally stupid. Dorcas to a T.

Dorcas It's true.

Alice There's almost nothing that a teacher can do.

Dorcas Alice says we're all the prisoners of our genes.

Alice When you actually try to engage their attention, you know that all they can really hear inside their heads is the great thump-thump of their ancestors fucking too freely among themselves.

Dorcas Nothing wrong with that.

Alice No?

Dorcas Stupid people are happier.

Alice Is that what you think?

They smile again. Brock watches.

Brock Well . . .

Susan Raymond, could you manage to make us some tea?

Brock Certainly, if there's time . . .

Susan I'm sure everyone's in need of it.

Brock smiles and goes out.

Alice rang me this morning. She said she was very keen we should meet.

Alice I didn't realize you were going back so soon.

Susan It's a problem, I'm afraid. My husband is a diplomat. We're posted in Iran. I haven't been to London for over three years. Then when I heard of Leonard's death I felt . . . I just felt very strongly I wanted to attend.

Dorcas Alice was saying he'd lost a lot of his friends.

Susan looks across at Alice.

Susan Yes, that's true.

Dorcas I didn't understand what . . .

Susan He spoke his mind over Suez. In public. He didn't hide his disgust. A lot of people never forgave him for that.

Dorcas Oh I see.

Pause.

What's . . .

Alice It's a historical incident four years ago, caused a minor kind of stir at the time. It's also the name of a waterway in Egypt. Egypt is the big brown country up the top right-hand corner of Africa. Africa is a continent . . .

Dorcas Yes, thank you.

Alice And that's why nobody was there today.

Alice looks up at Susan but she has turned away.

I got that panic, you know, you get at funerals. I was thinking, I really don't want to think about death . . .

Susan Yes.

Alice Anything, count the bricks, count the trees, but don't think about death . . . (*She smiles.*) So I tried to imagine Leonard was still alive, I mean locked in his coffin but still alive. And I was laughing at how he would have dealt with the situation, I mean just exactly what the protocol would be.

Susan He would know it.

Alice Of course. Official procedure in the case of being buried alive. How many times one may tap on the lid. How to rise from the grave without drawing unnecessary attention to yourself.

Susan Poor Leonard.

Alice I know. But he did make me laugh.

Susan looks at her catching the old phrase. Then turns at once to Dorcas.

Susan Alice said I might help you in some way.

Dorcas Well, yes.

Susan Of course. If there's anything at all. (*She smiles.*)

Dorcas Did she tell you what the problem was?

Alice There isn't any problem. You need money, that's all.

Dorcas Alice said you'd once been a great friend of hers, part of her sort of crowd . . .

Susan Are they still going then?

Alice They certainly are.

Dorcas And that you might be sympathetic as you'd . . . well . . . as you'd known some troubles yourself . . .

Alice Dorcas needs cash from an impeccable source.

Pause.

445

Susan I see.

Dorcas I'd pay it back.

Susan Well, I'm sure.

Dorcas I mean it's only two hundred pounds. In theory I could still get it for myself, perhaps I'll have to, but Alice felt . . .

Alice Never mind.

Dorcas No, I think I should, I mean, I think I should say Alice did feel as she'd introduced me to this man . . .

Pause. Alice looks away.

Just because he was one of her friends . . . which I just think is silly, I mean, for God's sake, I'm old enough to live my own life . . .

Susan Yes.

Dorcas I mean, I am seventeen. And I knew what I was doing. So why the hell should Alice feel responsible?

Susan I don't know.

Dorcas Anyway the man was a doctor, one of Alice's famous bent doctors, you know, I just wanted to get hold of some drugs, but he wouldn't hand over unless I agreed to fool around, so I just . . . I didn't think anything of it . . .

Susan No.

Dorcas It just seemed like part of the price. At the time. Of course I never guessed it would be three months later and, wham, the knitting needles.

Susan Yes.

Pause.

Dorcas I mean, to be honest I could still go to Daddy and tell him. Just absolutely outright tell him. Just say, Daddy I'm sorry but . . .

Alice Wham the knitting needles.

Dorcas Yes.

Susan looks across at Alice. The two women stare steadily at each other as Dorcas talks.

But of course one would need a great deal of guts.

Pause.

I mean I can't tell you how awful I feel. I mean, coming straight from a funeral . . .

Susan suddenly gets up and walks to the door, speaking very quietly.

Susan Well, I'm sure it needn't delay us for too long . . .

Dorcas Do you mean . . .

Susan Kill a child. That's easy. No problem at all.

Susan opens the door. She has heard Brock with the tea-tray outside.

Ah Raymond, the tea.

Brock I have to tell you the car has arrived.

Susan Oh good.

Brock The driver is saying we must get away at once.

Susan has gone out into the hall. Brock sets the tray down near Dorcas and Alice, and begins to pour.

It must be two years since I made my own tea. Persian labour is disgustingly cheap.

Dorcas I thought you said they . . .

Alice It's another name for Iran.

Dorcas Oh I see.

Susan has reappeared with her handbag and now goes to the writing desk. She folds the sheet back and lowers the lid.

Brock Susan I do hope you're preparing to go.

Susan I will do, I just need a minute or two . . .

Brock I don't think we have time to do anything but . . .

Susan walks over to him.

Susan I do need some tea. Just to wash down my pill.

A pause. Brock smiles.

Brock Yes, of course.

Susan takes the cup from his hand. Then goes back to the desk where she gets out a cheque book and begins to write.

Alice So, Raymond, you must tell us about life in Iran.

Brock I would say we'd been very happy out there. Wouldn't you, Susan?

Susan Uh-huh.

Brock I think the peace has done us both a great deal of good. We were getting rather frenzied in our last few months here. (*He smiles.*)

Alice And the people?

Brock The people are fine. In so far as one's seen them, you know. It's only occasionally that you manage to get out. But the trips are startling, no doubt about that. There you are.

Brock hands Alice tea.

Alice Thank you.

Brock The sky. The desert. And of course the poverty. Living among people who have to struggle so hard. It can make you see life very differently.

Susan Do I make it to cash?

Alice If you could.

Brock hands Dorcas tea.

Dorcas Thanks.

Brock I do remember Leonard, that Leonard always said, the pleasure of diplomacy is perspective, you see. Looking across distances. For instance, we see England very clearly from there. And it does look just a trifle decadent.

He smiles again and drinks his tea.

Susan I'm lending Dorcas some money.

Brock Oh really, is that wise?

Alice She needs an operation.

Brock What?

Alice The tendons of her hands. If she's ever to play in a concert hall again.

Brock Do you actually play a . . .

Susan gets up from her desk.

Susan Raymond, could you take a look at that case? One of those locks is refusing to turn.

Brock Ah yes.

Brock goes to shut the case. Alice watches smiling as Susan walks across to Dorcas to hand her the cheque.

449

Susan Here you are.

Dorcas Thank you.

Susan Don't thank us. We're rotten with cash.

Brock closes the case. Susan gathers the cups on to the tray and places it by the door.

Brock If that's it, then I reckon we're ready to go. I'm sorry to turn you out of the house . . .

Alice That's all right.

Brock Alice, you must come and see us . . .

Alice I shall.

Brock My tour has been extended another two years. Dorcas, I'm happy to have met. I hope your studies proceed, under Alice's tutelage. In the meantime perhaps you might lend me a hand . . . (*He gestures at the case.*) Susan's lifeline. Her case full of books.

Dorcas goes to carry out the smaller case.

Susan, you're ready?

Susan Yes, I am.

Brock You'll follow me down?

Susan nods but doesn't move.

Well . . . I shall be waiting in the car.

Brock goes out with the large case. Dorcas follows.

Dorcas Alice, we won't be long will we?

Alice No.

Dorcas It's just it's biology tonight and that's my favourite. (*off*) Do I put them in the boot?

Brock (*off*) If you could.

Susan and Alice left alone do not move. A pause.

Susan I knew if I came over I would never return.

She pulls the sheet off the desk. It slinks on to the floor. Then she moves round the room, pulling away all the sheets from the furniture, letting them all fall. Then takes them from the mirrors. Then she lights the standard lamps, the table lamps. The room warms and brightens. Alice sits perfectly still, her legs outstretched. Then Susan turns to look at Alice.

You excite me.

Brock appears at the open door.

Brock Susan. Darling. Are we ready to go?

SCENE NINE

Whitehall. January 1962.
From the dark the sound of a radio interview. The Interviewer *is male, serious, a little guarded.*

Voice You were one of the few women to be flown into France?

Susan Yes.

Voice And one of the youngest?

Susan Yes.

Voice Did you always have complete confidence in the organization that sent you?

Susan Yes, of course.

Voice Since the war it's frequently been alleged that

Special Operations was amateurish, its recruitment methods were haphazard, some of its behaviour was rather cavalier. Did you feel that at the time?

Susan Not at all.

Voice The suggestion is that it was careless of human life. Did you feel that any of your colleagues died needlessly?

Susan I can't say.

Voice If you were to . . .

Susan Sorry, if I could . . .

Voice By all means.

Susan You believed in the organization. You had to. If you didn't, you would die.

Voice But you must have had an opinion . . .

Susan No. I had no opinion. I have an opinion now.

Voice And that is?

Susan That it was one part of the war from which the British emerge with the greatest possible valour and distinction.

> *A slight pause.*

Voice Do you ever get together with former colleagues and talk about the war?

Susan Never. We aren't clubbable.

The Foreign Office. A large room in Scott's Palazzo. A mighty painting above a large fireplace in an otherwise barish waiting room. It shows Britannia Colonorum Mater in pseudo-classical style. Otherwise the room is uncheering. A functional desk, some unremarkable wooden chairs, a green radiator. An air of functional *disue. Two people. Susan is standing at one side, smartly dressed again with coat and handbag; **Begley** stands opposite by an inner door. He is a thin young man with impeccable manners. He is twenty-two.*

Begley Mrs Brock, Sir Andrew will see you now. He only has a few minutes, I'm afraid.

*At once through the inner door comes **Sir Andrew Charleson** in a double-breasted blue suit. He is in his early fifties, dark-haired, thickening, almost indolent. He cuts less of a figure than Darwin but he has far more edge.*

Charleson Ah Mrs Brock.

Susan Sir Andrew.

Charleson How do you do?

Susan and Charleson shake hands.

We have met.

Susan That's right.

Charleson The Queen's Garden Party. And I've heard you on the wireless recently. Talking about the war. How extraordinary it must have been.

Pause.

Susan This must seem a very strange request.

Charleson Not in the slightest. We're delighted to see you here.

Begley takes two chairs out from the wall and places them down opposite each other.

Perhaps I might offer you a drink.

Susan If you are having one.

Charleson Unfortunately not. I'm somewhat liverish.

Susan I'm sorry.

Charleson No, no, it's a hazard of the job. Half the diplomats I know have bad offal, I'm afraid. (*He turns to Begley.*) If you could leave us, Begley.

Begley Sir.

Charleson Just shuffle some papers for a while.

> *Begley goes through the inner door. Charleson gestures Susan to sit.*

You mustn't be nervous, you know, Mrs Brock. I have to encounter many diplomatic wives, many even more distinguished than yourself, with very similar intent. It is much commoner than you suppose.

Susan Sir Andrew, as you know I take very little part in my husband's professional life . . .

Charleson Indeed.

Susan Normally, I spend a great deal of time on my own . . . with one or two friends . . . of my own . . . Mostly I like reading, I like reading alone . . . I do think to be merely your husband's wife is demeaning for a woman of any integrity at all . . .

> *Charleson smiles.*

Charleson I understand.

Susan But I find for the first time in my husband's career I am beginning to feel some need to intervene.

Charleson I had a message, yes.

Susan I hope you appreciate my loyalty . . .

Charleson Oh yes.

Susan Coming here at all. Brock is a man who has seen me through some very difficult times . . .

Charleson I am told.

Susan But this is a matter on which I need to go behind his back.

Charleson gestures reassurance.

My impression is that since our recall from Iran he is in some way being penalized.

Charleson makes no reaction.

As I understand it, you're Head of Personnel . . .

Charleson I'm the Chief Clerk, yes . . .

Susan I've come to ask exactly what my husband's prospects are.

Pause.

I do understand the foreign service now. I know that my husband could never ask himself. Your business is conducted in a code, which it's considered unethical to break. Signs and indications are all you are given. Your stock is rising, your stock is falling . . .

Charleson Yes.

Susan Brock has been allocated to a fairly lowly job, backing up the EEC negotiating team . . .

Charleson He's part of the push into Europe, yes.

Susan The foreign posts he's since been offered have not been glittering.

Charleson We offered him Monrovia.

Susan Monrovia. Yes. He took that to be an insult. Was he wrong?

Charleson smiles.

Charleson Monrovia is not an insult.

Susan But?

Charleson Monrovia is more in the nature of a test. A test of nerve, it's true. If a man is stupid enough to accept Monrovia, then he probably deserves Monrovia. That is how we think.

Susan But you . . .

Charleson And Brock refused. (*He shrugs.*) Had we wanted to insult him there are far worse jobs. In this building too. In my view town-twinning is the *coup de grâce*. I'd far rather be a martyr to the tsetse fly than have to twin Rotherham with Bergen-op-Zoom.

Susan You are evading me.

Pause. Charleson smiles again.

Charleson I'm sorry. It's a habit, as you say. (*He pauses to rethink. Then with confidence*) Your husband has never been a flyer, Mrs Brock.

Susan I see.

Charleson Everyone is streamed, a slow stream, a fast stream . . .

Susan My husband is slow?

Charleson Slowish.

Susan That means . . .

Charleson What is he? First Secretary struggling towards Counsellor. At forty-one it's not remarkable, you know.

Susan But it's got worse.

Charleson You think?

Susan The last six months. He's never felt excluded from his work before.

Charleson Does he feel that?

Susan I think you know he does.

Pause.

Charleson Well, I'm sure the intention was not to punish him. We have had some trouble in placing him, it's true. The rather startling decision to desert his post . . .

Susan That was not his fault.

Charleson We were told. We were sympathetic. Psychiatric reasons?

Susan I was daunted at the prospect of returning to Iran.

Charleson Of course. Persian psychiatry. I shudder at the thought. A heavy-handed people at the best of times. We understood. Family problems. Our sympathy goes out . . .

Susan But you are blocking his advance.

Charleson thinks, then changes tack again.

Charleson I think you should understand the basis of our talk. The basis on which I agreed to talk. You asked for information. The information is this: that Brock is making haste slowly. That is all I can say.

Susan I'm very keen he should not suffer on my account.

Susan's voice is low. Charleson looks at his hands.

Charleson Mrs Brock, believe me I recognize your tone. Women have come in here and used it before.

Susan I would like to see my husband advance.

Charleson I also have read the stories in your file, so nothing in your manner is likely to amaze. I do know exactly the kind of person you are. When you have chosen a particular course . . . (*He pauses.*) When there is something which you very badly want . . . (*He pauses again.*) But in this matter I must tell you, Mrs Brock, it is more than likely you have met your match.

The two of them stare straight at each other.

We are talking of achievement at the highest level. Brock cannot expect to be cosseted through. It's not enough to be clever. Everyone here is clever, everyone is gifted, everyone is diligent. These are simply the minimum skills. Far more important is an attitude of mind. Along the corridor I boast a colleague who in 1945 drafted a memorandum to the government advising them not to accept the Volkswagen works as war reparation, because the Volkswagen plainly had no commercial future. I must tell you, unlikely as it may seem, that man has risen to the very, very top. All sorts of diplomatic virtues he displays. He has forbearance. He is gracious. He is sociable. Perhaps you begin to understand . . .

Susan You are saying . . .

Charleson I am saying that certain qualities are valued here above a simple gift of being right or wrong. Qualities sometimes hard to define . . .

Susan What you are saying is that nobody may speak, nobody may question . . .

Charleson Certainly tact is valued very high.

Pause. Susan very low.

Susan Sir Andrew, do you never find it in yourself to despise a profession in which nobody may speak their mind?

Charleson That is the nature of the service, Mrs Brock. It

458

is called diplomacy. And in its practice the English lead the world. (*He smiles.*) The irony is this: we had an empire to administer, there were six hundred of us in this place. Now it's to be dismantled and there are six thousand. As our power declines, the fight among us for access to that power becomes a little more urgent, a little uglier perhaps. As our influence wanes, as our empire collapses, there is little to believe in. Behaviour is all.

Pause.

This is a lesson which you both must learn.

A moment, then Susan picks up her handbag to go.

Susan I must thank you for your frankness, Sir Andrew . . .

Charleson Not at all.

Susan I must, however, warn you of my plan. If Brock is not promoted in the next six days, I am intending to shoot myself.

Susan gets up from her seat. Charleson follows quickly.

Now thank you, and I shan't stay for the drink . . .

Charleson (*calls*) Begley . . .

Susan I'm due at a reception for Australia Day.

Charleson moves quickly to the inner door. Susan begins talking very fast as she moves to go.

Charleson Begley.

Susan I always like to see just how rude I can be. Not that the Australians ever notice, of course. So it does become a sort of Zen sport, don't you think?

Begley appears.

Charleson John, I wonder, could you give me a hand?

Begley Sir.

Susan stops near the door, starts talking yet more rapidly.

Susan Ah the side-kick, the placid young man, now where have I seen that character before?

Charleson If we could take Mrs Brock down to the surgery . . .

Susan I assure you, Sir Andrew, I'm perfectly all right.

Charleson Perhaps alert her husband . . .

Begley If you're not feeling well . . .

Susan People will be waiting at Australia House. I can't let them down. It will be packed with angry people all searching for me, saying where is she, what a let-down. I only came here to be insulted and now there's no chance.

Charleson looks at Begley as if to co-ordinate a move. They advance slightly.

Charleson I think it would be better if you . . .

Susan starts to shout.

Susan Please. Please leave me alone.

Charleson and Begley stop. Susan is hysterical. She waits a moment.

I can't . . . always manage with people.

Pause.

I think you have destroyed my husband, you see.

SCENE TEN

Knightsbridge. Easter 1962.

*From the dark the sound of some stately orchestral
chords: Mahler, melodic, solemn. It is evening. The room
has been restored to its former rather old-fashioned
splendour. The curtains are drawn. At a mahogany table
sits Alice. She is putting a large pile of leaflets into brown
envelopes. Very little disturbs the rhythm of her work. She
is dressed exactly as for Scene One.*

*Brock is sitting at another table at the front of the stage.
He has an abacus in front of him and a pile of ledgers and
cheque stubs. He is dressed in cavalry twills with a check
shirt open at the neck.*

The music stops. The stereo machine switches itself off.

Brock Well, I suppose it isn't too bad. Perhaps we'll keep
going another couple of years. A regime of mineral water
and lightly browned toast.

*He smiles and stretches. Then turns to look at Alice.
There is a bottle of mineral water on the table in front
of her.*

I assume she's still in there.

Alice She paces around.

Brock gets up and pours some out.

Brock I told her this morning . . . we'll have to sell the
house. I'm sure we can cope in a smaller sort of flat.
Especially now we don't have to entertain.

He takes a sip.

I can't help feeling it will be better, I'm sure. Too much
money. I think that's what went wrong. Something about
it corrupts the will to live. Too many years spent sploshing
around.

He suddenly listens.

What?

Alice Nothing. She's just moving about.

He turns to Alice.

Brock Perhaps you'd enjoy to take the evening off. I'm happy to do duty for an hour or two.

Alice I enjoy it. I get to do my work. A good long slog for my charity appeal. And I've rather fallen out with all those people I knew. And most of them go off on the Aldermaston March.

Brock Really? Of course. Easter weekend.

He picks his way through the remains of an Indian takeaway meal which is on Alice's table, searching for good scraps.

Alice Except for Alistair and I've no intention of spending an evening with him – or her, as he's taken to calling himself.

Brock How come?

Alice Apparently he's just had his penis removed.

Brock Voluntarily? It's what he intended, I mean?

Alice I believe. In Morocco. And replaced with a sort of pink plastic envelope. I haven't seen it. He says he keeps the shopping list in there, tucks five pound notes away, so he says.

Brock I thought that strange young girl of yours would ring.

Alice looks up for a moment from her work.

Alice No, no. She decided to move on. There's some

appalling politician, I'm told. On the paedophiliac wing of the Tory party. She's going to spend the summer swabbing the deck on his yacht. Pleasuring his enormous underside. It's what she always wanted. The fat. The inane.

She looks up again.

If you've nothing to do, you could give a hand with these.

Brock takes no notice, casts aside the scraps.

Brock Looking back, I seem to have been eating all the time. My years in the Foreign Service, I mean. I don't think I missed a single canapé. Not one. The silver tray flashed and bang, I was there.

Alice Do you miss it?

Brock Almost all the time. There's not much glamour in insurance, you know.

He smiles.

Something in the Foreign Office suited my style. Whatever horrible things people say. At least they were hypocrites, I do value that now. Hypocrisy does keep things pleasant for at least part of the time. Whereas down in the City they don't even try.

Alice You chose it.

Brock That's right. That isn't so strange. The strange bit is always . . . why I remain.

He stands staring a moment.

Still, it gives her something new to despise. The sad thing is this time . . . I despise it as well.

Alice reaches for a typed list of names, pushes aside the pile of envelopes.

Alice Eight hundred addresses, eight hundred names . . .

Brock You were never attracted? A regular job?

Alice I never had time. Too busy relating to various young men. Falling in and out of love turns out to be like any other career.

She looks up.

I had an idea that lust . . . that lust was very good. And could be made simple. And cheering. And light. Perhaps I was simply out of my time.

Brock You speak as if it's over.

Alice I've no doubt it is.

Pause.

Brock How long since anyone took a look next door?

Alice That's why I think it may be time to do good.

Susan opens the door, standing dressed as for Scene One. She is a little dusty.

Susan I need to ask you to move out of here. I am in temporary need of this room. You can go wherever you like. And pretty soon also . . . you're welcome to return.

She goes off at once to the desk where she picks items off the surface and throws them quietly into cubbyholes. Alice is looking at Brock.

Brock You'd better tell me, Susan, what you've done to your hands.

Susan I've just been taking some paper from the wall.

Brock There's blood.

Susan A fingernail.

Pause.

Brock Susan, what have you actually done?

Brock gets up and goes to the door, looks down the corridor. Susan stands facing the desk, speaks quietly.

Susan I thought as we were going to get rid of the house . . . and I couldn't stand any of the things that were there . . .

He turns back into the room. She turns and looks at him.

Now what's best to be doing in here?

Brock looks at her, speaks as quietly.

Brock Could you look in the drawer please, Alice, there's some Nembutal . . .

Alice I'm not sure we should . . .

Brock I shan't ask you again.

Alice slides open the drawer, puts a small bottle of pills on the table. Brock moves a pace towards Susan.

Listen, if we're going to have to sell this house . . .

Susan You yourself said it, I've often heard you say, it's money that did it, it's money that rots. That we've all lived like camels off the fat in our humps. Well, then, isn't the best thing to do . . . to turn round simply and give the house away?

She smiles.

Alice, would this place suit your needs? Somewhere to set down all your unmarried mothers. If we lay out mattresses, mattresses on the floor . . .

Alice Well, I . . .

Susan Don't your women need a place to live?

Without warning she raises her arms above her head.

By our own hands.

Pause.

Of our own free will. An Iranian vase. A small wooden Buddha. Twelve marble birds copied from an Ottoman king.

Pause.

How can they be any possible use? Look out the bedroom window. I've thrown them away.

She opens the door and goes at once into the corridor. At once Brock crosses the room to the desk to look for his address book. Alice starts clearing up the leaflets and envelopes on the table in front of her.

Brock I suppose you conspired.

Alice Not at all.

Brock Well, really?

Alice That was the first that I've heard.

Brock In that case, please, you might give me some help. Find out what else she's been doing out there.

Susan reappears dragging in two packing cases, already half-full. She then starts gathering objects from around the room.

Susan Cutlery, crockery, lampshades and books, books, books. Encyclopedias. Clutter. Meaningless. A universe of things.

She starts to throw them one by one into the crates.

Mosquito nets, golf clubs, photographs. China. Marble. Glass. Mementoes in stone. What is this shit? What are these God-forsaken bloody awful things?

Brock turns, still speaking quietly.

Brock Which is the braver? To live as I do? Or never, ever to face life like you?

He holds up the small card he has found.

This is the doctor's number, my dear. With my permission he can put you inside. I am quite capable of doing it tonight. So why don't you start to put all those things back?

A pause. Susan looks at him, then to Alice.

Susan Alice, would your women value my clothes?

Alice Well, I . . .

Susan It sounds fairly silly. I have thirteen evening dresses, though.

Brock Susan.

Susan Obviously not much use as they are. But possibly they could be recut. Resewn?

She reaches out and with one hand picks up an ornament from the mantelpiece which she throws with a crash into the crate. A pause.

Brock Your life is selfish, self-interested gain. That's the most charitable interpretation to hand. You claim to be protecting some personal ideal, always at a cost of almost infinite pain to everyone around you. You are selfish, brutish, unkind. Jealous of other people's happiness as well, determined to destroy other ways of happiness they find. I've spent fifteen years of my life trying to help you, simply trying to be kind, and my great comfort has been that I am waiting for some indication from you . . . some sign that you have valued this kindness of mine. Some love perhaps. Insane.

He smiles.

And yet . . . I really shan't ever give up, I won't surrender till you're well again. And that to me would mean your admitting one thing: that in the life you have led you have utterly failed, failed in the very, very heart of your life. Admit it. Then perhaps you might really move on.

Pause.

Now I'm going to go and give our doctor a ring. I plan at last to beat you at your own kind of game. I am going to play as dirtily and ruthlessly as you. And this time I am certainly not giving in.

Brock goes out. A pause.

Susan Well.

Pause.

Well, goodness. What's best to do?

Pause.

What's the best way to start stripping this room?

Susan doesn't move. Alice stands watching.

Alice Susan, I think you should get out of this house.

Susan Of course.

Alice I'll help you. Any way I can.

Susan Well, that's very kind.

Alice If you . . .

Susan I'll be going just as soon as this job is done.

Pause.

Alice Listen, if Raymond really means what he says . . .

Susan turns and looks straight at Alice.

You haven't even asked me, Susan, you see. You haven't asked me yet what I think of the idea.

Susan frowns.

Susan Really, Alice, I shouldn't need to ask. It's a very sad day when one can't help the poor . . .

Alice suddenly starts to laugh. Susan sets off across the room, resuming a completely normal social manner.

Alice For God's sake, Susan, he'll put you in the bin.

Susan Don't be silly, Alice, it's Easter weekend. It must have occurred to you . . . the doctor's away.

Brock reappears at the open door, the address book in his hand. Susan turns to him.

All right, Raymond? Anything I can do? I've managed to rout out some whisky over here.

She sets the bottle down on the table, next to the Nembutal.

Alice was just saying she might slip out for a while. Give us a chance to sort our problems out. I'm sure if we had a really serious talk . . . I could keep going till morning. Couldn't you?

Susan turns to Alice.

All right, Alice?

Alice Yes. Yes, of course. I'm going, I'm just on my way.

She picks up her coat and heads for the door.

All right if I get back in an hour or two? I don't like to feel I'm intruding. You know?

She smiles at Susan. Then closes the door. Susan at once

goes back to the table. Brock stands watching her.

Susan Now, Raymond. Good. Let's look at this thing.

Susan pours out a spectacularly large Scotch, filling the glass to the very rim. Then she pushes it a few inches across the table to Brock.

Where would be the best place to begin?

SCENE ELEVEN

Blackpool. June 1962.
From the dark music. Then silence. Two voices in the dark.

Lazar Susan. Susan. Feel who I am.

Susan I know. I know who you are. How could you be anyone else but Lazar?

And a small bedside light comes on. Lazar and Susan are lying sideways across a double bed, facing opposite ways. They are in a sparsely furnished and decaying room. Lazar is in his coat, facing away from us as he reaches for the nightlight. Susan is also fully dressed, in a big black man's overcoat, her hair wild, her dress crumpled round her thighs. The bedside light barely illuminates them at all.

Jesus. Jesus. To be happy again.

At once Susan gets up and goes into what must be the bathroom. A shaft of yellow light from the doorway falls across the bed.

Lazar Don't take your clothes off whatever you do.

Susan *(off)* Of course not.

Lazar That would spoil it hopelessly for me.

Susan (*off*) I'm getting my cigarettes. I roll my own . . .

Lazar Goodness me.

Susan Tell you, there are no fucking flies on me.

She has reappeared with her holdall which is crumpled and stained. She sits cross-legged on the end of the bed. She starts to roll two cigarettes.

Lazar I am glad I found you.

Susan I'm just glad I came.

Lazar This place is filthy.

Susan It's a cheap hotel.

Lazar They seem to serve you dust on almost everything.

Susan You should be grateful for dust, did you know? If it weren't for all the dust in the atmosphere, human beings would be killed by the heat of the sun.

Lazar In Blackpool?

Susan Well . . .

Lazar Are you kidding me?

Susan reaches into the overcoat pocket.

Susan I was given some grass. Shall I roll it in?

Lazar Just the simple cigarette for me.

Susan nods.

I hope you didn't mind my choosing Blackpool at all. It's just that I work near . . .

Susan Don't tell me any more.

Lazar Susan . . .

Pause.

Will you . . . can you touch me again?

Susan facing away doesn't move, just smiles. A pause.

Do you know how I found you? Through the BBC. I just caught that programme a few months ago. They told me you were married and based in London now. They gave me an address . . .

Susan I left it weeks ago.

Lazar I know. I gather you've been out on the road. But . . . I went, I went round and saw the man.

Susan And how was he?

Lazar He looked like a man who'd spent his life with you.

Susan How can you say that?

Lazar (*smiles*) Oh I'm guessing, that's all.

Susan smiles again.

He said he'd only just managed to reclaim.

Susan Oh really? That's my fault. I gave the house away.

Lazar He said he'd had to fight to get back into his home. There'd been some kind of trouble. Police, violence it seems . . .

Susan Was he angry?

Lazar Angry? No. He just seemed very sorry not to be with you.

Pause. Susan stops rolling the cigarette.

Susan Listen. I have to tell you I've not always been well. I have a weakness. I like to lose control. I've been letting it happen, well, a number of times . . .

Lazar Is it . . .?

Susan I did shoot someone about ten years ago.

Lazar Did you hurt him?

Susan Fortunately no. At least that's what we kept telling him, you know. Raymond went and gave him money in notes. He slapped them like hot poultices all over his wounds. I think it did finally convince him on the whole. It was after Raymond's kindness I felt I had to get engaged . . .

Lazar Why do people . . .

Susan Marry? I don't know. Are you . . .

Pause.

Lazar What? Ask me anything at all.

Susan No. It's nothing. I don't want to know. (*She smiles again.*)

Lazar Do you ever see him?

Susan Good gracious no. I've stripped away everything, everything I've known. There's only one kind of dignity, that's in living alone. The clothes you stand up in, the world you can see . . .

Lazar Oh Susan . . .

Susan Don't.

Pause. Susan is suddenly still.

I want to believe in you. So tell me nothing. That's best.

Pause. Susan does not turn round. Lazar suddenly gets up, and goes to get his coat and gloves from his suitcase. Susan looks down at the unmade cigarette in her hands. Then she starts to make the roll-up again.

Susan How long till dawn? Do you think we should go? If we wait till morning we'll have to pay the bill. I can't believe that can be the right thing to do.

She smiles.

Is there an early train, do you know? Though just where I'm going I'm not really sure. There aren't many people who'll have me, you know.

Pause.

I hope you'll forgive me. The grass has gone in.

She licks along the edge of the joint, then lights it. Lazar stands still, his suitcase beside him.

Lazar I don't know what I'd expected.

Susan Mmm?

Lazar What I'd hoped for, at the time I returned. Some sort of edge to the life that I lead. Some sort of feeling their death was worthwhile.

Pause.

Some day I must tell you. I don't feel I've done well. I gave in. Always. All along the line. Suburb. Wife. Hell. I work in a corporate bureaucracy as well . . .

Susan has begun to giggle.

Susan Lazar, I'm sorry. I'm just about to go.

Lazar What?

Susan I've eaten nothing. So I just go . . .

She waves vaguely with her hand. Then smiles. A pause.

Lazar I hate, I hate this life that we lead.

Susan Oh, God, here I go.

474

Pause.

Kiss me. Kiss me now as I go.

> *Lazar moves towards Susan and tries to take her in his arms. But as he tries to kiss her, she falls back on to the bed, flopping down where she stays.*

> *Lazar removes the roach from her hand. Puts it out. Goes over and closes his case. Then picks it up. Goes to the bathroom and turns the light off. Now only the nightlight is on. Lazar goes to the door.*

Lazar A fine undercover agent will move so that nobody can ever tell he was there.

> *Lazar turns the nightlight off. Darkness.*

Susan Tell me your name.

> *Pause.*

Lazar Code name.

> *Pause.*

Code name.

> *Pause.*

Code name Lazar.

> *Lazar opens the door of the room. At once music plays. Where you would expect a corridor you see the fields of France shining brilliantly in a fierce green square. The room scatters.*

SCENE TWELVE

St Benoît, August 1944.
The darkened areas of the room disappear and we see a

French hillside in high summer. The stage picture forms piece by piece. Green, yellow, brown. Trees. The fields stretch away. A high sun. A brilliant August day. Another Frenchman stands looking down into the valley. He carries a spade, is in Wellingtons and corduroys. He is about 40, fattish with an unnaturally gloomy air.

Then Susan appears climbing the hill. She is 19. She is dressed like a young French girl, her pullover over her shoulder. She looks radiantly well.

Frenchman Bonjour, ma'moiselle.

Susan Bonjour.

Frenchman Vous regardez le village?

Susan Oui, je suis montée la colline pour mieux voir. C'est merveilleux.

Frenchman Oui. Indeed the day is fine.

Pause. Susan looks across at the Frenchman.

We understand. We know. The war is over now.

Susan 'I climbed the hill to get a better view.' (*She smiles.*) I've only spoken French for months on end.

Frenchman You are English?

Susan nods.

Tower Bridge.

Susan Just so.

The Frenchman smiles and walks over to join Susan. Together they look away down the hill.

Frenchman You join the party in the village?

Susan Soon. I'm hoping, yes, I'm very keen to go.

Frenchman Myself I work. A farmer. Like any other day.

The Frenchman works or starves. He is the piss. The shit. The lowest of the low.

Susan moves forward a little, staring down the hill.

Susan Look. They're lighting fires in the square. And children . . . coming out with burning sticks.

Pause.

Have you seen anything as beautiful as this?

Susan stands looking out. The Frenchman mumbles ill-humouredly.

Frenchman The harvest is not good again this year.

Susan I'm sorry.

The Frenchman shrugs.

Frenchman As I expect. The land is very poor. I have to work each moment of the day.

Susan But you'll be glad I think. You're glad as well?

Susan turns, so the Frenchman cannot avoid the question. He reluctantly concedes.

Frenchman I'm glad. Is something good, is true. (*He looks puzzled.*) The English . . . have no feelings, yes? Are stiff.

Susan They hide them, hide them from the world.

Frenchman Is stupid.

Susan Stupid, yes. It may be . . .

Pause.

Frenchman Huh?

Susan That things will quickly change. We have grown up. We will improve our world.

The Frenchman stares at Susan. Then offers gravely:

Frenchman Perhaps . . . perhaps you like some soup. My wife.

Susan All right.

Susan smiles. They look at each other, about to go.

Frenchman The walk is down the hill.

Susan My friend.

Pause.

There will be days and days and days like this.

FABER CONTEMPORARY CLASSICS

The Faber Contemporary Classics series
aims to provide a body of work, in collected form,
for all the Faber playwrights.

Alan Ayckbourn
Alan Bennett
Brian Friel
Trevor Griffiths
David Hare
Ronald Harwood
Sharman Macdonald
Frank McGuinness
John Osborne
Harold Pinter
Tom Stoppard
Nick Ward
Timberlake Wertenbaker